GURU OF NONE, DISCIPLE OF ALL

GURU OF NONE, DISCIPLE OF ALL

THE LIFE & TIMES OF DADA J. P. VASWANI

Anita Raina Thapan

HAY HOUSE INDIA

Australia • Canada • Hong Kong • India
South Africa • United Kingdom • United States

Hay House Publishers (India) Pvt. Ltd.
Muskaan Complex, Plot No.3, B-2 Vasant Kunj, New Delhi-110 070, India
Hay House Inc., PO Box 5100, Carlsbad, CA 92018-5100, USA
Hay House UK, Ltd., Astley House, 33 Notting Hill Gate, London W11 3JQ, UK
Hay House Australia Pty Ltd., 18/36 Ralph St., Alexandria NSW 2015, Australia
Hay House SA (Pty) Ltd., PO Box 990, Witkoppen 2068, South Africa
Hay House Publishing, Ltd., 17/F, One Hysan Ave., Causeway Bay, Hong Kong
Raincoast, 9050 Shaughnessy St., Vancouver, BC V6P 6E5, Canada
Email: contact@hayhouse.co.in
www.hayhouse.co.in

DADA VASWANI'S BOOKS
Visit us online to purchase books on self-improvement, spiritual
advancement, meditation and philosophy. Plus audio cassettes, CDs,
DVDs, monthly journals and books in Hindi.
www.dadavaswanisbooks.org

ISBN 978-93-84544-75-1

Printed and bound at
Rajkamal Electric Press, Sonepat, Haryana (India)

CONTENTS

THE MASTER

THE DALAI LAMA

FOREWORD

I am very happy to know that Anita Raina Thapan has written this biography of Dada J. P. Vaswani, which will be published on the occasion of his 97th birthday.

Dada Vaswani is a fount of inspiration for his followers. I have warm memories of my visit to his ashram in 2013 on his 95th birthday and of sharing his interaction with his followers.

Dada Vaswani has lived a life of dedication to the service of society, helping the poor and downtrodden. The schools and social institutions he has set up during his lifetime have benefited many people enormously. His spiritual advice has likewise helped many to lead meaningful lives. He has also worked to foster inter-religious harmony that is so important in our increasingly interdependent world.

I congratulate the author for compiling this biography, which will allow readers to better appreciate Dada Vaswani's many achievements.

March 31, 2015

Preface

Several years ago I was part of a team that was working on a project of the Sadhu Vaswani Mission. Knowing that on my own I would never be able to gain the profound insights I needed, I asked Dada Jashan, one day, if he would bless me so that I could become a worthy instrument of his work.

Dada looked deep into my eyes with his clear, laser-like gaze, and gently asked:

'What time do you get up in the morning?'

'At 4:45 a.m.,' I replied.

'Alright. At 5:00 a.m., I will be thinking of you and you can tune in to me.'

I felt that the work was as good as done, because Dada had taken the responsibility of working through me. Upon returning to Delhi, I faithfully did what he told me, for a while. My output was inspired and my writing became a joyous prayer. However, there were delays and obstacles in the working of the whole team, and within a couple of months, the project came to a temporary standstill. Slowly, I dropped the practice of tuning in to Dada. In sheer ignorance and foolishness, I lost my connection with a living saint. Mundane and meaningless preoccupations gained precedence in my life. Without realizing it, I had let go of the rope that had been given to me to pull me out of a life of stress, fear, and limitation.

Several months later, I revisited Pune for some personal work. I was, instinctively, drawn to meet Dada. Standing with a crowd of people near the sacred Samadhi one evening, I saw the familiar figure, dressed in white, with a radiant face, captivating smile, and hands joined together in greeting. I experienced the same surge of inexplicable joy and love that his presence always seems to evoke. Suddenly, I felt that I had dissolved in the crowd and had become part of one strong wave of aspiration, rising to be engulfed in his divine presence; to imbibe the purity, the goodness, and the timelessness that he radiates; to drink in his words and perhaps touch the hem of his garment as he passed by.

The prayers at the Samadhi brought tears to my eyes. I recalled how every day of his life, morning and evening, Dada bows down before His beloved Master and invokes His Grace. His devotion, dedication and faith are so simple and touching; yet they are the key to his phenomenal spiritual power, ethereal majesty, his all-encompassing love and healing.

After the prayers, Dada passed by the numerous devotees who yearned for a smile, a touch, a blessing. I wondered whether he would remember me. For some reason, I also felt a discomfort, which I could not quite understand then. Dada stopped before me. Clasping my folded hands with both of his, he said my name. There was delight in his voice. Then looking deep in my eyes, he said with his gentle tone, 'I remembered you but you broke faith with me. Yes, yes.' He moved on to the next person.

I was stunned. He had known that I had stopped tuning in to him! And by turning away, my inspiration had slowly dried up; all that I had sought to change in my life was back to what it had always been.

I remained at the Samadhi long after he had left and the crowd had melted away. I prayed that I be given a second chance; that I be allowed to experience, once again, that connection with the Source. I fervently beseeched him, in my mind, to let me regain that state when work becomes an expression of a profound inner joy; when thoughts of the divine imbue one with great reserves of enthusiasm, optimism and faith; when creative ideas flow out in an endless stream.

In his infinite compassion, Dada gave me the opportunity once again, of doing some work for the Mission. This time I asked him nothing, as I had understood that he knows everything. I merely invoked him in my prayers every day. Sure enough, I felt the same familiar exultation and inspiration that I had experienced earlier. The work was completed. But this time, I had gained something immensely valuable. Invoking Sadhu Vaswani and Dada Jashan had become an intrinsic part of my daily *sadhana*. Turning back to Dada has been a turning back to God. And turning back to God is what Dada emphasizes is the vital need of the day. As he puts it:

> The modern world has everything but it needs this small message of four words TURN BACK TO GOD. I have but one tongue. If I had a million tongues, with every one of those million tongues, I would still say: Turn back to God! Turn back to God! The cure to our present ills lies in turning back to God.
> We have thrown God out of our educational institutions and out of our homes. We have everything, but we don't have the spirit. Nietzche in the 19th century went so far as to write, 'Haven't you heard? God is dead!'

The life of Dada J. P. Vaswani is a testimony to the effulgence and glory of a life lived in God. To read about it is to journey to the source of that Supreme Power; to be able to draw the energy and wisdom of the Universe through that connection with the Supreme. It is to understand the immense power of faith and surrender; and the transformative, and healing capacity of love. It is an affirmation that strength and gentleness go hand in hand, as do truth and fearlessness.

To the numerous individuals who want to change themselves but are not clear about what to change and how to go about it, the life of saints such as Dada Jashan is the key. Entering into the world of Dada's words, actions, and his sacred silence, is like taking a dip in the river of divine Grace. One emerges purified and sanctified. One is made aware of, and inspired to strive for, the real purpose of life which is to realize one's divine potential, use it in the service of all sentient beings and, thereby, reach a state of abiding plenitude and fulfilment.

1

THE CHOICE IS MADE

'Jashan's heart belongs to Sadhu Vaswani,' thought Krishnadevi, 'and I cannot hold him back.' Much as she had tried to shut it out of her mind, she had finally accepted that this exceptionally gifted son of hers, with his rare abilities of head and heart, had a calling that was far beyond the ordinary. Rare is the child who becomes a spiritual aspirant at a tender age; who looks deeply at what is around him and what is within him. Jashan had, at every stage, been different from his peers. Intuitively, she knew that he was born for some higher purpose; he had a mission to fulfil.

Just the other day he had returned to her in Karachi at the bidding of his uncle and Guru, Sadhu T. L. Vaswani. On seeing him she had broken down and wept. Putting his arms around her he had said, 'Ma, please don't worry. I will do whatever you wish.'

She had replied, 'Son, someone in the neighbourhood told me that he would get you a good job. I wish for you to attain a high position and status.'

'I will do as you say,' Jashan had assured her.

Obediently he went about applying for a job in the Customs Department, as suggested by her. He did not complain or protest. But he was silent and withdrawn. His deep anguish and resignation were evident, even though his words were, as always, gentle and loving.

'Are you sure it is all right?' she asked him again. Then, without waiting for a reply, she continued, 'How will you then belong to God, dedicate your life to Him?'

'Don't worry,' he had replied. 'God is not just in one place. God is everywhere. You just give me your order and tell me what you want of me.'

The more she observed, the clearer it became to her that he appeared like a bird in a cage. And it was her maternal love and possessiveness that caged him. She had to set him free, for it was clear that he yearned to soar to the realms that only a few ever aspire to.

Resolutely, she entered his room and found him bent over a book. Putting her arms around him and cradling his head against her heart, she whispered, 'Go my child. Go to your Guru. I will not keep you. I know that you will never find meaning in a life here.'

Jashan looked up, with sad eyes and said, 'He won't take me back now, after what you've told Kaka Shamdas.'

'I will write to him,' Krishnadevi gently assured him. 'I will tell him that I have sent you, for always, with my blessings. I will tell him that I am happy at your dedicating your life in his service.'

Krishnadevi took a deep breath because she did not want to spoil this sacred moment with any emotional display.

'You see, Jashan,' she continued keeping her voice steady, 'at the time when I spoke to Kaka Shamdas, I was thinking of myself. Now, I am thinking of you, and that makes all the difference. Your happiness is more important to me than anything else.'

Jashan's eyes shone. 'Oh! Ma!' he whispered, hugging his mother with gratitude and love. He seemed to transform immediately. His joy was palpable.

Then, suddenly, filled with fear, she had asked, 'But you are mine, aren't you?'

'Yes, of course, I am your son,' he had replied.

'Go then, and belong to God. In His service seek the fulfilment of your life. I will go and write the letter,' said Krishnadevi, fighting back her tears as she left the room.

Shutting the door behind her, she sat down and silently wept. There! She had done it! She had opened the door to Jashan's cage. And very soon, this son, the most beloved of all her children, would fly away. How much she had dreamed of his great future – a brilliant career, marriage and children, wealth and fame. He seemed to excel in everything he did. He was well loved by his family, teachers, and peers. Everything desirable seemed within his easy grasp. How blessed she had always felt, for he had only brought her joy and pride. And, as her eldest son, she had taken for granted that she would live with him in security and comfort until her call came. But now, she did not quite know what to expect from the future.

Krishnadevi thought of her late husband, Pahlajrai. He had been gone so many years, but she knew that wherever he was, he would be proud of her. After all, had not Pahlajrai been the staunchest supporter of his younger brother, Thanwar, when the latter, as a college student, had expressed his desire to become a *fakir*?

For the first time, Krishnadevi appreciated what her mother-in-law, Varandevi, must have felt when her son declared his most unusual aspiration to her. Varandevi, too, had become a widow at an early age. And Thanwar had been the most brilliant of her five children. But Varandevi had resisted her son's impulse to renounce the world. She had made him promise that, as long as she was alive, he would continue in his career and help her repay her debts; that he would also bring her fame, and some comforts in the evening of what had been a hard life. Thanwar Lilaram Vaswani had fulfilled all her wishes, and her last words to him had been, 'I die a happy woman, for now I realize that you, my son, are a saint of God!'

That very day, Sadhu Vaswani had sent in his resignation as the principal of Mahendra College, Patiala. Discarding his robes of a principal and his brilliant career, he had walked out into the unknown, to pour his life out in love and sacrifice to the God he saw in suffering humanity. Sadhu Vaswani was barely forty years old when he found the freedom to live the life of his choice.

Krishnadevi did not want Jashan to wait until her death in order to be free to follow his heart. It was better to let him go his way and realize his dreams while she was still around to see it. But, it was not something that she had been able to accept easily. To reassure herself, she had taken Jashan to a renowned astrologer. He had pored over Jashan's horoscope and then minutely examined his palms and even the soles of his feet. Then he had announced, triumphantly, that, within a year, the young man would be married. Jashan, in a soft but adamant tone, had insisted that that would not be. But the astrologer had seemed confident.

Krishnadevi understood that Jashan was very clear about what he wanted. She came away from the astrologer with a lingering doubt. Perhaps, in her mind, there also lurked some resentment at the power her brother-in-law had over her son. She had even complained to a family friend that she had brought up Jashan with so much of struggle, only to see him taken over by his uncle. This friend had repeated those words to Sadhu Vaswani in Hyderabad, and he had sent Jashan right back to Karachi to serve his mother.

Jashan was just twenty-one years old. Closing her eyes Krishnadevi prayed fervently that she would live to see this beautiful flower bloom and spread its fragrance while she was still alive. This was the greatest sacrifice that she would ever make. This was her *seva*, her *tapas*, her *dana* to humanity; this was her surrender to the Supreme Will. Jashan was brilliant. He was pure and truthful. He was firm of resolve. His compassion for all creatures knew no bounds, and his yearning for the spiritual had only grown stronger with each passing year. He was drawn to a Master who, although his uncle, was also one of the most revered, admired, and sought-after figures, not only in Sind but in other parts of India as well. Surely, then, she had nothing to fear. Only good could come from all this. Besides, there was a higher power at work, compelling the events in which she was just one player. Of that she was certain.

Taking up her pen, Krishna Devi wrote a note to Sadhu Vaswani entrusting her greatest treasure to him. That letter Sadhu Vaswani was to keep with him until the end of his days.

It is said that the force that brings the Guru and the disciple together is more tremendous than the force of gravitation. Without any coaxing or supplication on his part, Jashan received the permission of his mother to serve his Master. And that was vital, for without her unconditional blessings, his Master would never have accepted him. Letter in hand, he left for Hyderabad at once.

Sitting in the train, Jashan was lost in reverie. His heart felt light. He did not think of the future and what it would bring. All he knew was that he wanted to serve his Master with every breath in his body, at every moment of his life. For him, fulfilment was to be in the sacred presence of his Master, to drink in his nectarine words, to learn from his every gesture, as also from his silence.

Sadhu Vaswani had said, 'True life is that which is lived in the depths. It is life in the spirit.' And this life in the spirit was not some life tucked away in a cave in the mountains. It was a life of dynamic action, rooted in compassion and courage, as lived by Sadhu Vaswani himself. Having renounced his family, home, and career, Sadhu Vaswani was better able to dedicate himself, single-pointedly and selflessly, to the welfare of others.

Sadhu Vaswani had chosen to serve the nation through awakening the youth to the ideals of the rishis, through the emancipation of women, and through service of the poor and suffering, which included animals, birds, and fish. Above all, he sought to awaken people to life of the spirit and become truly free. For true freedom, he emphasized, was only for him who had mastered himself. Gradually, an ever-widening circle of devotees and disciples had grown around him in Hyderabad, Sind.

Jashan knew that no government service or profession would enable him to serve and contribute to national life as much as the spiritual path would. Had Sadhu Vaswani not repeatedly stressed, 'Share the best in you with others. Some day this body, this earthly house, will perish, but it has been built for spiritual ends. The spiritual values of life will persist when all else has passed away. Share them with others! Alexander and his kingdom have passed away. On the other hand, the great ones like Plato, Jesus, Buddha, Sri Krishna, Sri Rama, Guru Nanak, Sri Chaitanya, and Mahavira, their kingdoms endure: they conquered the mind.'

Jashan understood that his own life would be one of abundance and richness, of joy and fullness, if he dedicated himself to his highest ideal – Sadhu Vaswani. He also knew that his death would be, in the words of his Master, 'Richer, nobler, and more serene than it could ever be otherwise.' The quest that had begun in childhood had evolved in the most natural way to culminate at the feet of his Master. Sadhu Vaswani was the Pole Star that would continue to guide his voyage on the stormy sea of life.

THE SEEKER

Love the world, and you become worldly.
Love the Lord, and you will grow Godlike!

J. P. Vaswani

2

THE EARLY YEARS

*If there is a language, which the deaf can hear and the
blind can see, it is the language of love!*

J. P. Vaswani

According to the Hindu belief, a *jiva* (embodied soul) chooses the family that it takes birth in because of the environment that it will provide for its mission or evolution on the earth plane. The Vaswani family was well-known for three things – learning and erudition; social service and social reform; and, simplicity and love for God. It was in this family that Jashan Pahlajrai Vaswani was born on 2nd August, 1918.

On a hot afternoon, while the sun beat down relentlessly upon the dusty lanes of Hyderabad, Sind, Krishnadevi gave birth to her first son. Pahlajrai, the young father, anxiously waiting in the adjoining room, heard the cry of the infant and murmured a prayer of relief and thanksgiving. It was 2:00 p.m. Taking his two little girls, Shakuntala and Hari, by the hand, he tiptoed into the chamber where Krishnadevi lay, exhausted but blissfully happy, holding the precious bundle beside her.

Pahlajrai held his newborn son in his arms and gazed at him in rapture. How serene and radiant he looked. The little girls gently touched their brother's head in a loving gesture. 'Jashan,' whispered Krishnadevi, 'he is our little jashan (celebration).' Pahlajrai nodded in agreement. This was, indeed, reason for celebration and festivity. His heart seemed to be overflowing and he thought of what he would offer the poor in order to share his joy with them and express his gratitude to the Lord.

As per the custom, six days later, the Brahmin was invited to name the baby and to prepare his horoscope. The child was named Veeru, which means brave. But the family continued to call him Jashan. The name was to stick with him because he was exceptionally loving, joyful, and the beloved of all the members of the family. Even though Krishnadevi had four more children after him (three sons and a daughter) Jashan always occupied a very special place in her heart.

When Jashan was born, Pahlajrai was working at the Hyderabad Training College for Teachers. Unlike many of his contemporaries, he was fluent in English and wrote well. His Sindhi was of a highly literary level, and he revelled in the poems of the great Sindhi poets, such as Shah Abdul Latif. Pahlajrai was also proficient in Persian, and he loved reading the works of Rumi and Hafiz, the mystic poets of Iran. Because of his gift of oratory, he was often asked to address various meetings, which he did with ease and pleasure. He was outgoing and easy to be with.

When he was not teaching, Pahlajrai was a devoted social worker and reformer. He started the Social Service League in Karachi shortly after Jashan's birth. It was the only important institution of social work in the city at that time. Among other things, it ran a night school for the underprivileged, particularly for male domestic workers who sought to better their prospects. At other times, he would organize aid for those stricken by flood or famine, the two recurring natural disasters, which perennially affected one or the other part of Sind. Pahlajrai would visit these areas with a band of young people, despite the fact that his own health was delicate. Imbued with the ideal of service, he refused to rest when urged by his well-wishers, declaring that the body would itself take rest, when the time came. Because of his many initiatives in social work, Pahlajrai came to be highly respected in the community, and was looked upon as a role model by many.

Jashan's birth brought great joy to another very special member of the family – the beloved younger brother of Pahlajrai, Thanwar Lilaram Vaswani. Professor Vaswani was then principal of Mahendra College, Patiala. He had established a formidable reputation for himself in many parts of India as a scholar, orator, and teacher. He was widely published and greatly respected by students and faculty members alike, for his erudition and his great spiritual inclination. Above all, he was loved for his great compassion and kindness towards everyone including birds and animals.

Pahlajrai shared a very deep and close bond of love and friendship with his brother. This had only strengthened with the loss of their father when they were both still in school. Professor Vaswani had been overjoyed at receiving the news of his nephew's birth, but it was only some months later, during the vacations, that he could visit Hyderabad and see the child.

Baby Jashan was put in his loving uncle's lap as the family looked on with pride and joy. The uncle gazed at his nephew intently while the little one looked back at him with his bright serene eyes. For one brief, shining moment, there was complete silence and stillness. A gentle smile played on Professor Vaswani's lips, and he seemed to murmur something. A divine moment, thought Pahlajrai; there could be no better gift for the child than the benedictions of this man of God, his brother. Little could Pahlajrai have fathomed then, how destiny's plan had already begun to unfold. Did some wordless communication take place at this moment between the Guru and his future disciple?

Professor Vaswani put his hand on the child's head invoking the Lord's Grace on him. In the tiny hands, he placed a hundred-rupee note, a great fortune in those days. Years later, J. P. Vaswani would jokingly claim that, with that hundred-rupee note, Professor Vaswani had actually bought him.

Jashan grew up in a happy and loving home. Visitors were many and frequent – teachers, social workers, and neighbours, seeking advice or guidance from Pahlajrai, or simply in search of solace. Pahlajrai received everyone with warmth and sympathy. Each one was given a patient hearing. His reserves of energy and goodwill seemed endless. Krishnadevi was, naturally, expected to extend hospitality to one and all, which sometimes proved very daunting. But she always rose to the occasion, and the children learned the ability to juggle many activities at the same time from their parents.

Krishnadevi found in her husband, a great support. Pahlajrai encouraged her to give up the purdah and the traditional long skirts that Sindhi women wore. Instead, he urged her to wear the sari and go about without her head covered. Although, initially shocked and hesitant, Krishadevi gradually grew in self-confidence because of the support and open-mindedness of her husband. When she did go out in the streets, people would come out onto their balconies to look at her, for she represented a rare sight indeed. Women secretly admired her for the freedom that she enjoyed.

Pahlajrai considered the Sindhi women of his time to be bound in chains and he felt those chains needed to be broken. He advocated that women who were often more gifted than their menfolk, needed an opportunity to develop their talents for the benefit of society. As the supervisor of all the primary schools in Karachi, he encouraged women to work as primary school teachers. He was convinced that they would do a better job than men who, at that time, mainly fulfilled that role. Therefore, whenever the occasion presented itself, Pahlajrai filled in such vacancies with women. Several such women became the heads of primary schools.

As the eldest son, Jashan was indulged by all. His two older sisters doted on him and sought to include him in all that they did. That, sometimes, unwittingly, led him into trouble. Once, on the occasion of Durga Ashtami, a puja was being performed in a neighbour's house. All the little girls, *kumaris*, of the locality were invited to be present and they were told that each of them would receive a two-anna coin. Shakuntala and Hari, eager that their little brother, too, should get the two annas along with them, decided to dress him up as a girl. So, three-year-old Jashan was dressed in a skirt and blouse, and, being tiny and delicate, he looked like a pretty little girl. Feeling immensely pleased with himself because of the compliments his sisters paid him, he accompanied them enthusiastically to the puja.

When the puja was over, all the little girls lined up to receive their coins. As Jashan moved ahead in the line and received his coin in the palm of his hand, his sisters behind couldn't help giggling. This made the host suspicious. He stared hard at little Jashan and then catching hold of him, shook him and said, 'You think you can fool me? How dare you come here dressed as a girl! That is cheating.' He snatched the coin back and gave Jashan a slap.

Jashan felt humiliated and, with tears smarting in his eyes, he rushed outside. His sisters could do nothing to console him. From that moment, there arose in his mind a great distaste for money. He associated it with humiliation, with deceit and violence. It left a deep impression on his very sensitive young mind.

As the son of the supervisor of the Municipal Primary Schools in Karachi, little Jashan was allowed to join the T. C. Sindhi Medium School, unofficially, at the tender age of three, as a special case. Miss Castellino, the nursery school teacher, affectionately nicknamed him 'chuha' (mouse) because he was so tiny and ever alert. What was supposed to be fun and play turned out to be a revelation for Pahlajrai and Krishnadevi, as well as for Miss Castellino. The boy appeared to have an extraordinary ability to grasp things. And he seemed to have an exceptionally focussed mind for his age. Above all, he endeared himself to all with his loving nature.

The child's remarkable aptitude for learning led to two double promotions, enabling him to finish his primary education in three years instead of the usual five. Seeing the abilities of his son, Pahlajrai engaged a tutor to coach him in the English language so that he could be educated in an English medium school. Jashan then joined the Rosary School where he again excelled and received a triple promotion enabling him to join St Patrick's High School at the age of eight.

Although Pahlajrai appreciated the importance of being fluent in English, he was, nevertheless, a great patriot. Heeding the call of freedom fighters such as Aurobindo Ghosh, Lokmanya Tilak, Bipin Chandra Pal, and others who launched the Swadeshi Movement, Pahlajrai abstained from buying goods made in England, as they were detrimental to the Indian cottage industry. He always dressed in traditional Indian clothes made from handspun khadi. None of his children ever wore any article of Western clothing or anything made from cloth manufactured in Britain. This posed no problem for the family, until the day young Jashan developed a fascination for the tie. He thought that the tie was the smartest article of clothing for a boy. It added the final touch of sophistication. Pahlajrai, however, would not hear of it. As far as he was concerned, the tie was a symbol of slavery.

Krishnadevi understood her little boy's longing for the tie and felt that it was just a passing whim. The desire would be out of his system if he were allowed to wear it a couple of times. Knowing the strong views of her husband, though, she, one day, said to Jashan, 'If you are so keen to wear a tie, go ahead and do it, but make sure that you go out from the back staircase, so that your father does not see you.'

'Are you sure that will be alright, Ma?' asked Jashan.

'Of course it will. I know that you will not feel like wearing it more than a couple of times.'

With great excitement, Jashan rushed to his room and put on a tie that a friend had given him. Admiring himself in the mirror, he felt ready to go out and make his mark among his peers. Picking up his school bag, he was about to head for the spiral staircase when he hesitated. A little voice deep within said that this, too, was a form of deceit. 'Should I or shouldn't I?' he debated silently. He paused, and then decided that it wasn't worth it. If he could not do it openly, he was not going to do it at all. Taking the tie off and flinging it aside, he left for school as usual, from the main door.

The value of self-reliance was ingrained in the children in the Vaswani household. Although there was one full-time domestic helper and one part-timer, Pahlajrai expected his children to do their own work. They were expected to fold their own clothes, make their beds, and fetch and carry for themselves. Once, he overheard Jashan ordering the helper to bring him a glass of water. Feeling that such habits should be nipped in the bud, he asked Jashan, 'Have you hurt your hands or feet?'

'No, Baba,' replied Jashan feeling sheepish.

'If you are in perfect health, then please help yourself. And please don't ever order the helper around.'

'Yes, Baba.'

Years later, Jashan was to appreciate this lesson from his father; for self-reliance leads to great inner strength. His parents had, in fact, empowered their children by making them perform little tasks for themselves at home. It would prove handy during the years of struggle that the family would one day have to pass through. But, of course, none could have imagined such things during these happy years of early childhood.

Unlike most Sindhi homes of the time, the Vaswani household was purely vegetarian. Pahlajrai, like his brother, T. L. Vaswani, strongly believed that animals were the younger brothers and sisters of men. They, therefore, needed to be nurtured, rather than slaughtered for the mere gratification of the palate. Eating flesh went against their grain. Jashan grew up with the idea that compassion was not limited to human beings. It extended to every sentient being. At an early age, he saw all creation as sacred, pulsating with life and joy. He understood that human beings could either join in that universal celebration of life, or create disharmony and discord by destruction and violence. This conviction was to become the cornerstone of his teaching later in life.

Another striking feature of the Vaswani household was that the prophets and saviours from all traditions of the world were venerated. Hung on the walls of the home were pictures of Sri Krishna, Sri Rama, of Buddha and Zoroaster, of Guru Nanak and Jesus Christ, among others. Pahlajrai, as a Theosophist, believed in all religions and considered them all as pathways to the same great goal. Moreover, the kind of people that both he and T. L. Vaswani had been exposed to while growing up had also opened their minds and hearts. Pahlajrai had written a number of pamphlets on religion and on many great spiritual figures. He was fond of reading the scriptures of different religions.

Every picture had a story that Jashan would hear from his father or his uncle. The young boy would marvel at the heroism of the Sikh Gurus, of the infinite tenderness and love of St Francis of Assisi. He would marvel at the spirit of renunciation of the Buddha, and the supreme sacrifice of Jesus Christ. Very soon he developed a relationship with each figure on the wall and would often talk to them and share his thoughts with them. However, one among the pictures was within easy reach of little arms, that of Rishi Dayaram, a noble social reformer of Sind and a devout man of God. For him Jashan developed a special affinity.

Often, when everyone in the family would be out of the house, Jashan, who even as a young child loved to be alone, would take the picture down and lie down with it on the cot. Delighting in his solitude, the child would talk to the rishi. Years later he declared to the family that the rishi had taught him three things: simplicity of dress and demeanour, silence, and humility. This familiarity with multiple religious figures and traditions was another trait that was to remain with Jashan throughout his life, making him at ease with people from anywhere in the world. An open mind, a universal outlook, and reverence for all life were gifts that he imbibed from his enlightened parents.

Life in the Vaswani household was the epitome of simplicity, bordering on austerity. Pahlajrai believed that whatever money flowed in was to be shared with the needy. As a result, the family lived with the bare minimum, but what was available in abundance was love. Another thing available in abundance was books. A friend of Pahlajrai owned a bookshop, M. H. Punjabi Booksellers, where Jashan and his siblings were free to go and pick up as many books as they liked. The owner of the bookshop was told that the children had *carte blanche* to do so and Pahlajrai regularly settled the bills. The condition set by Pahlajrai, however, was that all the books would be read and there would be animated discussions on them.

Jashan eagerly looked forward to birthdays, Christmas, and other festive occasions, because he knew that he would receive a collection of books as gifts. Books became his first love and they were to bring him great joy throughout his life. They were the doorway to countless voyages of discovery through time and space, into myriad cultures and phenomenal minds. Books enriched his life, sharpened his thinking, and kept him connected with heroes and ideals that shaped his aspirations and goals. They also enforced a mischievous streak in him.

If there was one thing that young Jashan could not bear, it was arrogance and boastfulness. Nor did he easily accept being compelled to do something that genuinely did not make sense to him. For instance, whenever an elder member of the community visited the house, Krishnadevi would ask Jashan to bow down and touch her/his feet. This just did not make sense to him and he disliked having to do so.

One day, an acquaintance who had a pronounced stammer and who Jashan did not particularly admire, visited their home. As usual, Krishnadevi asked Jashan to touch his feet. Jashan obediently bent over low and discreetly pinched the foot of the visitor. As he straightened up with a very sober expression on his face, the visitor started spluttering and stammering in a most agitated and wild manner. Of course, he was completely incoherent. All that Krishnadevi could make out was that he seemed very angry about something. She felt offended. How dare this man make such a song and dance about a noble gesture made by her young, respectful son. Since the poor man simply could not articulate what had troubled him, Krishnadevi resolved that she would never ask her son to touch anyone's feet again, as it was not even appreciated.

Another time, a neighbour dropped in to visit Jashan's parents. The gentleman would only visit when he needed an audience to listen to his boasts of successful business ventures. He was not in the least interested in anyone of the Vaswani family. All the same, in Pahlajrai he found a kind and sympathetic ear. That evening, Jashan was engrossed in some homework in Geography, when he heard the same familiar voice that he was quite tired of. Feeling sorry for his parents, who out of politeness, felt compelled to waste their time, Jashan walked up to him with his atlas. In all innocence he asked the man, 'Uncle, can you point out your row of buildings on this map of India?'

'What's that?' asked the visitor nonplussed.

'Here is Karachi,' said Jashan pointing to a dot on the map of India. 'Can you show me where is your row of buildings?'

The man evidently got the message, for, shortly thereafter, he left.

The remarkable promise that Jashan had shown in primary school continued in high school, which he joined at the age of eight. His parents recognized that their son was a genius. His English was flawless and fluent. Whatever he heard or read even once was committed to memory and easily recalled whenever required. But what was also clear was that he did not spend any time preparing for exams. As a result, when the exams were at the doorstep, Jashan would get a little concerned and would approach his mother.

'Ma, wake me up early tomorrow morning.'

'At what time shall I wake you up, my darling?'

'At 5:00 a.m.'

In the morning, Krishnadevi would gently shake Jashan. When there was no response, she would remove the blanket and say, 'It's 5 o'clock. Time to wake up!' A very sleepy voice would respond, 'I am waking up!' And Jashan would continue to sleep.

Half an hour later Krishnadevi would discover that he was still asleep. So she would shake him again, this time a little more forcefully, until, irritated, Jashan would sit up in his bed and complain, 'Why are you shaking me like that? I am not some plank of wood!'

Then getting out of bed, he would pick up his books and start studying. Everything else would fade out of his mind as he applied himself with single-pointed attention. It was a wonder that he managed to pass with such minimal study. When the results would be declared, Jashan would rush to Krishnadevi and joyfully announce, 'Ma our efforts did not go in vain. I passed in my examinations!'

Jashan was as young as eight years old when he understood that to achieve something good one had to forego some comfort and ease. Giving up his sleep and waking up earlier than usual was the price to pay for passing exams, without preparing for them throughout the year. It was clear that Jashan always secured high marks in subjects that required intelligence, but did not fare quite so well in those that required detailed study. His father was patient with him, recognizing that his son had an insatiable thirst for knowledge, and that his learning was not restricted to the classroom.

Pahlajrai often took Jashan along to meetings and to talks that he was invited to give in the various leagues with which he was associated. The young boy, whose mind was developed way beyond his eight years, was a keen observer at all these events. His constant questions to his father about the Theosophical Society, about his social work and about the books that he had read, showed how much he reflected upon all that he saw and heard. The father found in him a wonderful little companion. People who saw the young boy, ever so often, alongside his father called him jocularly, 'The Prince of Wales.'

Jashan would also sometimes accompany his father to the night school. On one such visit he had his first experience of fear. Pahlajrai settled the young boy in a room while he went to check the class. Left to himself, Jashan explored the room and found a typewriter. Feeling very grown up, he sat down before it and began moving his fingers on the keys. Suddenly the keys stopped moving and Jashan froze in terror. He felt he had broken the typewriter. His initial reaction was to run away. But then he realized that that would not be the correct thing to do. Meanwhile, the principal of the school happened to look into the room. On seeing Jashan and the expression on his face, he kindly asked him, 'Why do you look so confused and unhappy?'

'I have broken the typewriter,' blurted out Jashan, close to tears.

'Don't worry,' came the reassuring reply, 'there is a

mechanic on the premises attending the night school. He
will repair it.'

Jashan heaved a sigh of relief. As he sat back in his chair,
he realized that when one faces fear and acknowledges the
problem, the solution invariably comes.

Waiting for his father, he leaned out of the window and
saw someone with a lighted torch in his hand lighting the
lamps on the road. Karachi, in those days, had no lights on
the roads. After dark, lanterns were lit. Jashan observed how
from one flame so many lamps were being lit. And how the
man carrying the flaming torch, after having completed his
task, suddenly disappeared into the night.

Jashan was lost in reverie. He decided that when he grew
up, instead of being a tram driver, he would be the lighter of
lamps. Having lighted many lamps, he would then disappear.

3

THE INFLUENCE OF
SADHU VASWANI

All good things come from God!
And they come like the tide
At their own right time!

J. P. Vaswani

The greatest influence on Jashan, while growing up, was that of his beloved uncle, Professor Vaswani. Destiny seemed to link the two from the very beginning, for, shortly after Jashan's arrival in the world, Sadhu Vaswani, too, was born into a new life. This happened when Varandevi, mother of Sadhu Vaswani and paternal grandmother of the baby Jashan, passed away, releasing Professor Vaswani of his pledge to her. Renouncing his career, Professor Vaswani had taken to the life of a fakir. For the next couple of years he would wander from place to place, but always spend time in Karachi with his brother and his family, every now and then. Eventually, because of his role in the Freedom Movement, and his dedication to social service and the spiritual upliftment of society, he came to be addressed as Sadhu Vaswani.

Jashan and his siblings loved it when Sadhu Vaswani was around, for he played games with them, and listened, with love and patience, to their little woes. And, best of all, when they were scolded by one or the other of their parents, they were sure of finding in him a staunch supporter, who would see things from their point of view. Sadhu Vaswani loved children. He would say, 'Does God not come in the little ones to teach our hard and wayward hearts? God is radiant in the roses and in the rosy faces of little children.'

The children admired and worshipped their uncle. Jashan could never remember an instance when his uncle had been impatient or cross with them. He seemed like a perennial fountain of love.

One evening, Jashan and his sister were playing their favourite game of word-making (an earlier version of scrabble) with their uncle. In the course of the game, Jashan had made the word 'man'. When Sadhu Vaswani's turn came, he drew the letter 'E'. Jashan's heart beat fast. He knew that his uncle would now take his word and improve upon it. But, to his surprise, Sadhu Vaswani did not even look at his word. Instead, he looked at the alphabets that were lying at the centre and made another word without using his 'E'. The moment he had done that, Jashan cried out triumphantly:

'It's so simple, Dada, you could have taken my word and made m-e-a-n.'

'Not only m-e-a-n, I could have made n-a-m-e.' And he gave examples of other words that had been possible with that 'E'.

'Then why didn't you do that, Dada?' asked Jashan, quite taken aback.

'Because, my child, Dada never takes, Dada only gives,' said Sadhu Vaswani with a loving smile.

Those words made a deep impression on the eight-year-old Jashan. Later that night, as he lay in bed, his mind kept repeating those words: 'Dada never takes, Dada only gives.'

He began to understand that while it is easy to receive, it requires true greatness to give. He, too, felt that he wanted to be a giver. But what did he have to give? How he wished that he could have an opportunity to give something meaningful to someone.

Such an opportunity soon presented itself. Every day on his way to school and back, Jashan would pass by a toyshop and pause to admire a toy train displayed in the shop window. How he wished he could purchase it. Once, he had even dared to enter the shop and ask how much it cost. The shopkeeper had said that it was for fourteen annas. That was a small fortune and Jashan knew that it was way beyond his means. The toy train had made such an impression on him that the desire to own it grew steadily stronger. It was like a seed that had sprouted and seemed to be growing bigger day by day.

On August 2nd, his birthday, his mother gave him a one-rupee coin as a gift. Instantly, he thought, with glee, that the toy train would now be his. Rushing out he made a beeline for the shop. As he rounded the corner and reached the shop, he saw a distraught beggar woman with a sick child in her arms. 'Oh give me a rupee, little sahib, just one rupee so that I can get treatment for my child. Have pity, little sahib, on this innocent one who is so sick and who will die if not treated.'

For a split second Jashan felt exasperated. Why did she have to be there just on that one day when he was going to fulfil his heart's desire? Ignoring her, he rushed into the shop and declared that he wanted to buy the toy train. Would the shopkeeper give him a demonstration of how it worked?

Jashan was thrilled when he saw the engine chug along the rails, pulling its many bogeys behind. How smoothly it sped round and round the tracks. Then he looked up and saw the woman through the shop window. She was weeping and begging from all who passed by. None paid any heed to her. He could not bear it. How pitiable! Here was a mother weeping for the life of her child and no one seemed to care. Mumbling something to the shopkeeper, he rushed out and put the one-rupee coin in her hands. Her face lit up with so much gratitude and relief. She blessed him over and over again with her head bowed and palms joined together. Suddenly, Jashan realized that her joy was a far more precious gift than the toy train could ever be. He walked home feeling light and happy. He had lost his one rupee and the toy train, but a child had probably gained a new lease of life.

Sometimes, Jashan's generosity proved to be very trying for his mother. One Sunday, Krishnadevi, while preparing curry, discovered that she had run short of jaggery. Calling out to Jashan, she said, 'Take this two-anna coin. Run across to the nearby shop and bring some jaggery, soon!'

Briskly walking towards the bazaar, Jashan saw a crowd of people. Curious to know what was happening he made his way into the crowd and found a man entertaining the crowd with his pet monkey. The crowd clapped and cheered, as the pert little monkey performed its clever tricks. Totally engrossed in the show, Jashan lost track of the time and completely forgot about the jaggery.

At the end of the show the man lifted up the little monkey on to his shoulder, and came around with his bowl. He told the people that his little monkey was ill and required immediate treatment. He also needed to buy food for it so that it could be healthy and strong. Would the generous people who had watched it perform, offer something for the poor creature?

Jashan's tender little heart melted at those words. If he had a hundred-rupee note then, he would have happily given it away for the monkey. As it happened, he only had with him the two-anna coin clutched tightly in his little hand. He opened his hand and looked at it, momentarily forgetting how it came to be there. Happily parting with it when the man brought his bowl around, he headed home and only remembered the jaggery when he saw his mother waiting impatiently at the door.

Krishnadevi was most annoyed, but seeing Jashan's expression so full of dismay and regret, her heart soon melted. She could never remain angry with him for long. She knew that he wore his heart on his sleeve. Was his father not exactly like that?

Krishnadevi had also begun to notice how her beloved son would frequently give away foodstuffs and other articles from the house to a passing beggar or a needy one. He would even go as far as giving away his own portion of food if he heard the cry of a hungry man on the street when he was about to start eating. She never questioned him, being large-hearted as she was. But she observed his qualities of head and heart and, deep within, was proud of his sterling character.

It also became increasingly clear to Krishnadevi that Jashan and his sister Hari were growing extremely attached to Sadhu Vaswani. Every time the latter had to depart after a visit, Hari would weep her heart out. To humour and console her, Sadhu Vaswani would lovingly extend his stay by a day or two. Jashan, on the other hand, would become pensive and silent, as though withdrawing into himself to reflect on the many long conversations he had begun to have with his uncle.

Sadhu Vaswani had a rich inner life, and his stories of great men and women from all periods of history, and from all places around the world, were endless. These stories evoked wonder and admiration in the hearts of his nephews and nieces. It was so easy to talk to him.

'Dada, why do they call you 'sadhu'?' asked Jashan one day.

'Well that only they know, who address me as such. I am not worthy of that title.'

'But they must have a reason. What is so special about a sadhu?' persisted Jashan.

'Well, generally, a sadhu or a fakir is one who has devoted his life to God. He has no career and no family, and so he is not tied to any place and to anyone. He wanders from place to place helping those who are in need, for he sees God in everyone and everything.'

'But are we not your family?' asked Jashan in surprise.

'Yes, my child, you are, but so are all the others – the poor, the suffering, the birds, the animals, and fishes in the sea. They, too, are my family and I love them all equally.'

'Did you meet many sadhus when you were little like me?' asked Jashan.

'So many.'

'Like who, for example?' continued Jashan.

'Well, one extraordinary one was Sadhu Hiranand,' began Sadhu Vaswani. 'I met him when I was eight years old. He was the principal of the school I went to called The Academy.'

'Why was he extraordinary?' asked Jashan, sitting up with full attention.

'You see, when he graduated from college in Calcutta, Sadhu Hiranand did not seek a well-paid job as all young men would do. Instead, he returned to Sind because he wanted to do something for his people. He established a new school, where he gave the greatest importance to character building. "Studies are important," he would say, "but good character is far more vital. If you have a good character, you will always do great work in life, and it will benefit not only you but all those around you.'"

'And what did he make you do to develop good character?'

'Well, Sadhu Hiranand taught us that the most important thing in life was truthfulness and honesty. He taught us the importance of daily prayer. He made us understand that if we prayed everyday we would never be afraid of anything.'

'Hmmm,' said Jashan.

'He made us understand how important it was to help those who were less fortunate than ourselves. He would say that prayer is not complete without service to the poor,' continued Sadhu Vaswani.

'How did he serve the poor?' asked Jashan.

'Well, he created a group called the Band of Hope and many of us young boys became members. We would go around the city creating awareness against the evils of drinking and gambling. So many families were unhappy because of these terrible habits among their menfolk. Money, instead of being used to pay school fees, or to buy food and clothing, was diverted to drinking and gambling. So families were unhappy.'

'Then,' continued Sadhu Vaswani, 'because he wanted to help the sick, he studied homoeopathy. Then he would visit the homes of the sick and the poor giving free medicine to those who were suffering. In 1892, an epidemic of cholera broke out in Hyderabad and thousands of people died. Sadhu Hiranand went around comforting and consoling the people, giving them medicines and other kinds of help.'

'And did he cure all the people?'

'Many. When he could not cure, he consoled them and shared their grief. He also cured me of an eye ailment which was troubling me, and I have never had problems with my eyes again, even though I read and write all the time,' replied Sadhu Vaswani.

'Is that why he became a sadhu?'

'He never *became* a sadhu. It is people, who out of love and reverence for him, started calling him sadhu. Unfortunately, he died when he was only thirty years old.'

'How old were you, Dada, when he died?'

'I was fourteen. I can never ever repay the debt that I owe him. For he touched my life and it was never the same again.'

'What is the difference between a sadhu and other great men?' asked Jashan.

'You see, my child, a sadhu is a very humble soul. He does everything for others in a simple and quiet way. He never looks for praise and recognition and he lives for others. Other great men shine as meteors. They flash in the firmament of life and then pass away. But the sadhu's life is like a flame that continues to burn brightly. He gives of himself generously to everyone and so, even when he leaves his body, he continues to live in the hearts of others.'

'And how can you tell when someone only lives for others?' asked Jashan.

'When a person dedicates himself to a cause and not to a career!' said Sadhu Vaswani, softly.

With that, Sadhu Vaswani lapsed into silence with a far-away look in his eyes. Jashan, too, was silent. His heart felt drawn towards Sadhu Hiranand. For days on end, Jashan thought about all that he had heard of this noble man. He repeated to himself what Sadhu Vaswani had said about those who live for others – '*When a person dedicates himself to a cause and not to a career!*'

Such stories inspired Jashan to resolve to do at least one good deed a day. An occasional good deed was simply not enough. Once, after a very hectic day at school, he returned home very late and completely exhausted. As he slipped into his cozy bed, he recapitulated the events of the day. To his surprise, he found that he had not done a single, selfless, good act the whole day. Springing up from bed, he went out of the house in search of an opportunity to serve. Weary and tired, he could not think of any good turn he could render to someone in need. Just to keep up his vow, he picked up an ant very carefully, put it in a puddle of water then, very benevolently, he placed his finger under the struggling ant and rescued it! He realized that it was just a mock situation he had created, but at least he had kept his word.

On another occasion Sadhu Vaswani spoke to Jashan about Dr Annie Besant. He described how he had been so impressed and inspired by her oratory, as a young lad, that he had wanted to become a public speaker of her stature. In order to get started, he had gone alone to the banks of the Phuleli River in Hyderabad and given his first talk to the wind and waters. He described how he had, thereby, discovered his natural gift of eloquence. Jashan listened with fascination. He, too, wished he could be a powerful and inspiring speaker like his father and his uncle.

The opportunity to make such a beginning came soon enough. An elocution competition was announced in school and Jashan was asked to take part. He prepared a well-worded speech but felt that he must practice speaking it aloud. Feeling the need for some privacy, he created a tent for himself by draping his mother's saree around the four legs of a cot. Settling himself inside and thinking that no one could see him or hear him, he raised his voice imagining that he was speaking to a huge audience.

He thought that no one was listening to him. But those at home could not help hearing him, and they were amazed at the clarity and conviction with which he spoke. His voice was loud and clear.

On the appointed day, young Jashan walked onto the stage with courage and confidence to give the most marvelous speech that the faculty and students had ever heard. Little did the audience know that this young boy would one day become one of the most acclaimed speakers in the world. Naturally, the first prize went to him. Pahlajrai beamed with pride and joy. He knew that Jashan would go far. Krishnadevi offered silent gratitude to the Lord for this son, who was turning out to be exceptional in more ways than one. He was just eight years old, but his manifold talents were slowly unfolding. And, best of all, they were being acclaimed by his teachers and peers.

Pahlajrai did not shower too much praise on their son. Instead, he would tell Jashan that his success was because of the blessings of his elders, or because of those of his uncle. Or, that it was because of the Grace of the Lord. This he did deliberately, for he recognized that the ego is the most insidious enemy and it must be reigned in from the very beginning.

One evening, while gazing at the picture of Jesus Christ hanging on the wall in his home, Jashan remembered his conversation with Sadhu Vaswani:

'I only learnt about the greatness of Jesus Christ from my Sanskrit teacher in school,' began Sadhu Vaswani one day.

'I thought that the Christians spoke only English,' interrupted young Jashan.

'Well Upadhyay Brahmabandhav had been born a Hindu. He was a Brahmin from Bengal and he had studied all the

Hindu scriptures like the Upanishads and the *Bhagavad Gita* that are written in Sanskrit. Then, later in life, he discovered Jesus Christ and his heart was so filled with love and yearning for Jesus that he converted to Christianity.'

'Would you say that he, too, was a sadhu?' enquired Jashan.

'Absolutely. He was a Christian *sanyasi*.'

'What did he tell you about Jesus Christ?'

And Sadhu Vaswani had gone on to describe the story of Christ who died on the cross, forgiving the sins of those who crucified him. The part about him begging for water in his dying agony, with none to quench his thirst moved Sadhu Vaswani to tears. He would tell the story so vividly and with so much feeling that even Jashan could hardly hold back his tears, so moved was he.

'But uncle, are there many Hindus who worship Jesus Christ?'

'A true Hindu worships everything and everyone. So does a true Christian. For the man of God sees God in everyone and everything. The great Ramakrishna Paramahamsa always kept a photograph of Jesus on his altar.'

'What else did Upadhyay Brahmabandhav* teach you?' continued Jashan, fully tuned in to what his uncle was saying.

'He introduced me to the greatest literature of the world, the *Bhagavad Gita* and also the Upanishads. What inspiration and exultation have I derived from these texts!' And Sadhu Vaswani was overcome with emotion and lapsed into silence once again.

In the evenings, Pahlajrai, Sadhu Vaswani, and the children would often go for a walk along the sea on Clifton

---

*This exceptional man, later in his career, helped establish the Chair of Hindu philosophy at Oxford University.

Beach. While walking, Pahlajrai and his brother would talk about the message of the *Gita* or the *Sukhmani Sahib*. All this flowed from them most naturally and the children, particularly Jashan, absorbed it in the most effortless fashion. The thirst for such knowledge only grew stronger in young Jashan's mind. Everything else would be forgotten in those glorious, unforgettable moments of pure, undiluted bliss.

Krishnadevi began to notice that Jashan was given to prolonged periods of silence. Many a times she would find him sitting quietly in a corner with a far away look in his eyes.

'What are you thinking of, my dearest one?' she would enquire tenderly.

'So many great men ... such great things they have done. How wonderful for those who knew them and walked with them'

'What else?' gently asked Krishnadevi.

'What is the purpose of my life, Ma?' Why have I come here?'

And Krishnadevi never quite knew what to respond to that. 'You will discover that as you grow older,' was all she could say.

The Hindu scriptures emphasize that the foundation of a child's personality are laid in the first seven years of life. The samskaras or values imbibed at this stage become the core of his or her character. Jashan Vaswani was exposed to the highest and the best from his very infancy. Above all, he was shaped and moulded by a living saint. The ideals that took root in his young heart were those that were to determine his future attitudes and aspirations.

4

THE STRUGGLE

Everyday I must try to do something I think I cannot do. That is the way to develop strength, courage and confidence.

J. P. Vaswani

Jashan's carefree childhood came to an abrupt end when he was just ten years old. On 17th April 1929, on the auspicious Ram Navami day, his beloved father, Pahlajrai, passed away. Krishnadevi was left, bereft, with seven young children: sons Jashan, Ram, Hiro, and Harkrishin, and daughters Shakuntala, Hari, and Sundri. The youngest child, Harkrishin, was only six months old.

While Krishnadevi was inconsolable, she also had to deal with her grieving children. Jashan had already experienced the death of his dearest friend, a fellow cub scout called Prem, the previous year. His death had been a great shock to the young boy and had made him even more introspective. Now, the death of his father raised many questions in his mind and there seemed to be no one to answer them. At an early age Jashan came to understand the ephemerality of life. All that he had taken for granted – his father's loving presence, a sense of security and well-being, a happy family – was snatched away in one moment. Was there anything permanent in this world? Was human life all about suffering?

Yet, there had been so many happy moments. Jashan pondered over these questions in the stillness of the night.

The children would keep asking their mother whether she was certain that their father would never return. To console them, Krishnadevi would say, 'If you stay awake the whole night and repeat the holy name, 'Rama! Rama! Rama!' then your father will come. Innocently believing what she said, the children would resolve to do that. But sleep would invariably overtake them, try as they did to resist it.

It was not that Krishnadevi was particularly devoted to Sri Rama. It was just that, shortly before he died, Pahlajrai had ordered a book on Sri Rama, the write-up of which he had read in a newspaper. The author of the book claimed that all those seeking *mukti* were sure to find the means to it by reading this book. So Pahlajrai had promptly sent for it. Upon opening it, he found, on every one of its numerous pages, the sacred name 'Rama' written 108 times. He had commented on it to his wife, amused that a whole book should be devoted to just one word. Moreover, Pahlajrai had also started writing a *Ramayana* in Sindhi especially for the youth. It was a project very dear to his heart. So Sri Rama had figured constantly in his conversations at home. For that reason, Krishnadevi could think of no better way of keeping her children connected with their father. Eventually, all of them, except one, came to terms with the fact that they would not be able to bring their father back.

Of all the children, Shakuntala, the eldest child in the family was the most affected by the father's death. 'How can we live without Father?' she would keep asking. She steadily pined away in grief, and passed away in February 1930, ten months after her father. She was barely sixteen years old.

Many years later Jashan described how, through her, he had realized how sweet the experience of death could be. As she was about to pass away, Shakuntala said to her mother who stood by her side, that Sri Krishna had come to fetch her in a chariot. He invited Shakuntala to get into it and sit by His side.

Krishnadevi wept her heart out for days on end. To console her, kindly neighbours and well-wishers introduced her to Sant Gurmukh Singh, a Punjabi preacher, who would visit Karachi quite often. He persuaded her to keep a *Guru Granth Sahib* in her house and to do *paath* every day. Until then she had not had any special religious routine, but after the demise of her husband, she became an ardent devotee of Guru Nanak. She would spend all her spare time reading the sacred scripture of the Sikhs, which occupied a place of honour in many Sindhi homes.

After Pahlajrai's death, the family was plunged into a severe financial crisis. With his generous heart and many philanthropic activities, Pahlajrai had left little by way of material wealth. Jashan, who had completed two years of high school at the Jesuit English medium St Patrick's School, had to be withdrawn from there as his mother could no longer afford the fees. He was transferred to the N. J. V. High School, a government school, where the medium was both English and Sindhi. Disappointed though he was, Jashan took consolation in the fact that his beloved uncle, Sadhu Vaswani, had also once studied in this school. Sadhu Vaswani had moved from Hyderabad to Karachi with his elder brother, Pahlajrai, after the death of their father. While Pahlajrai taught in a Teacher's Training College in Karachi, Sadhu Vaswani had continued with his schooling in this very school.

The adolescent Jashan had to adapt to much that was new. For one, he could no longer travel in comfort whenever he took the train. All his friends and classmates travelled by the second class or the inter class, which existed in those days. Jashan alone had to take the third class, for that was all that Krishnadevi could afford. Jashan knew he could not ask his mother for more money because he saw how bravely she struggled to make both ends meet. Every penny counted. But third class travel did make him feel inferior to the other boys. Little did he realize at that point that whatever life throws up is a preparation for one's onward journey. It is to equip us for what we are meant to face in the future.

Jashan could never have imagined then, that one day he would find the greatest of joy and pride in travelling the third class, in the company of his revered Master, Sadhu Vaswani. But that was still in the distant future. He was just eleven years old and had to pass through the ups and down of adolescence which is, invariably, a difficult phase. In his case it was compounded by the absence of his father and great financial difficulties at home.

Another change at home was that Krishnadevi no longer kept any domestic help. That ensured that the children had to assist her by running errands more often. Although Jashan was very happy to help his mother, he did go through a brief phase when he resisted some of the things she asked him to do. For instance, he had become very conscious about his 'image' and one of the things he felt to be detrimental to this image was to carry anything heavy while walking on the road. For some reason he felt that it would make him look undignified! He had entered the painful stage of adolescence with its many conflicts and confusions.

One day, Krishnadevi asked him to fetch a tin of ghee from the grocer. Jashan was most embarrassed at the thought of having to walk on the road carrying the tin of ghee, so much so that he refused his mother. It did bother him, though, because he knew in his heart that what he was doing was not something that would have been appreciated by his father.

A few days later, Vishnu, the young son of a family friend, arrived in the house with a large tin of ghee. It was from their family farm and his mother had sent it for Krishnadevi and her children. Krishnadevi thanked Vishnu and, taking Jashan aside, put a coin in his hand to offer as a tip to Vishnu's servant for having carried the tin.

When Vishnu got up to leave, Jashan accompanied him to the door and asked, 'Where is your help?'

'Which help?' asked Vishnu, looking blank.

'The man who carried the tin of ghee. My mother asked me to give him a tip.'

'Why would I need someone to carry the tin for me? I am quite capable of carrying it myself. It's not even heavy!' replied Vishnu with a laugh.

Jashan was shocked when he heard this. He even felt a little ashamed of himself. Vishnu was smart and clever, and Jashan respected him. He also realized that Vishnu did not appear smaller in his eyes for having carried the tin of ghee. On the contrary, he greatly appreciated Vishnu's attitude. Jashan resolved that he, too, would try and inculcate a similar attitude. He recognized that his own attitude was one of false pretension and that was not something to be proud of.

Jashan started questioning everything in his life. When his mother made preparations for her four sons to undergo the sacred thread ceremony (*jania*), Jashan wanted to understand its significance. Having understood that the three threads symbolized the three ideals of compassion, truthfulness, and purity, he refused to wear them unless he was sure that he could bear witness to these ideals. The hapless Krishnadevi did her best to persuade him telling him that it was a sacred tradition that had been followed by his father and grandfather before him. She scolded and pleaded but Jashan refused to wear the thread. Finally, Krishnadevi went ahead with the ceremony for the three younger boys.

Krishnadevi observed these adolescent struggles in her son. In her wisdom she knew that they were but a passing storm and that the rainbow would inevitably appear thereafter. Jashan had never been a source of trouble or anxiety. But he was, after all, a child, and growing up without a father had its very obvious challenges. What she did realize, however, was that a new character trait was manifesting in him, that of strong determination and the ability to remain steadfast to his convictions.

Playing cards had been taboo in the Vaswani household. 'Occupy your mind with more worthwhile things,' Pahlajrai would tell his children. Yet, it was a pastime that was popular with most families. In Jashan's school there was a huge, massively built Pathan who stood outside the school, selling a popular sweet called *gubeet*. He would always encourage the boys to gamble and many, alas, did succumb to the temptation. For several weeks Jashan would pass him resolutely by, tempted neither by the sticky sweet nor by the excited cries of the boys who were gambling with him. One fine day, however, he was irresistibly drawn to see what it was all about. His eager mind, ever ready to learn new things, felt curious. He wanted to see for himself what all this excitement was about and whether he, too, would be affected by it. He played his first game of cards. Much to his great surprise he won the first game; and the second; and the third. Five paise became ten paise, one anna became two annas. Success went to his head. He felt that he was as good at this as he was in his academic work.

Jashan started enjoying the thrill of the game. He became more daring. The game became more exciting and addictive. After a few more wins, Jashan began to lose. And how he lost! He lost as much as fourteen annas which in those days was a considerable fortune, considering that he received just one paisa a day as pocket money (25 paise made four annas and 100 paise made sixteen annas or one rupee). Suddenly, fear and anxiety gripped him. How was he ever going to repay such a large sum? He felt full of remorse. How could he, a scout leader, an outstanding student, and a favourite of his teachers, have let himself be carried away in this fashion? How had he, son of the noble Pahlajrai, succumbed to this temptation? And now he had to face the ruthless threats of the Pathan, impatiently demanding his money. Who was he going to turn to?

Jashan spent some sleepless nights. Had he not already experienced, when he was little, how money was associated with deceit and violence? That incident of the slap had never been forgotten. Then why, oh why had he let himself be carried away thus? He begged the Pathan to give him some more time. But the days went by and Jashan kept avoiding the Pathan. One day, however, the merciless fellow waited for Jashan at a corner. Pouncing on him as he arrived, he shook him by the scruff of his neck. Giving him one last ultimatum, he threatened the frightened boy with dire consequences if he did not stick to the final deadline.

In sheer terror, Jashan went home and quietly took the money from his sister's piggy bank. He felt terrible doing that but he made a solemn promise to himself that he would put every penny of his pocket money back into the bank and slowly repay the whole amount. This he did eventually do, but as an endowment in his sister's name some years after her early demise.

Handing over the required sum to the Pathan the next day, Jashan resolved that never again would he succumb to temptation. It was not worth it. His father in his wisdom had insulated him from such dangerous hobbies. Jashan thought how heartbroken his mother would have been had she known what had happened. And how let down his father would have felt had he been around, for had he not always stressed that playing cards and gambling only whetted the appetite and encouraged greed and risk-taking?

Through his own experiences, young Jashan realized that there are always two choices in life. One is the path of quick gratification which is easy, and which is taken by most people. But it invariably leads to pain and sorrow. The other is the path of resistance, which is hard, and often makes one feel deprived, but it is the path of long-term good. It is the path of self-control and self-discipline but it ultimately leads to peace and contentment. He knew that it was the latter that he sought, and that implied remaining truthful and honest. There was no other way.

Jashan also understood that temptations only serve to strengthen character. Just as the physical muscles are strengthened through daily exercise, so is the mind made strong through resistance to temptation. They help enhance one's hidden spiritual strength and unlock the slumbering powers of the spirit.

Slowly the family adapted to a life without Pahlajrai. The latter's former colleagues created a post for Krishnadevi in the best primary school in Karachi. Since Krishnadevi had no specific qualifications, they started a new subject in school: cookery. Since it was a school only for girls, Krishnadevi found considerable joy in teaching cooking to eager and enthusiastic young girls. This she was to continue doing until her eldest daughter, Hari Devi, joined as an assistant of a school in Sukkur.

Jashan also began to understand how those who live for others continue to live on in the minds of those whose lives they have touched. Although his father was no more, his name continued to command love and reverence. In Jashan's school, there was a peon named Ram Prasad. Much to the surprise of Jashan and his classmates, one fine day they found Ram Prasad seated in the teacher's chair. He had been the most dedicated and sincere student at the night school run by the Social Service League founded by Pahlajrai. Thanks to such an institution, this man had taken a giant step forward in life. Jashan felt a renewed sense of reverence and deep admiration for his beloved father.

5

THE NEED FOR SOLITUDE

The source of energy is within you! It is inexhaustible.
It is the Divine within you!
To contact it, practice silence everyday!

J. P. Vaswani

'Have you ever wondered what makes you unhappy, discontented, dissatisfied, and restless?' asked young Jashan one day, of some of his classmates.

'No. Tell us,' came the prompt response.

'It is a combination of various things. It can be jealousy, resentment of others' success and prosperity; or it may be a persecution complex, the unhealthy attitude that people are deliberately placing obstacles in our path to prevent us from achieving what we desire; it could be an obsessive desire for perfection, the inability to be content with what we are and what we do; and, most importantly, it is due to the needless regret over past decisions, a futile wishing to change the past, which cannot be changed.'

'To put it simply,' continued Jashan, 'we are unhappy because we cannot accept life as it is. We are not satisfied with what we have; we live in the past or fantasize about the future; and, finally, we resist change or, in some cases, we want to change conditions around us.'

Jashan was sharing what he had heard at the Theosophical Society. He had grown up in a home where discussions and conversations had always been conducive to thought and reflection. With the passing away of his father, he acutely felt the absence of such discussions and was, thus, drawn to the regular discourses offered to the public by the Theosophical Society. Pahlajrai had been a regular visitor here but had never specifically encouraged his children to go there. They had been far too young. However, Jashan's Scout Master was connected with the Theosophical Society and had managed to get some space on its premises for the scout meetings. In this way, Jashan had his weekly scout meetings on Saturday after which he would attend the weekly lectures on the *Bhagavad Gita*. These teachings appealed immensely to his reflective and sensitive mind.

Another trait of Jashan's personality that became more evident at this stage was the need for solitude. The sea became his first love. He would go on the weekends to the Manora Islands (small islands at the south of Karachi, forming a protective barrier between the Karachi harbour and the Arabian Sea), where he would sit and watch the heaving and crashing of the waves for hours on end. They seemed so full of anguish, as though yearning to reach somewhere. He compared his mind to the ocean. He, too, was yearning and searching to go somewhere, but where? It was not quite clear. Perhaps it was the search for an understanding about death. If only he could understand what death really meant.

As he continued to gaze at the waves, Jashan also recognized that the turbulence of the waves was only at the surface. Deep within was silence and stillness. So it was with him, he felt sure of it. He only had to reach that depth, but how? There was a growing awareness in him of something deeper and more meaningful to life than what was apparent, but what it was and how it could be experienced was not quite clear. The whole day seemed not enough to spend in contemplation of the sea. The only food that he would eat during the day would be the prasad of *dhodho* (unleavened bread) and chutney offered at midday at the little temple on the island. This he would relish in silence.

What Jashan also enjoyed doing on his own was walking in the Gandhi Gardens. He would often sit by the small stream that flowed through it. Across the stream was a suspension bridge, which shook when anyone walked on it. Jashan loved crossing over the bridge. The swaying movement reminded him of the fragility of life, of the temporality of all things.

Once, when he arrived at the garden he found the entrance to the bridge blocked by a barricade. The bridge had become weak and needed repair. Jashan settled down beside the stream, his eyes scrutinizing the bridge when, suddenly, he saw a nest under it. A little bird darted to and from it, quite oblivious of the danger of the bridge collapsing. Happy and full of faith, she nurtured her newly hatched family in the nest. Jashan watched her with love and fascination and then whispered, 'Little one, do you not know that your life is in danger? The bridge can collapse any time.'

He felt he heard the bird chirp a reply, 'What danger? If something happens to the bridge we will just spread our wings and fly away!'

How wonderful, he thought, to be able to live with such faith and trust. Was there not a Lord above who took care of all His creation? Jashan remembered the saying of the great Roman thinker, Marcus Aurelius, 'If you are disturbed, made unhappy by external things, it is not they that disturb you, but your judgment of them. And it is in your power to wipe out that judgment now.'

Jashan was awestruck. We can escape from unhappiness

and misery. All we have to do when conditions are unfavourable and we cannot change them is to change our attitude, and, thereby, change our life! Jashan wished he could change his attitude and, like the little bird, spread his wings and fly away from sorrow and pain. He wanted to fly away somewhere where he would find answers to his questions, where he would feel the bliss and peace he had seen in the eyes of his father and in those of his revered uncle, Sadhu Vaswani.

The first year after his father's death had been tough. At school there had been another heartbreak, or what Jashan initially perceived as one. It was the day on which the examination results were announced. He had missed the first rank by a whisker, and felt quite despondent.

Walking alone on the beach in search of solace, Jashan met one of his classmates who had secured the 29th rank in a class of thirty. The latter's face shone with joy and a sense of achievement. Enthusiastically, he offered Jashan a sweet. 'I am celebrating my success,' he declared with pride.

'Success?!' inquired Jashan, quite taken aback. 'What are you so happy about?'

'I am so grateful and so relieved that I have passed,' he replied. 'I really thought that I was going to fail. Just a few marks less and I would have had to repeat the year. So don't you think I am lucky?'

'Yes, of course,' stammered Jashan, quite at a loss to understand this reaction.

Taking the sweet that was offered to him, and wishing his classmate a happy evening, Jashan proceeded to the beach. Sitting there and reflecting on what had just happened, he, once again, realized that everything depends on how you perceive things. Here he was so dejected because he had not come first. And there was his classmate who was jubilant simply because he had scraped through his exams. He had wanted nothing more. So it was not the outside circumstances that determined happiness, but how one looked at those circumstances that mattered.

Jashan resolved to be happy, regardless of outside circumstances. He understood that he alone was responsible for his happiness or unhappiness. He had been wasting his time praying for outside circumstances to change. Outside things could never be controlled nor changed. Did not every family and every individual have their share of sorrow, setbacks, and challenges?

There was one thing, however, which always made him feel good. That was doing a deed that would benefit some poor, helpless person. Jashan was acutely conscious of those less fortunate than him. A former classmate of his remembers the following incident:

I was rather the gregarious sort and had many friends. I sat next to Jashan because he had a calm and soothing effect on me. Before the teacher came to class all the other boys would create a mayhem shouting and screaming, but Jashan would sit quietly, absorbed in his book. Even after school was over, all the other children would crowd at the door trying to rush out at the same time, but Jashan would patiently wait, with a smile on his face, for everyone to leave. Our homes were in opposite directions so I never got the chance to see him on the road walking home.

One day, a friend of mine who lived four houses away from Jashan's invited me home for lunch. It was then that I noticed Jashan walking with his head lowered, watching the ground as he walked. Suddenly he bent down and picked up something. My friend and I were right behind him and were curious to see what he had picked up. A man, who had been standing close by watching him, suddenly moved towards the child and demanded that he open his fist.

'Have you picked up some money?' he asked sternly. 'You young boys must learn not to pick up money that is not yours. It is like stealing. You look like a good boy from a good home then why did you do that?'

'Huh, it is nothing,' replied Jashan, acutely embarrassed.

'No you must show me what you have in your hand. I insist.'

Reluctantly, the small fist was opened only to reveal a sharp piece of glass.

'Glass! Why did you pick this up?' asked the man in surprise and disbelief.

The tears quickly gathered in young Jashan's eyes and his tremulous voice said, 'Sir, I was afraid it might pierce the bare feet of some poor man.'

My friend and I were speechless. We never forgot this incident and even now when we recall it, our throats feel choked. Years later, we wondered what had become of Jashan, whether he had become a saint.

That Jashan was different to other children became increasingly clear to his teachers and peers. Yet, few could actually understand the deep insights into life that the young boy was developing.

Jashan and his group of cub scouts would often enact plays. In one such play, the group had to sing a prayer song. While eight members of the group sang in tune, Jashan was

Krishnadevi and Pahlajrai Vaswani, parents of J. P. Vaswani.

12th Karachi Cub Pack, Winners of Jamshed Mehta Shield, 1927.
Little Jashan seated on chair (extreme left).

Professor T. L. Vaswani (later Sadhu Vaswani),
beloved uncle and confidante of Jashan and his siblings.

With the Cub Scouts (Karachi, 1927).
Jashan standing and leaning out of second window from right.

Hyderabad
From left: Sati Thadani, Kala Hathiramani, Shanti, Sadhu Vaswani,
Sundri (Jashan's younger sister), Stanley Jones, Jashan, Gangaram Sajjandas.

Hyderabad (Sind), 1942-43
Spinning khadi as all patriotic Indians did.

Love for solitude and reflection amidst nature.

Ever alert and ever smiling.

completely out of tune. H. R. Lalwani, who was in charge of the group, therefore, asked Jashan to remain silent and merely move his lips. As the Cub Master, Jashan could not be left out of the group altogether. To young Jashan, this pretense amounted to deceit, something that he was not comfortable with. So he decided to approach a music teacher and try to improve his singing.

On the very first day of his singing class, the teacher taught Jashan the scale – *sa-re-ga-ma-pa-dha-ni-sa*. In a sudden flash, Jashan had a profound experience, which he described years later in the following words:

> I was ten years old when I learnt the musical scale, *sa-re-ga-ma-pa-dha-ni-sa*. A strange occurrence took place within me at that time, like a bolt of lightning. I experienced the knowledge of what is the duty of my life.
>
> Each individual is on the level of 'sa'. I told myself, 'Jashan, you are also on the level of 'sa'. 'Sa' comes twice – once at the beginning of the scale, and the other at the end. One 'sa' raises you higher, and the other brings you down. You tell me which 'sa' you are going to hold on to? Many are on the descending 'sa', wherein the mind runs wherever it finds enjoyment. The mind makes us fall. One 'sa' lifts up the man. One should check oneself: am I going up or coming down? Animals are unable to do this. A dog will continue to be a dog. But a man can decide which 'sa' to hold on to.

Along with deep insight, what was also growing in young Jashan was the power of intuition. Once, he misplaced a ten-rupee note that had been given to him as a gift. Despite searching for it high and low he was unable to find it. Finally, he decided to forget about it for a while, certain that it would eventually be found, safely tucked away somewhere.

That night Jashan had a dream in which someone was telling him, 'Child, do not be disturbed. Your note is safe. It will be found at the appropriate time.' On waking up he wondered why he had had such a dream. At the talks he attended at the Theosophical Society, he had once heard said that dreams are due to indigestion. Perhaps it was simply due to that.

As it turned out, some days later, Jashan required money urgently but had no one who he could ask. At the same time, he felt like reading a particular book and decided to look for it. Finding it, he happily opened it and there, among the pages, lay the ten rupees which had been misplaced a few days earlier. This sum of money was of tremendous value in those days. In fact, five rupees was enough to provide good quality groceries for a month.

Sitting back in amazement and gratitude, Jashan reflected on the fact that there always was a higher, guiding power that took care of each one of us. Whatever one needed would come one's way at the appropriate time. There was no point in getting upset over things.

It is at this stage, too, that the seed of a spiritual life was sown in the mind of the young boy. This seed would, one day, grow into a magnificent, towering tree, under which countless men, women, and children, would seek refuge. It happened during a journey from Karachi to Hyderabad that Jashan undertook in the company of one of the teachers of the Sindhi Medium School in which he had studied. He later recalled the incident thus:

When the train began pulling out of the station in Karachi, the Master began talking to me and kept me entertained. We stopped at Drig Road Station, where the halt was a very long one, making it very boring.

It is then that the Master asked me, 'What is the purpose of life?' In the midst of that long and tiring halt, the Master also provided the answer to his own question, 'Attaining God is life's purpose and goal.'
The Master had brought with him *puris* (fried roti) and potato bhaji. We fell upon it with gusto. I don't think I have ever eaten such delicious puris since then.

He continued, 'If one does not attain God, then no matter what good deeds one does – opens institutions, constructs rest houses, digs wells, performs pujas, fasts – it is all in vain. Till then we are no better than animals.'
'We are born first from our mother's womb,' he continued. 'Then we are born again, thanks to the Guru and it is he who shows us the way to God. Till we don't attain God, we are trapped in the lower self, to be smashed and ground in this world. We have to bear a lot due to the law of karma – what you sow, so shall you reap. If something bitter is sown, one cannot expect to reap a sweet mango from it!'

6

THE TEENAGER

Debates and discussions cannot prove the truth of life.
Only experience can. You know whether a shoe fits you
only by wearing it!

J. P. Vaswani

In 1931, at the age of thirteen, Jashan Vaswani joined D. J. Sind College to begin his undergraduate studies. He was three years younger than his classmates. Because of his short stature, and the fact that he continued to wear shorts as he had done in school, he stood out among his classmates who were physically far more mature than him.

Jashan Vaswani also stood out for another reason, one that he felt very proud about. His uncle, Sadhu Vaswani, had made a great name for himself in this very college thirty years earlier. He had topped in English and had been the first student from Karachi to win the honour of being awarded the Ellis Scholarship to pursue his MA degree. Some years later, in 1908, at the age of twenty-nine, T. L. Vaswani had joined the faculty of the college as Professor of Philosophy. The Principal of the college, an Irishman called Dr Jackson, had asked Professor Vaswani to substitute for other professors when they were absent. So Professor Vaswani often had occasions to give lectures on History and English as well. The students simply loved his classes. In addition to his regular classes, Professor Vaswani had also started holding evening classes on the *Bhagavad Gita* and the *Sukhmani Sahib*. Gradually, a large group of young admirers formed around him.

With his spiritual bent of mind, Professor Vaswani soon became an able guide for those who had even the slightest spiritual yearning. On popular demand, he set up an ashram in rented rooms in a crowded quarter of Karachi. Here he prepared students to live a life of self-discipline and prayer so that they could eventually become worthy servants of India and humanity. Sitting in silence everyday, in order to attune the spirit to the stillness within, was an essential part of daily life. He taught them to make each word a prayer and each deed a sacrifice.

In 1910, while he was still on the faculty of the College, Professor Vaswani had been invited as a speaker on Hinduism at the World Congress of Religions at Berlin. The speech he gave at that forum on The Four Pillars on which Spiritual Life Must be Based (Self-discipline, Meditation, Serenity and Satsang or the Fellowship with Noble Souls) made a lasting impression on the minds of his Western audience. Professor Vaswani spent six months travelling in Europe meeting scholars, intellectuals, social workers, and men of God. His many public discourses were widely acclaimed.

When he returned to Sind, he had become quite famous all over the country. He was hailed as a scholar and philosopher, as one who was able to put across the teachings of the Upanishads and the *Gita* in a simple, profound, and inspiring way. A growing number of people, officials, scholars, and others, began to attend his lectures. They started referring to him as a rishi and a sadhu. During his six years as faculty of the D. J. Sind College, Professor Vaswani influenced the lives of numerous students and citizens of Karachi.

By the time Jashan joined the college, however, Professor Vaswani's life had taken a different course altogether. Having renounced his career and possessions, Sadhu Vaswani had become a fakir, visiting places of pilgrimages and other holy sites. He was particularly drawn to sacred sites in the rural areas of his native Sind.

In 1920, when Gandhi launched his Non-Cooperation Movement, Professor Vaswani wholeheartedly got associated with it thinking that the new movement would spiritualize the political life of India. He gave it his wholehearted co-operation and promoted the movement through the columns of the *New Times*, a paper that he wrote for. Professor Vaswani organized *hartals* in Karachi and then travelled to various parts of India propagating the message of Mahatma Gandhi. His numerous articles and talks during this period were published as forty short books by Ganesh and Company in Madras in the 1920s. Thus, Professor Vaswani became one of the earliest advocates of the Freedom Movement in Sind. When Lokmanya Tilak and Acharya Karve visited Sind, it was Professor Vaswani who presided over their public meetings and talks.

Professor Vaswani looked at the Freedom Movement as something more than just the ousting of the colonial ruler. To him it included the spiritual upliftment of India, the freeing of the masses from the shackles of poverty, and restoring to them a sense of human dignity. But, when he eventually saw that the actions of politicians and the activities of citizens were far from those inspired by Gandhi's lofty ideals, he turned his focus away from politics. Instead, he turned his attention to education, and other spheres, emphasizing that 'character building is nation building'. It was at this time that people started calling him Sadhu Vaswani, out of love and reverence. He would often say, 'I pray each day that I may be true to the title of Sadhu.'

Jashan Vaswani knew that with such an uncle, much would be expected of him. However, in his heart, he firmly believed that no one could be like Sadhu Vaswani, a towering figure both spiritually and intellectually. Sind definitely had not witnessed such a personality. While fakirs and holy men were plenty, they were not intellectuals and scholars. Similarly, while there were many scholars, they were not men of God. So, Sadhu Vaswani was an exception and he stood out like a lighthouse in the academic and spiritual life of Karachi.

The first year at college was memorable for Jashan in more ways than one. To begin with, he was elected to a student office that gave him access to the library whenever he wanted. He was not restricted by the timings that other students had to adhere to. Moreover, there was no limit to the number of books that he could borrow. Given his voracious appetite for books, this was the most exciting thing in his life. At the same time, Jashan also found another source of reading material, which kept him well supplied with a variety of articles and essays on all kinds of subjects.

In those days, dealers imported vast quantities of foreign newspapers, which, once read, would be made into paper bags for use in shops. Jashan made friends with one such dealer and persuaded him to separate the magazine sections of the old newspapers and sell them to him by weight. As a result, Jashan always had an enormous amount of reading material, which he was able to acquire with the very limited means at his disposal. Not only did his English become impeccable but his powers of expression, too, were honed to a highly literary level.

Jashan was still in his first year of college when the Literary and Debating Society announced an elocution contest. The topic was 'The Life and Work of Mahatma Gandhi'. His friends urged him to take part, confident that he would win the prize. Their enthusiasm was, however, somewhat dampened when they learnt that the debate was open to even the MA students. Among the latter was a reputed debater by the name of K. N. Vaswani. Jashan prepared as well as he could. The topic was interesting and it implied reading and researching, which he relished anyway. So it was the preparation more than the actual event that excited him.

K. N. Vaswani gave a brilliant speech and received a resounding applause. It was clear that he would, as usual, walk away with the first prize. Then young Jashan went on stage. The hall was packed and, having heard the best, many students now seemed to have lost interest. They watched this first-year student, who hardly reached up to the mike. They knew who Jashan Vaswani was but they had not heard him speak before. And then Jashan began his speech. His voice was strong, each word was a message conveyed with clarity and perfect diction. Watching Jashan speak was to witness a transformation before one's eyes. With every sentence he seemed to grow taller. His understanding of Gandhi seemed well beyond his years. It was as though he knew Gandhi intimately. With passion in his voice, intensity in his eyes, he spoke words that seemed to come from the very depths of his heart. Listening to him, the audience felt that these were his own ideas and convictions being given out with urgency and insight.

There was a complete hush in the hall. Nobody wanted to miss even a word, for such power and feeling brought tears to the eyes. No one remained untouched. At the end, Jashan received a standing ovation. He had carried the day and so, the first prize and gold medal went to him. With that first speech, Jashan Vaswani established a reputation for himself in college as an exceptional orator. His seniors looked at him with new respect. He was the outstanding nephew of an outstanding alumnus.

Winning the prize for the talk on Gandhi was gratifying. But, more powerful was the impact that the study and research on the Mahatma had on Jashan's mind. He was deeply impressed by one incident when a man had said to Mahatma Gandhi:

'You are a Mahatma. You have nothing to do with worldly affairs. Why don't you go to a *tapovan* (forest of austerity) and live there? Why are you unnecessarily troubling us, living in this world with your unworldly ideals?'

Mahatma Gandhi smiled and replied, 'My dear brother, I carry the peace of the tapovan within me. I am all the time in the midst of a tapovan. No one can disturb that peace within. No matter how disturbing the external forces are; no matter what criticism or slander is hurled at me, the peace of my tapovan remains within me, always.'

Jashan often repeated to himself the words of Gandhi: 'The seeker after Truth must conquer all fears.' Gandhi emphasized how fear had no place in our hearts when we have shaken off all attachment for wealth, for family, and for the body. All these are not ours but God's. Nothing, whatever, in this world is ours. Even we ourselves are His. Why then, should we entertain any fears?

Jashan was also very moved by some of the things that he read in a biography of Benjamin Franklin. The episode when the nine-year-old Benjamin, travelling on a steamer, sees many fish caught in a net, left a lasting impression on Jashan's mind. Shocked by the panting and wriggling of the fish, Benjamin exclaimed that he never knew that what he ate everyday caused so much agony to the poor creatures. He, then, firmly resolved to be vegetarian. Returning home, he informed his mother never to serve him non-vegetarian food. The mother protested saying that she is not going to be able to cook vegetables for him everyday. Undeterred, he said he will just eat bread. With the few cents his father gives him, Benjamin bought potatoes and ate them with bread everyday until, one day, his mother took pity on him and promised to cook vegetables for him.

Jashan was also impressed by how young Benjamin Franklin had woven self-discipline into his daily life. As a young man, he had prepared a chart on which he divided each hour of the day into four parts of fifteen minutes each. After reserving a certain number of hours for sleep, he assigned a particular activity such as studying, eating, or playing to each of these divisions. He thereby, regulated his life and enhanced his productivity. Best of all, he was able to stick to this discipline.

Throughout college, Jashan won several writing contests announced by local magazines. The first prize would often be a meagre five rupees; but for Jashan who had very limited pocket money and who lived a frugal life, this was always welcome. Five rupees enabled him to buy five books, and sometimes more, if he went to the second-hand bookstores of Karachi. Frugal living did not deter Jashan in his quest for knowledge. Nor did it deny him the pleasure of buying and reading books.

Jashan's prodigious memory, reading habit, and insatiable thirst for knowledge made him, alas, prone to arguments. He found it difficult to accept ideas that appeared foolish, or superficially thought out. Interaction with people around him was an opportunity for him to share what he was constantly acquiring by way of ideas, concepts, and information. But the argumentative side of him proved to be a source of great annoyance to his mother. As he recalls:

> One day, my mother asked me to go out and buy her some coriander powder. I had barely walked a few steps when I met someone I knew on the road. We got into a conversation, and soon, it turned into an argument. Neither he nor I was willing to compromise. I forgot all about the coriander. By then it was afternoon and my worried mother sent my brother to look for me. He finally found me in the lane and urged me to come home. I told him, 'You go, I'm coming.' Once again, we resumed our argument, which continued till the evening. Finally, my mother, in sheer despair, came and, shaking my arm, said, 'Now come home right away. How much will you argue?' She dragged me home.

Sind, at that time, was part of the Mumbai Presidency (from 1847–1935) and the college was, therefore, affiliated to the University of Mumbai. Students from Sind would travel to Mumbai to appear for the Intermediate Arts and Final BA Examinations. The journey by ship took four days.

The first time Jashan travelled to Mumbai was in itself a great experience. The return journey, however, turned out to be unforgettable. Suddenly, a terrible storm arose. Thick clouds appeared in the skies and the day became almost as dark as night. Furious waves lashed against the steamer, making it toss like a paperboat. All the passengers trembled with terror. Were they doomed to a watery grave? In the midst of this dreadful scene sat a little child, barely six years old. He was calm, serene, and undisturbed by the raging storm.

Jashan, who was trying to remain calm, marvelled at this six-year-old's unruffled serenity in the face of death. He went up to him and asked, 'The steamer is about to sink, are you not afraid?'

With a cherubic smile the child answered, 'Why should I be afraid? My father is the captain of the ship!'

Jashan was deeply touched by that reply. Despite the raging storm and the violent tossing of the ship, the child had so much faith in his father. Jashan's mind went back to the time when he was still in primary school. He had been fond of knitting and, one day, his wool had got entangled and knotted all over. Try as he did, he could not set it right. Finally, he had handed it over to his mother and begged her to sort it out for him. How easily she had solved his problem. She had smilingly told him to run out and play and that she would set it all right.

And so it was! When he returned from his play, happy and relaxed, the ball of wool was neatly rolled up, and a neat row of stitches had been added to the needles, to help him begin his knitting anew.

Looking back on that incident Jashan realized that his surrender to his mother had been exactly the same as the surrender of this little boy to his father, the captain of the ship. The secret to a serene life was surrender; surrender to the Divine Father or Mother above, who was the real burden bearer. The power of faith was vital if one wanted to sail the sea of life and not drown. It was essential to strive and do one's best, but fears and anxieties needed to be surrendered. For, did not God have a plan for each one of us? As Swami Vivekananda expressed it so powerfully, 'On my own, I cannot even cross the threshold. But with

God as my support and strength, I can cross the seven seas!'

After one year in the arts stream, which he found quite boring, Jashan moved to the science stream. He chose physics, chemistry, and mathematics as his main subjects and was awarded a distinction in mathematics in the second year. In his final year, he stood first in physics in the whole university.

Krishnadevi could not stop reminding Jashan of the great future that awaited him and how much she looked forward to the day when he would step out into the world and gain name and fame. She felt that the best career for him would be the Indian Civil Services (ICS). The ICS exam was particularly challenging and only the brightest and most gifted of Indian students even attempted it. Jashan's family and teachers believed that Jashan had every chance of making it because of his exceptional track record right through school and college. Moreover, the exam was taken not before the age of twenty-one. Since Jashan would finish college at the age of seventeen, he would have four years to prepare for the exam, giving him an even better chance of success. It was widely accepted that Jashan would do the family proud.

7

The Search for Meaning

*Men are so busy changing conditions and circumstances
that they have no time to change themselves. Until man
learns to change himself, all other change is futile!*

J. P. Vaswani

While Jashan established himself as an outstanding
student in college, excelling in dramatics, debate, and
in the literary society, there was a side to him that hungered
for things of the spirit. The burning need to understand
the deeper meaning of life, which had manifested while
he was still a schoolboy, now became more intense. The
many encounters that he had with holy men, all left a deep
impression on his mind and he would recall each experience
with extreme clarity and precision.

One such memorable encounter took place when he was
just eleven years old. He had been on the train in the same
compartment as a sadhu. Recalling that incident, years
later, J. P. Vaswani described it thus:

I found the sadhu's appearance fascinating. I simply
could not take my eyes off him.

Soon the train stopped at a small station, and
beggars gathered at the window of our compartment.
The saint opened a basket of fruits and gave them all

to the beggars. As I watched, open-mouthed, the basket of fruits was emptied, and the beggars were eating bananas and apples happily, and blessing him aloud. He had not eaten a single fruit himself, but had given them all away.

'May be he doesn't *like* fruits,' I thought to myself, in my childish innocence.

Soon, the train halted again. It was a passenger train, and it moved slowly, stopping at every station. Here, too, beggars surrounded the compartment. This time, he opened a box of sweets and distributed them. And so it went on, at the third and fourth station, more sweets were given away. At the next station, he began to give his food away. So much for my childish notion that he was going to eat all that food on the journey! In truth, he did not eat a thing. All that he had been given, he gave away to the poor and needy, before we had passed six stations!

He sat down in a corner of the berth, and was soon lost in meditation. By now, I was utterly fascinated by him. I moved to sit right opposite him, for I had heard that when people went into meditation, a great power akin to electricity, came into their being, and when they opened their eyes at the end of the meditation, this electric power would emanate from their eyes and be passed on to those who looked into their eyes. And so I sat eagerly before him, waiting to be touched by his magic.

He opened his eyes, and I will never forget the encounter that followed. It was indeed a magical, memorable experience, which left a lasting impression on me. He spoke to me kindly, sweetly, and eloquently. *Sant Bani* and words of wisdom and goodness flowed from his parted lips. It was my earliest introduction to philosophy and mysticism. The hours flew by, and soon, the saint prepared to alight from the train. Alas, I could not get off with him, although I longed to do so!

I got down to see him off, and when he was about to leave the station I touched his feet. In a flash, he too, touched my feet. Reluctantly, I boarded the train, still watching him. A porter approached him and offered to carry his bag. He gave the porter some money, but carried the bag himself.

Suddenly, I remembered a piece of advice given to me by my revered father, 'Whenever you meet a man of God, you must never, ever forget to take a teaching from him.' Here I was, on the train which was about to move, and I had not taken a teaching from this magnetic man of God.

'Swamiji,' I called out to him hastily. Without the least hesitation, he came near the compartment and said, 'Tell me, my child, what can I do for you?'

'Swamiji, I forgot to take a teaching from you – a simple teaching which I can treasure in my heart and bear witness to in daily life,' I said to him.

'But I am not a Swamiji. I am but a simple man,' he interrupted. 'However, I am touched by your piety and reverence, and so I shall share with you the simple teaching that my Guru gave to me.'

'Your Guru!' I exclaimed. 'You are so wonderful, and your Guru must have been a truly great soul.'

'Far from it,' he said. 'My Guru was a humble peasant and this is the teaching he gave me. *Seek only to please God.* I try to live by this teaching, and if you do so too, you will be richly blessed.'

'Thank you, thank you!' I exclaimed, clasping his hands through the window of my compartment. 'By what name shall I refer to you?'

'They call me Narumal Narsinglal Navani,' the man of God replied. 'And remember, in all your affairs and activities, always seek to please God!'

One question that had intrigued Jashan for quite a while was how to pray. He understood that prayer was important, but no one had really explained to him the best way to pray. His mother simply read from the *Guru Granth Sahib* and that did not appeal to him. Other elders in the family were ritualists. They had nothing to offer by way of explanation for what they did. So that, too, was a dead end.

In college, Jashan became a member of a small group called the 'Prayer Circle'. The group met every evening and would collectively study a treatise on prayer written by some authority on the subject. It was intellectually very satisfying. They would discuss the types of prayer; levels of prayer; degrees of prayer; the difference between prayer, meditation, and contemplation. But Jashan never got to the heart of the subject: What did prayer, as a practice, imply in daily life? In other words, while he had gathered a ton of theory, he was zero in practice. Earlier, he used to simply talk to God, in his own words, as he would talk to his late father or his beloved uncle. But now, he felt he was always analyzing his manner of praying and becoming completely self-conscious and stilted. He quit the prayer group and decided that it had only made him realize how intellectual knowledge was a great obstacle to spiritual progress.

Then, one day, Jashan happened to meet a holy man on the outskirts of Karachi. Sitting under a tree, he seemed lost in contemplation. It was his serene countenance that drew Jashan to him. Approaching him, Jashan sat down and gazed upon his face with admiration and longing. The man opened his eyes. They were kind and gentle.

'O teach me to pray!' Jashan beseeched him.

'If you would learn to pray, just go and pray,' came the simple reply.

'But what is the best way to pray?' asked Jashan, determined to find an answer.

'There is no best way, just go and pray.'

'What is the best time for prayer?' continued Jashan. 'And the best place?'

'The best time for prayer is *now*, and the best place for prayer is *here*,' came the reply.

The wise man went on to explain that no learning or education was required to be able to pray. Some of the greatest saints had been completely illiterate. Sri Ramakrishna Paramahamsa, for example, had not even known how to sign his name. Yet he was able to pray for hours together.

Jashan felt humbled. There was much that he gained from books. But there was also much that would never be available in them. It was the book of life that had to be read. Sincere prayer was not dependent on wealth, strength, special rooms and temples, or books. All that was needed was a loving desire to commune with the Lord, in words and thoughts that were spontaneous and sincere.

Many unforgettable encounters happened because of Jashan's love for walking. As a college student he went everywhere by foot. He knew the whole of Karachi because he had visited different parts of the town on foot. As a result, he was always alert to life on the streets. He describes one such incident:

One day, I was caught in a sudden downpour, soon after I set out from home. It was raining in torrents, and I had to seek shelter somewhere. I saw a garden near by and the gardener's cottage, a little hut, stood near the gate. It was invitingly open. I approached the door and asked hesitantly, 'May I come in?'

An old, feeble, dark-skinned gardener sat at a *chulah*, cooking food. Some dal was boiling in an earthenware pot on the smoke fire. The old man was kneading dough.

'Come in, my child,' he greeted me warmly. 'Come and dry yourself. I hope you won't catch a cold.'

I wiped my face and head with my handkerchief and looked around. It was a humble cottage, and there was little to see.

'Will you eat with me?' he asked, kneading the dough vigorously.

I was acutely embarrassed. I hesitated before replying, 'I'm only here for a short while, I shall have to go home when the rain stops.'

'But the food will be ready in no time!' he insisted. 'The dal is nearly done. I have kneaded the *atta*, and the rotis will be ready in a few minutes.'

I stared at the fire. How could I eat dal cooked in a mud pot, and rotis rolled on the floor of the hut? But the gardener was loving and persistent. He would not let me go without eating.

'You have blessed my home by your arrival today. Do you know that our *shastras* tell us that a house is blessed when a guest arrives. Alas, I don't get many guests. And how can I let you go without eating? How can I send Sri Krishna away without offering Him food?'

'I am not Sri Krishna,' I tried to explain politely. 'Actually, my name is Jashan.'

'Yes, dear son,' he laughed. 'you are Jashan; but you carry Sri Krishna within you.'

Puzzled, I said to him, 'How can Sri Krishna be in me? I can't see Him!'

'Well, there are two Jashans in you,' laughed the kind old man. 'One who is looking at the outside world: he is looking at me now. The other is face-to-face with Sri Krishna all the time. Look with the real Jashan and you will see Sri Krishna within!'

I stood speechless with amazement at this startling revelation.

'I think that perhaps, you don't like dal and roti. But just eat this humble meal I am offering you and you will change your mind.'

The gardener and I sat down together to eat a hot meal of *dodo* (thick roti) and simple dal. He served me with great love and affection. I can tell you honestly that the food tasted wonderful! As I ate, I wondered if it was I, Jashan, who was eating it, or Sri Krishna, whom the gardener had seen in me.

'Can I have some more?' I asked him, when I had eaten one roti. He smiled and offered me a second helping of that delicious food. The taste of that food, so lovingly offered, still lingers in my memory. As for his teaching – that Sri Krishna dwells within us – it is etched in my memory forever!'

Unlike boys of his age, who looked forward to vacations away from the city and trips to unknown places for recreation, Jashan longed to commune with fakirs, dervishes, and other holy men. There were periods when his mother would have to go out of town and Jashan would use these opportunities to visit the villages that formed the rural hinterland of Karachi. He would go in search of fakirs and yogis. Jashan would carry no luggage, trusting himself wholly to the loving care of God. He would sleep under a tree and eat a meal at the home of the village headman. It was the custom, then, that any visitor to the village would be treated as a guest by the village *mukhi*. Jashan would think of Sadhu Vaswani who had renounced everything, for always, and he felt happy at being able to experience this temporary renunciation. He yearned to experience that intoxication that the men of God talked of in their poetry, and that he had sometimes seen in the eyes of his beloved uncle.

Once, while walking down a country lane, he saw a man seated by the side of the road. The man observed him carefully as he approached. Jashan felt that he was curious to know the man's thoughts. So, coming up to him, he said, 'Please give me some teaching.' Promptly came the reply, 'Be a lion and not a dog.'

Jashan was quite taken aback. What could such a statement mean? Then, being quick at repartee, he said, 'I am a lion already. My zodiac sign is Leo!'

The man smiled patiently and said, 'The difference between a dog and a lion is that if you throw a ball or a stone at the dog it will run after the ball or the stone. But, if you throw something at the lion, the lion will come and pounce on you. He will not pay attention to what you have thrown.'

'I'm not sure that I understand what you mean, Baba,' said Jashan.

'It means that you don't have to think of all the balls and stones that come your way. In other words, you don't have to flinch at the worries and difficulties that come to you and weigh you down. You have to ask yourself, 'Where are they coming from?' If you ask this question, you will know that everything comes from the holy hands of the Lord. If you become a lion, you will go and catch hold of the Lord. You will not look any further.'

Then came a time when Jashan had the opportunity to actually live for a whole fortnight in the company of a wise one. Convalescing from a serious illness, Jashan had longed to go somewhere for a change of climate but did not know where to go. In answer to his desire, a friend, who knew a man of God, arranged for the latter to invite young Jashan to stay with him. Jashan received a loving letter from his potential host stating that he would be very happy to serve Jashan, share his room and meals with him, and be blessed!

Although astonished to receive such a letter from someone unknown, Jashan, nevertheless, felt intuitively that the meeting was ordained. It was to be with someone who had been a part of his life in some earlier life. He bought his ticket and left with the faith that this vacation would be something meaningful and rich.

As the train steamed into the platform, Jashan looked for his host and recognized him without having ever met him. He knew it was him, for as he looked at him long and deep, a flame kindled in him and he recognized him.

The man greeted Jashan as a father would greet his son and involuntarily, Jashan addressed him as 'Baba'. His abode was clean but spartan. His life was peaceful and humble. A small circle of devotees visited him every evening. Jashan felt that, after many years, he was with someone with whom he could have long meaningful dialogues about life.

One day the holy man suddenly asked Jashan, 'What are you thinking of my son?'

'I don't know, Baba,' cried Jashan, 'I do not know what I am thinking and I do not even know what I need in this wide wonderful world.'

The man looked deep into Jashan's eyes, as though reaching into his heart and reading his deepest concerns.

'May I tell you, my son, what it is that you need? Your need, your greatest need, your one and only need is God.'

'How may I reach Him?' asked Jashan in an anguished tone.

'If you want to draw near to God, turn away from all that stands between you and Him. God and God alone: let that be the watchword of your life. You can't have both things – God and the world. The world will give you many things but will rob you of the peace of mind without which life, even in a palace, becomes a burden. Blessed, indeed, is he in whose heart there is room for nothing save God and whose mind revolves around Him as a planet around the sun.'

'What must I do to be worthy of God?' asked Jashan.

'Two things: one, you must die to all creatures; and two, you must die to your passions,' answered Baba.

'And what is the mark of one who has died to all creatures and to his passions?' continued Jashan, feeling the blood pounding in his veins.

'The man who has died to creatures is free from the least taint of attachment. Such a man expects nothing from anyone. He passes through life asking for nothing, claiming nothing. He is full of gratitude for all that comes to him. And the mark of him who has died to his passions is that he has risen above the pairs of opposites. Pleasure and pain, loss and gain, sunshine and rain, success and failure, praise and censure, health and sickness, heat and cold, mud and gold, all are alike to him. He rejoices in the will of God and is not concerned about himself. His will has been merged in the will of the Divine.'

This teaching was not just some idle talk, for Jashan saw how the Baba lived every word of what he said. One of Baba's sons had fallen in evil company. Baba had tried his best to draw him to the right path, without any success. One day, news came to Baba that the boy had been sent to jail for some petty crime that he had committed. Baba was unperturbed. His face showed not the slightest mark of sorrow or anxiety. One of his friends, who had influence over the police, offered to help, but Baba would not hear of it.

'If the boy remains in jail, the reputation of the family would suffer,' the friend warned.

'Whose family?' Baba calmly asked, 'And whose reputation? These things are as shadows on the wall, bubbles floating on water. One thing alone is real. It is the will of God. And whatever He wills is for our good. If God's will takes the boy to jail, it will surely do him good.'

As it turned out, the jail did, indeed, do a lot of good to Baba's son, for the boy eventually settled down to an honourable life. He married and became a devoted householder.

Living in the uplifting company of Baba, was a continuous learning for Jashan. On one occasion, Jashan asked him, 'You eat just once a day, and that too, so little. Do you not feel hungry?'

'What I share with others,' replied Baba, 'comes back to me tenfold, and I feel full!'

Not only was Baba frugal with his eating, but he also spent very little time sleeping. He was awake for the greater part of the night. Sometimes he would sit in silence, lost in contemplation. At other times he would read aloud from the *Sant Bani*. Jashan, too, tried to stay awake but sleep would invariably overpower him. How he marvelled at Baba and wondered if he, too, would ever be able to make do with such little food and sleep.

When Jashan questioned him about his ability to forego sleep, he laughed and said that being awake had a deeper meaning.

'You should wake up from the slumber of the senses in which you are now mired. The night must come to an end. Do you not realize, my son, that with each passing moment, someone is passing out of the body and starting upon the inevitable journey? Whose turn will come next? Who knows? Wake up! Beware of the temptations of this transient life, and direct your mind and heart to God!'

Jashan felt grateful for all that Baba told him. There was so much to understand, to reflect on. But, before he went back home, he needed to have some guidelines for his daily spiritual practice. He was not quite clear how to put everything that he was listening to into practice. So, one morning, he approached Baba, 'Give me some simple, practical rules whereby I may regulate my daily living and enrich my inner life.'

'I will give you three simple rules. If you follow them faithfully, your life will bloom as a garden in spring, blessing all who cross your path:

1. Talk little or not at all. And when you open your lips, see that your talk is concerning God.
2. Judge no one! Behold the good in all. Everyone whom you see or meet has something to teach you. Learn from him in all humility. Criticize no one! Give

your love to all and give the service of love to all. And, even in your secret thoughts, wish well to all.

3. Do not depart from truth. Though you are cut into pieces, do not flinch in your loyalty to truth.'

That night, Jashan went over these rules over and over again. How inspiring and uplifting it all was. The first rule about talking little or not at all, was perhaps particularly challenging for him, given his inclination to argue. The next morning, he had yet some more questions.

'I feel so restless, again and again,' he confessed. 'Give me some magic formula whereby I may attain the peace of mind.'

Without pausing even for a brief moment, Baba said, 'It is simple. Just keep repeating to yourself:

Whatever has happened is for the best!
Whatever is happening is for the best!
Whatever is to happen is for the best!'

'If you can live by this you will always have inner peace. You see,' he continued, 'the basis of inner tranquility is a child-like trust in God who is our all-loving Mother. Whatever she does is for our good, even though it may sometimes seem to the contrary.'

Baba went on to give an example of a child whose arm needs to be amputated. If the operation is delayed, the child's life is in danger. The mother does not hesitate: she takes him without delay to the hospital. The child does not understand. He weeps and wails and considers his mother to be so cruel. Years later, he realizes the wisdom of his mother's action. He realizes that if the arm had not been amputated, he would have died. He appreciates his mother for having done what she did.

At other times, Jashan learnt to sit in silence with the Baba. For long periods, Baba would be lost in a world beyond the realm of time and space, absorbed in the Beloved. He taught Jashan how to repeat His name and go into the depths within and be absorbed in it.

Reminiscing about him, J. P. Vaswani would later say, 'His words are graven upon the tablet of my heart as with a chisel.'

The world saw Jashan as an exceptionally brilliant, all-round student who stood poised on the threshold of a glorious future. Few, at this point, recognized how the spiritual quest in him had intensified and how destiny was shaping him and preparing him on the journey to the great crossroads, where he would have to choose. One road led him to worldly success. It would be all-consuming. The other was of spiritual success. That, too, would accept no compromise.

8

THE QUEST INTENSIFIES

This is the experience of the time when I used to go and live in silence. I alone know of the disturbance there was in my mind during that time. On the one hand there was the heat of summer, along with the burning of the sun. In that extreme heat, I would wrap myself up in a blanket and go to sleep. Within me was intense restlessness. My insides would burn … I was also filled with anger. I would perspire in the heat and not even eat. One day, mercy was bestowed on me; the sun peeped through the clouds. I beheld a glimpse of that light of the Divine.

It dawned on me, what am I wasting my time on?! I have been given this special jewel in the form of a human birth. What am I losing it on? This human birth is not easy to attain. Human birth comes through good fortune, like drawing lucky lots. All of us have received this human birth through these lucky draws, and are unnecessarily wasting them.

What good deed brought me this gift beautiful,
Don't waste it in being forgetful.
In longing, grab ecstasy's flow
Sing Hari, Hari, Hari Bol.
Make this birth worthwhile.

J. P. Vaswani recalls this phase of his life and explains, 'Seekers of the Spirit often pass through a period of intense anguish. During this evolutionary phase of their spiritual growth, perhaps, they themselves do not know for certain what it is that they are seeking. But seek they do, on the highways and byways of life, for that something that will put an end to their dark night of despair.'

The hand of destiny brought many men of wisdom on Jashan's path. Whereas earlier encounters with holy men had been a source of inspiration and wonder, the encounters that this young seeker now began to have were those that resulted in his adopting specific spiritual practices. These helped him on his journey inwards.

One important encounter was with Anmol Baba, as he was known. He was an eccentric man who talked and behaved in a manner that led most people to think that he was not quite right in the head. His ways were unpredictable, but there was something in his eyes that drew Jashan to him. He had recently moved into town and Jashan would see him every now and then. On an impulse, Jashan had once mentioned to him that if he needed anything he should let Jashan know. It was in the middle of the hot summer and the man had seized the opportunity to say, 'Yes, there is one thing you can do for me. I would like to eat some curd every afternoon. Can you bring me a bowl of curd every day? The condition is that you must make sure that you bring it to me on foot. I don't want you to take the tram or a taxi. Now, when you walk, for every step you take, you must repeat the name of God. If you forget to repeat that even once, then you must retrace your steps. Go back and start again from the point where you are sure you last uttered the name divine.'

This turned out to be a greater challenge than Jashan could have ever imagined. Little had he realized until then, how easily and consistently the mind wanders? Holding on to one thought seemed virtually impossible. As a result, he would spend an extraordinary amount of time everyday to reach the Baba, a distance of three miles by foot. Being honest and sincere, Jashan would always retrace his footsteps. But, sometimes, he even forgot at what point he had stopped repeating the name of God.

Anmol Baba would say, 'Going on pilgrimages and taking baths in sacred waters and other rituals do help the seeker but these are all nothing compared to the repetition of the name of God which is easily accessible to all of us. All you have to do is to repeat it with deep love and longing of the heart, with sincerity and with faith, and it will work wonders. It is the best penance that I know.'

Jashan realized that the Baba was not really interested in curd. He had seen the sincerity of the true seeker in young Jashan and had, in his own way, wanted to help him along on his spiritual quest. He had given him an exercise in concentration and self-awareness. It helped Jashan understand the fickle nature of the mind and how it was not by physical torture that the mind would calm down. It had to be trained in a gentle way; it had to be coaxed and persuaded over and over again to form new habits.

In order to keep the mind focussed, it helped if one felt some love towards God, for the mind naturally dwells on that which it loves. Jashan learnt to repeat the name with sincerity and longing and realized that it was a great way to grow spiritually. Over and over again, Jashan offered gratitude to this simple man who was pure, humble, and true. No one paid any attention to him for he seemed just so ordinary. And no one guessed that, despite the ordinary tasks he did, he was, in fact, a truly holy man. He was God-intoxicated and wanted nothing other than the love for God in his life.

The name of God became Jashan's source of strength and support. Through periods of adversity, of trial and tribulation, the name of God became his refuge.

The practice of *japa*, or repetition of the holy name, was intensified thanks to the influence of yet another holy man. As J. P. Vaswani recalls:

I was young when I received the company of a devotee of God. I became close to this holy person. He had bound me with his love. Anything he would say, I would never find it strange. He made me crazy in his love. The day I did not meet him, I felt I had lost something.

One day he said, 'Dear child, will you do something for me?' I replied, 'Anything you say. I will even pluck the stars for you.' He said, 'Dear one, I don't need anything. But for my sake keep repeating the name of the Lord. Sing His name, meditate on His name. Lose yourself in His name.'

Thus, he forcefully tied me to the habit of recitation of His name. Since then I learnt to regularly do japa.

Once I went to spend the night with him. All night he stayed awake and recited the holy name. Through the name he helped so many. He would say, 'Jesus Christ comes to me; Sri Krishna comes to me; Guru Nanak comes to visit me.' Guru Nanak Dev was his 'Ishta Devata'. He would say, 'God has books of accounts sitting open. Some of the sorrow Ram will remove. Some of the pain Krishna will remove, and some of the difficulties Guru Nanak will destroy.'

He would stay awake and repeat God's name. 'The name holds within it unusual glory and power,' he would say. 'That is why, repeat the holy name more and more. Connect your heart to it. There are sages, who by encouraging people to do japa, have removed all their sorrow. There is a unique power in it. The name removes any type of sorrow and pain. Bind your heart to the *naam*. Unfortunately, our hearts are attached to the world instead.'

If one commits any sin, one repents. But sin also has its own value. When we fall in its trap, we take the support of the Name. Sin is God's weapon. Through it He first strikes the individual, and then He lifts him up. Hence, do not laugh at the sinner, don't hate him. One does not know how Krishna comes and makes him His own. Sing His Name, meditate on His Name Lose yourself in His Name.

Jashan also understood how men of wisdom are like mirrors. They reflect back to us our moods and state of mind. The incident below is one such example, captured in one of his later writings:

I had gone to a dervish, a holy man. Usually this man of God would meet me with a lot of love. But on that particular day, he spoke very rudely to me, and ordered me to leave at once.

Though I was aghast at his rudeness, I obeyed him and left immediately. Within me, though, I wondered at the cause of this behaviour of the dervish towards me. How could this same person, who usually has so much love in his heart, behave like this today?

On analyzing my reaction and feelings towards this attitude, I realized that today was the day when hatred for another had taken seed in my heart. Hence, the dervish on receiving these negative vibrations from me had behaved the way he had.

It took me two hours to pacify my mind and make myself understand. Finally, I was able to calm my mind, remove the turmoil and in the ensuing peace, make it agree. I approached the brother for whom hatred had arisen in my heart. I bowed down to him and then gave him a big hug.

After some time, I went back to the dervish. This beloved of the lord, with a lot of love, warmly greeted me. He showed me that on the spiritual path, it is necessary that feelings of enmity and hatred should be completely eliminated from the heart. The one who genuinely walks on this path is the one who understands and empathizes with the pain of another.

Your suffering is my suffering.

Your joy is my joy.

Jesus Christ says: If you have hatred in your heart for another, you are upset with another, then just go to that person and make amends. Only after that can you come and sit in prayer with me.

Another important learning for the young and ardent Jashan was the lesson of obedience. In his own words:

There was another holy man who showered his grace upon me. This man of God would say to me, again and again, '*Pyare* (dear one), if you wish to walk the path of the aspirant, walk in utter, complete obedience.'

I am afraid my nature was very different, at that time. It was not easy for me to practice obedience. I had a tendency to question, to argue over what I thought was not acceptable. However, the holy man's words set me thinking. I had made up my mind that the path of the seeker was to be my chosen path; therefore, it was incumbent upon me to practice the virtue of obedience, however, difficult it would be.

After a few days of struggle, I made up my mind to follow his advice in letter and spirit. I went to see him. I sat at his feet and said to him, 'Baba, I am ready to walk the path of obedience.'

The holy man smiled and said, 'May I put your obedience to test?'

'I am waiting to carry out your every behest,' I replied earnestly.

He told me to go and tell a fellow disciple a few harsh truths: that he was doing the wrong thing and that he had to mend his ways. Now this gentleman in question was much older than me. How could I go up to him and tell him to his face that his actions were causing displeasure to the holy man? I shrank from this task. My courage and resolution failed me utterly. Was it so tough to walk the path of obedience?

But I had told the saint that I would walk the path of obedience and I was determined to keep my word. My mind turbulent, but my determination firm, I made my way to this brother's house.

It was the longest, hardest walk I took. Every step I went forward, I seemed to withdraw two steps mentally. As I drew near his house, my reluctance grew manifold.

But the physical distance was easily covered. And very soon, I found myself knocking at the brother's door, my hands actually trembling.

The door opened, and I was face-to-face with his

mother. I greeted her politely, and asked to see her son.

'Come in, come in, *beta* Jashan,' said the mother warmly. 'How long since we saw you last! As for my son, I am afraid you cannot see him today; he left for Shikarpur just last evening.'

I can't tell you how happy and relieved I felt on hearing those words! A huge burden seemed to be lifted from my shoulders. 'God,' I whispered in my heart of hearts, 'you have saved me for the time being, at least!'

After making polite conversation with the mother and her family members, I returned to the holy man and said to him, 'I went to meet this brother, as you suggested. But he is away at Shikarpur today.'

I paused, swallowed my reluctance, and continued in a small voice, 'Tomorrow, when he gets back, I shall call upon him again and convey your message.'

'There's no need for that now,' said the saint nonchalantly. 'There's something else I want you to do ….' And I was assigned some simple tasks, which I carried out meticulously.

Once he called me and said to me, 'I want you to go to the press which is printing this series on the lives of saints, which I am reading. Their next edition is about to be printed shortly. Please tell them to use a better quality of paper and a larger print size.'

I was taken aback when I heard him. I knew nobody from the press or the publishers. How could an unknown young student go to a well-known press and tell the printers how to do their job?

Determined as ever to keep my vow of obedience,

I found my way to the press, where I asked to see the manager. I was requested to wait in his office.

My heart beat rapidly, and my hands trembled at the thought of what I was about to do. I could visualize the scene: upon hearing my 'suggestions' the manager would abuse me freely, tell me to mind my own business and show me the door. May be, this entire test of obedience was to teach me to bear insults and abuse!

Shortly afterwards, the manager entered the cabin and took his seat. 'What can we do for you, young man?' he enquired pleasantly.

'Actually sir, it is about the next edition of your series on the lives of saints,' I began diffidently.

'Ah yes, our new edition,' he beamed. 'Here is a brand new copy of the book, hot from the press. Would you like to take a look?' And he offered a hardbound copy of the book which was on his table.

'Do you mean to say the book has already been printed?' I stammered.

'Yes, indeed!' he said happily. We are ahead of schedule, for a change. Oh, please do keep the copy with our compliments. It is nice to know that youngsters like you are taking an interest in our series.'

I almost collapsed with a sense of relief. I thanked him for the book and hastily left the press.

'God you have saved me!' I thought with gratitude. 'I could not have gone a step further on the path of obedience, without your grace.'

I returned to the holy man's abode and reported the details of my visit to the press.

'What should I have done under the

circumstances?' I asked him anxiously. 'Should I have passed on your suggestions to him despite the fact that the edition has already been printed?'

The saint smiled lovingly and made me sit down near him. 'My son,' he said affectionately, 'you worry too much; you take things easily to heart. All you needed to do, you have done. You obeyed me implicitly. The instructions and suggestions were only meant to help you destroy your ego, your personal pride; no more, no less. You have, indeed, passed the test. You readily agreed to do things you did not like, to carry out instructions, which you found unpleasant. This is all I expected of you.'

Little did Jashan realize how the growing radiance of his face and the light in his eyes were magnets that drew men of God towards him. Once, such a man approached him and said that he was very different from others of his age. Blessing him, he said, 'From now on, when you look at anyone's palm, I shall speak through you. You will be able to read accurately, the past and the future of the people you meet.' The blessing came true and though Jashan made no study of palmistry, whenever he saw anyone's palm, he would tell them precisely of their past and would predict things about their future, which came true.

In later years, when troubled devotees came to Sadhu Vaswani he would often refer them to J. P. Vaswani, who would read their palms and guide them accordingly. One day, however, Sadhu Vaswani called Jashan and said to him, 'My child, reading others' palms is an obstruction to your spiritual evolution. It will hamper your growth. It is a practice you should avoid in the future.' From then on, the gift of reading palms was taken away from Jashan.

Jashan was shaped and moulded by the men of God for that great, glorious moment when he was ready to become a disciple. The scriptures declare that no person need search for a Guru, for when the disciple is ready, the Guru himself comes into his life. Thus, when the moment was ripe, the hand of destiny brought Sadhu Vaswani back to Karachi.

9

THE GURU APPEARS

The Guru loves all: but he who loves the Guru and surrenders himself to him, serving him day and night, will attain the Highest!

J. P. Vaswani

In 1934, after an absence of five long years, Sadhu Vaswani revisited Karachi. When Jashan first beheld him, he felt a powerful surge of emotion. Never before had he experienced such joy and exultation. The very presence of his uncle seemed to flood the home with spiritual vibrations. Suddenly everything appeared as though tinged with a heavenly hue. The trees seemed to stand taller; the flowers appeared to be smiling. Even the wind seemed to shiver in anticipation of some great impending event. Jashan felt a tremendous expansion of consciousness and everything was forgotten in that bliss.

Fifteen-year-old Jashan observed his uncle closely, and noticed many things that he had not paid attention to before. Sadhu Vaswani wore home spun khadi garments. His curly hair looked dishevelled for he did not comb or brush it any more. He lived and moved as a common man, travelling in the crowded and uncomfortable third class railway compartments. Yet, the radiance on his face and the divine expression in his eyes spoke of his inner state. This man, whose dress and mannerisms were so simple, moved as a king among men, towering above them with the confidence of one who has found his purpose in life, and has received the divine grace to fulfil it.

During his five years of absence, Sadhu Vaswani had established himself as a reputed social and spiritual reformer. He had launched the All India Youth Movement with a view to spiritualizing the daily life of the youth; he had begun work for the emancipation of women, and for the awakening of people to the life of the spirit. With Hyderabad as his base, an ever-growing group of followers had gathered around him. He held weekly classes at the Brahmo Samaj as well as at the Theosophical Society on the Upanishads and the *Bhagavad Gita.* Around the same time, one of his disciples started a fortnightly English Journal called *Dawn* to spread the teachings of the Master.

In 1931, when thirteen-year-old Jashan had joined college, Sadhu Vaswani's special classes for women and girls had evolved into the Sakhi Satsang, a fellowship for women. Sadhu Vaswani told members of this satsang about the great women from the world over, with a view to broadening their horizons, and inspiring in them aspirations beyond the mundane. Sadhu Vaswani also spoke out actively against dowry. One of his close women devotees, Sati Thadani, was asked to start a magazine in Sindhi, called *Shyam* specifically for women. Sadhu Vaswani himself started another monthly magazine in Sindhi called *Sant Mala.*

Two years later, in 1933, Sadhu Vaswani launched the Mira Movement of Education in Hyderabad. It aimed at offering girl students modern education while inculcating in them a love for the Indian ideals and culture. A weekly journal, *Mira*, containing news and articles in both English and Sindhi was also launched for the young girls. The movement grew rapidly, and soon Mira schools opened in Larkana, Rohri, and Sukkur.

The purpose of Sadhu Vaswani's visit to Karachi in 1934 was to attend a function organized by a newly opened branch of the Sakhi Satsang in the city. Young Jashan observed how Sadhu Vaswani's whole life energy was poured out in stirring the hearts of youth, and inspiring in them the love for simplicity, service, and sacrifice. Every moment was spent in kindling devotion for the motherland, and for spreading the message of prophets and saints of the East and West. Sadhu Vaswani sought to awaken a generation of young men and women to lead India from the darkness of poverty and servility into the greatness and light that had been hers in centuries gone by.

Krishnadevi observed how much Jashan and his sister Hari were drawn to their uncle. Jashan's face looked transformed. The sparkle in his eyes and the radiant smile on his face offered a striking contrast to his pensive look of late. He accompanied his uncle everywhere. He drank in every word his uncle uttered and was ever attentive to his every wish or demand. It was as though everything else in his life had been temporarily suspended.

Sadhu Vaswani spent a few days in Karachi before returning to Hyderabad. Thereafter, his visits became more regular. The days he spent in Karachi became the highlights of Jashan's life. When Sadhu Vaswani would depart for Hyderabad, Jashan would seek solace in the library. As one of the students in charge of the library, he had free access to it at any time of the day or night.

Jashan would often remain in the library until the wee hours of the morning, as he loathed leaving a book unfinished once he had started it. Whenever he felt tired, he would stretch himself out for a short nap on one of the long tables. He read everything and anything. There was no favourite author or topic.

One night, when all was still and silent, and Jashan was engrossed in a novel, there came a knock on the door. Taken aback that anyone should visit the library at such a godforsaken hour, he ignored it. The knock was repeated. Jashan hesitated. The third knock was stronger and more insistent. Getting up, Jashan went and opened the door. On the threshold stood Sadhu Vaswani.

'What are you doing here, at this hour of the night?' he asked.

'I was reading this book and wanted to finish it before going home.'

Looking at the book in Jashan's hand, Sadhu Vaswani said, 'This book does not merit the time that you are spending on it. If it was something more elevating, I would understand.'

'What kind of books should I read?' asked Jashan.

'Read biographies of noble people. They can change your life and make you a new man.'

From that day on, Jashan became very selective about what he read. Biographies became a priority. The only exceptions were stories by Arthur Conan Doyle and P. G. Wodehouse.

Once, during his visit to Karachi, Sadhu Vaswani led a protest for a socio-religious cause against the British authorities. As a result, he was arrested along with a few others and sentenced to fifteen days in jail. Jashan who had joined the *satyagraha* was determined to go to jail with his uncle. It had become a matter of pride and self-respect for patriotic Indians to court arrest and to spend a few days behind bars. All the freedom fighters had had several stints in prison. Some of the most outstanding works by Lokmanya

Tilak were written in jail, as also the memorable books by
Pandit Nehru.

Sadhu Vaswani and some others were rounded up, while
young Jashan was pushed aside by the police. As the leaders
of the protest were being herded into a lorry, Jashan noticed
a tall giant of a policeman standing with his back to the lorry,
legs apart, gesticulating to a crowd on his right. Jashan made
a dash, and, being small and nimble, he slipped through the
legs of the tall policeman and jumped into the lorry. In the
jostling that was going on, no one seemed to notice him.
And, thus, with a sense of national pride, he entered the jail
in the company of his uncle.

In the jail, Sadhu Vaswani was not treated as a common
criminal, for the superintendent and other jail staff knew
of him. They went out of their way to make his stay as
comfortable as possible, within the circumstances and the
facilities available. At his request, Sadhu Vaswani was given
permission to move around and meet the other prisoners.
He greeted them with love and compassion and blessed
them all. Many shed tears and opened their hearts to him.
They begged him to ensure that they were forgiven in the
eyes of God, if not in those of society. The whole atmosphere
in the prison seemed transformed. 'They are my friends and
brothers,' Sadhu Vaswani said to Jashan, 'and to them I fain
would reveal the boundless love and mercy of God.'

Being in jail gave Jashan a greater opportunity to be in
constant contact with his revered uncle. Early one morning,
when Sadhu Vaswani came out of his meditation, his
eyes opened and his gaze fell on young Jashan. He said,
'Sometimes, a feeling of sadness fills me when I think of the
things men run after: pleasures, possessions, power. They
are shadow-shapes. Alas! Men live in forgetfulness of the
reality of life.'

Sadhu Vaswani referred not just to the prisoners in the jail but also to the rest of society: the prisoners of their desires, their addictions, and their passions.

'But Dada,' said Jashan, 'how many can attain to God-realization and escape desire and passions? It is only for a few chosen ones.'

'My child,' replied Sadhu Vaswani, 'I love to think that God-realization is not the monopoly of a privileged few. It is open to all, to all who would practice certain *sadhanas* (disciplines), to all who would truly seek the Lord.'

'I have been practicing sadhanas, Dada, so can I hope to attain that state?'

'A person gets what he seeks: God or wealth or power. To get God you must seek Him sincerely. Earnestness will sustain you in the practice of spiritual disciplines. Long must you struggle in the water before you learn to swim. He alone realizes God who renounces everything for His sake. Renunciation means renunciation of the false self, the ego. Renounce the ego and you announce the Eternal.'

Jashan thought over it in the course of the day. Renunciation did not mean turning one's back to the world. It simply meant renouncing the ego. That was what real transformation was all about.

A little later in the day, Sadhu Vaswani asked Jashan how he wanted to live his life. Suppressing his real desire, Jashan replied what he believed was expected of him by his mother, his extended family, and his teachers; he answered what he felt duty-bound to answer. His mother continually reminded him of her great dream of his joining the Indian Civil Services. As the eldest son of a widowed mother and with several siblings, Jashan felt that a great responsibility was upon him.

'Well, after my BSc, I will prepare for the ICS,' he replied softly.

'And then?'

'Then, hopefully, I will join the ICS and make a name for myself in the service.'

'And then?'

'Well, I will have a promising career and will be able to make a difference in society.'

'And then what?'

'I will continue to write ...' Jashan's voice trailed off. None of this really set him on fire. It was hopeless to pretend. Any life, other than that of the spirit, seemed equally meaningless. He just did not feel enthusiastic.

'You may make money, receive honours but what then? What then? What then? What is the purpose of life? What is its goal?' persisted Sadhu Vaswani.

'You tell me, Dada, what is the ultimate purpose in life?'

'Go into silence and see what answers you get,' replied Sadhu Vaswani. 'Sit in meditation regularly. It clarifies the mind and it enables you to find the answers you seek from within. Inside you is an enormous *shakti*, an eternal powerhouse of energy. You only have to enter into silence, go deep within to set that powerhouse in operation.'

'But what does it mean to meditate?' asked Jashan, wondering how his dilemma would be solved through meditation.

'To meditate is to navigate; each day be thou a navigator and each day discover a new region of the light within thy soul. The infinite universe is within thee. The wisdom of the Atman is profound, but it cannot be intellectually attained; wisdom is intuited, not conceptually formulated. The soul communes with wisdom when the intellect, the imagination, and the will go into silence. To meditate is to renounce the 'fragments' and enter into communion with the whole.'

Jashan knew very clearly that acquiring degrees, amassing a fortune, gaining approbation, and the applause of crowds was not what beckoned him. His ideal was Sadhu Vaswani himself, who had turned his back to a career, and was still leading a life of tremendous, invaluable service to society. Because he walked alone, this great man of renunciation could serve others with single-pointed attention, at every moment of his life. His life was a wholesome blend of meditation and action.

Another morning, when Sadhu Vaswani had come out of his meditation, Jashan confided in him. 'Why do I feel such restlessness? I have met several holy men and have tried to live by their many teachings, yet I remain restless.'

'People remain restless for different reasons,' explained the Master. 'One type of seeker, the *aarta*, is restless because he is discontent with all that material life can give. He wants something more. Another type of seeker, the *jignasu*, feels restless because although he feels the presence of the great Truth, he cannot understand it intellectually. Then there is the *arthaarthi*, who is restless because he is discontent with his present condition. He believes that some material change in his life will make it better. All three experience restlessness because their devotion is of a lower type.'

'What is the highest form of devotion, then?' continued Jashan.

'That of the *jnani*. He experiences the supreme peace of the Highest, which puts an end to all the restlessness. He becomes one with the Self where he sees nothing else, where he hears nothing else. He experiences that he and the Beloved are one. The jnani is one who has gained a perfect identity with the Lord.'

'So what does freedom from restlessness imply?' asked young Jashan.

'It implies freedom from desire and fear.'

'And what must one do to attain that state?'

'One must take refuge at the feet of an Enlightened One, a Holy One. The teacher's grace is needed to attain to that state.'

Jashan became silent. The conversation continued the next day.

'Talk to me about death, Dada. How does one overcome grief?' asked Jashan of him whom he now looked upon as his Master.

'Grief is due to attachment,' replied Sadhu Vaswani. 'And attachment is due to ignorance. Why is a man sad? Because he clings to forms. The essence is not the form. The wise man does not grieve because he understands that, at death, only the form departs, the Atman lives on. The wise man knows that the departed ones are still alive in another sphere of consciousness.'

'Does the wise man, then, never feel grief at all?'

'He does, but he also understands that overcoming grief is the way to develop spiritual power and win. He thinks, "Krishna walked, and Jesus walked through the valley of the shadow of death. Who am I to say that I must escape sorrow and anguish? I too, must bear my cross, bear and bleed; only let me remember that when I bear and bleed, the will of God is working though me: and through suffering and pain, the will of God is purifying me and preparing me for the vision of transfiguration, the *visvadarshanam*, the vision of the one Lord of life and light and love in all that is around me, above me, below me, within me!"'

Sadhu Vaswani paused for a moment. Jashan remained still, waiting for him to continue. 'Grief, then, is sacred,' continued Sadhu Vaswani. 'It is God's gift to the seeker; it is the benediction He pours upon him to whom He would reveal the meaning of His infinite mercy, to reveal Himself, His wisdom, and His love.'

When suddenly Sadhu Vaswani and his group of followers were released after a mere four days in prison, instead of the scheduled fifteen days, Jashan was deeply disappointed. Prison had been a heaven for him, for he had spent all his time with Sadhu Vaswani. Moreover, there had been long moments when he had had his uncle's undivided attention. Here was a master of masters. He could quell every doubt, every misgiving in Jashan's mind. His words were a balm to his troubled mind. Jashan realized that he would have to make some important choices in the not-too-distant future.

Of the experience in the jail, J. P. Vaswani was to later write:

It was then that I felt drawn to him. His love was boundless. I cannot describe it in words. It was as though he was built of love. His eyes were radiant with love. His words were vibrant with love. As I often say, the tips of his fingers thrilled with love. It was this love that enveloped me. This love had the power to attract and to draw people like me.

Once out of prison, there was a lot of work to be done. Sadhu Vaswani had to issue statements to the press. He needed somebody to type those out immediately. Jashan knew typing; his English was impeccable. He was a gifted writer and he was only too happy to help his uncle in all his work. Slowly, he started taking on more of such work.

A thought came to him that he would not study any further than his BSc. That he would live with his Master and serve him. Sadhu Vaswani drew him as a magnet draws a piece of iron. But did the Master consider him a worthy disciple? What did the Master feel about him?

Eventually, mustering up the courage, Jashan opened his heart to Sadhu Vaswani. The latter would not hear of Jashan giving up his education. First he had to finish his BSc. After that, it was important for him to do a master's degree. Then, alone, should he think of anything else!

10

THE DILEMMA

Think little! Feel Less! Love more!
J. P. Vaswani

Jashan topped the university in Physics in his final year of BSc. Thirty years earlier, Sadhu Vaswani had topped the university in English. While Sadhu Vaswani had been awarded the Ellis Scholarship to pursue his MA degree, young Jashan was made a Fellow of the D. J. Sind College. This implied that he would teach undergraduate students, while pursuing his work for an MSc degree.

At this point, however, Jashan ran into a difficulty with the principal of the college. The latter insisted that a tie was part of the dress code for all male faculty members. As a fellow of the college, Jashan needed to observe the dress code when teaching the undergraduate students. However, as a matter of principle, Jashan only wore clothes made from Indian homespun cotton. In fact, all patriotic Indians wore khadi in those years prior to independence. So Jashan refused to wear a tie remembering how his father had always considered it a form of slavery to the British. The principal would not relent and neither would Jashan. Six months passed and Jashan was not allowed to teach any classes. Krishnadevi despaired.

Finally, the principal, Mr Butani, had a personal problem. Professor Paldhikar, head of the Department of Physics, who had recommended Jashan for the fellowship, was able to offer him some invaluable assistance and, in the bargain, he was able to persuade the principal to yield to Jashan's stand. The young man was finally allowed to start teaching. Dressing in his usual khadi trousers and shirt, Jashan broke what he considered to be a meaningless tradition.

During this period, on the insistence of his mother, Jashan also joined evening classes for LLB. Krishnadevi believed that the knowledge of law would be an asset for the tough civil service entrance examination. Jashan thus led a very busy schedule: research and study for the MSc degree; teaching undergraduate students; and then two-hour law classes in the evening.

Despite this gruelling schedule, Jashan always found time for assisting Sadhu Vaswani in whatever way he could, whenever he was in town. This led him to do things that he had never dreamt of doing before. For instance, when a devotee decided to build a house for Sadhu Vaswani, and found that cement was a scarce commodity, Jashan proved to be most resourceful. Approaching proprietors of a cement factory, he arranged to get the requisite supply. Then, sitting in a truck loaded with cement bags, he arrived at the building site. Sadhu Vaswani was very touched. In every way, Jashan was always in the forefront to assist or facilitate things for him. It was clear that a very special bond had developed between the Master and his young nephew.

Sadhu Vaswani named his new home Krishta Kunj. It had a spacious assembly hall and here he started fellowship meetings twice a day. In addition, he would also hold a class on the *Bhagavad Gita* every Saturday evening, whenever he was in town. To this class came the educated and the elite of

Karachi, belonging to all religions and castes. When Jashan was not attending his own classes at the college, he would be at Krishta Kunj. It became his home during the days that Sadhu Vaswani was in Karachi.

Jashan was the first in Sind to do his masters by research. He would often talk about his work with his Master, only to discover that the latter was extraordinarily well informed on every conceivable subject. It would be no exaggeration to say that Sadhu Vaswani had a truly phenomenal mind. And he took interest in everything.

One evening, Jashan requested Sadhu Vaswani to come and bless his X-ray machine in the college laboratory. During the visit, Sadhu Vaswani asked the young man if he had a telescope through which he could gaze at the stars above. On the windowsill was one such instrument. Fascinated, Sadhu Vaswani looked through it. Then he asked Jashan to look through it. The stars were dazzling. Sadhu Vaswani then blew his breath against the lens of the telescope and asked Jashan to look through the lens once more. This time Jashan was unable to see anything.

'A thin film of moisture can conceal all the stars,' said Sadhu Vaswani. 'So also can pride, ego, and selfishness cloud the face of the omnipresent God. Wipe the lens of your inner eye and you, too, will behold the Lord, face to face!'

Sadhu Vaswani became the focus of Jashan's life. Increasingly, the world and its allurements, an academic career, friends and family, all paled into insignificance when he sat at the feet of his Master. The hunger for acquiring further degrees was replaced by an insatiable desire to serve the Master. Yet, whenever Jashan raised the topic, Sadhu Vaswani never said anything. Jashan hoped that once his MSc was over, the Master would agree. With this hope in mind, he did not take his LLB examinations at the end of the second year. Acquiring a law degree would have only brought family pressure upon him to take up the legal profession as a career, as an alternative to the ICS. Quietly, he chose to forego that option. At the same time, his MSc thesis, *The Scattering of X-rays by Solid,* had still to be submitted. The research work was complete but the process of writing had not yet begun. He had lost interest in it. Meanwhile, nothing had been clearly discussed with Sadhu Vaswani. The Master knew what was in Jashan's heart, but Jashan did not quite know what the Master felt about it.

After giving his MSc exams, Jashan went to spend some time with Sadhu Vaswani in Hyderabad. Here, he had full exposure to the life his Master led. He saw how Sadhu Vaswani, a combination of erudition, wisdom, sacrifice, and service, had created a magic web to which were drawn men, women, and the youth from all walks of life. His sacred presence was awe-inspiring, for he radiated a divine peace around him. Jashan took over all the secretarial duties of Sadhu Vaswani. In addition, he would do all the administrative and other sundry tasks as and when required.

Krishnadevi saw that the ICS did not seem to interest Jashan at all. However, his academic record was so exceptional that she was confident that he would be offered a teaching job in his alma mater. Soon enough, a temporary post came up and Jashan accepted it, for teaching was closer to his heart than the ICS. Everyone seemed confident that Jashan would soon become a permanent member of the faculty. The job ensured that he could be in Karachi where Sadhu Vaswani was a regular visitor. Holidays would be spent in Hyderabad.

Inspired by Sadhu Vaswani's work with the youth, Jashan and two of his friends decided to publish a monthly English journal. Its objective was to bring about an awakening in the youth of Sind. When approached by Jashan for a title, Sadhu Vaswani named it *Excelsior*, which means to go forward. When Jashan added a spiritual dimension to the magazine, the two friends backed out. Single-handedly, Jashan worked on the *Excelsior*: writing articles, correcting proofs, looking after the printing, advertisements, circulation, packing, posting, and so on. Jashan already had considerable expertise in writing and editing because ever since he had been in college he had been contributing stories and articles to local magazines. He took the nom de plume Nav Juan and, later, Vidya Vinaya. Writing under these pen names he won several writing contests and competitions.

To launch *Excelsior* and give it a profound spiritual message, Sadhu Vaswani agreed to contribute, every month, a portion of the *Gita* in translation and in rhyme. The first issue came out in 1939.

In May 1939, Sadhu Vaswani was invited to speak at an International and Inter-Religious Retreat and Conference in Colombo, Ceylon (now Sri Lanka). Although his health had deteriorated considerably, the doctors felt that the sea air would do him good. So Sadhu Vaswani accepted the invitation and since it was the period of summer vacations, he agreed to take Jashan along.

After thrilling the hearts of his listeners at the conference with the message of the Indian rishis, Sadhu Vaswani visited Nuwara Eliya where, instead of the planned four days, he remained, instead, for four long months. It was here, in Nuwara Eliya, that Jashan made a crucial decision.

The college reopened in June. Jashan needed to head back to Karachi. A letter arrived for him from Professor Paldhikar, head of the Department of Physics in D. J. Sind College, Karachi. The post of a lecturer had fallen vacant and the professor wrote to tell Jashan, his favourite student, that the post could be his for the asking. Could he, therefore, return to Karachi by June 20?

Jashan understood that, finally, he had come to a crossroads in his life. On the one hand was stability, a steady income, security for his mother, and a brilliant academic career. On the other hand was a life with his beloved Guru.

Jashan thought of all the things he had wanted to do as a child. His very first ambition had been to become a tram driver. Some years later, he had wanted to become a sailor. He loved the sea and felt that he would love nothing better than to be on board a ship all the time. When a Dufferin Course – training course for cadets in the Merchant Marine – was advertised and Jashan wanted to take it up, his mother was aghast at such an ambition. 'Dufferin is for duffers,' she had exclaimed. 'How can I permit my bright and gifted son to ruin his future?'

Jashan had felt deeply disappointed at that time. He had prayed fervently for his mother to change her opinion but Krishnadevi did not relent. So Jashan had gone on a fast as a way of putting pressure on her. Finally, Krishnadevi, who knew that Sadhu Vaswani was expected, had told Jashan that they would leave the decision to him. Jashan had been delighted, thinking that his uncle would take his side, as he had always done when Jashan was little. Sadhu Vaswani heard the matter out and very lovingly told his nephew, 'Greater things await you in life. Let the matter rest for now. At the right time, you will surely steer your own ship.' And so the matter had rested there.

Outwardly, Jashan had everything that any young man could wish for. He was intelligent, good looking, and a high achiever. In college, his friends used to call him 'a gentleman and a scholar'. Several of his stories and thought-provoking articles had been published in Indian journals. He had a prodigious memory for facts. He had studied law and had a logical mind. Besides being blessed with a great sense of humour, he also possessed the gift of repartee. A fluent speaker, he had won many prizes in debating societies. Academically, he was several years ahead of his peers. Despite all this, his heart yearned for nothing other than Sadhu Vaswani.

Had Sadhu Vaswani himself not said, 'Truly great among men is he who hath renounced desires and possessions and all fruits of action and is rich only in dreams and aspirations and never would turn them into silver and gold!'

Had Sadhu Vaswani not stated, just the other day, in one of his talks, that there are three things which never come back? One, the arrow which the *kshatriya* sends forth from his station on the battlefield; two, the spoken word which also goes forth like the arrow, blessing or wounding human hearts; and three, opportunity – it comes and may prove to be a blessing, or it may be lost forever, leaving behind, a pain, a feeling of sorrow.

Here was Jashan's opportunity. The decision had suddenly come upon him and the choice had to be made.

Jashan spoke to his beloved Master of the letter from Professor Paldhikar, and sought his guidance. He told the Master that he had no wish to pursue a worldly career. He was neither interested in money nor in fame. He wanted nothing more than to serve Sadhu Vaswani and spend his life at his sacred feet.

Sadhu Vaswani listened. 'You must do the bidding of your beloved mother,' he said. 'She has made all the efforts to educate you and bring you to this level. Now you must act according to her wishes. Therefore, please consult her. Tell her what you have told me and seek her permission.'

Jashan was in a dilemma. How could he write to his mother and tell her that he had no desire to pursue a career, in fact, no desire to go back home at all? How could he make her understand that he wished to devote his life to the service of his beloved uncle and Guru? The last thing he wanted to do was to hurt her. At the same time, he did not wish to live a meaningless life.

Finally, Jashan chose a well-considered way out of the dilemma. He wrote to his brother, Ram, telling him of the offer from the college, adding that he personally wished to continue to be with Sadhu Vaswani. Could Ram please talk to their mother and ask her what she felt about it? If she said no, he would come back home to Karachi. If she did not say anything, would Ram still please let him know? No response would mean that she was not against the idea.

Ram's reply arrived a few days later. Their mother had consented to Jashan's wish to stay with his Guru. Jashan was overjoyed. He enthusiastically communicated the message to his Master, who heard it with a gracious smile but without uttering a word. Immediately, thereafter, Jashan wrote to the college authorities resigning from his temporary job, and declining the offer of the post of lecturer.

Despite Jashan's response, the college was not yet ready to let go of its star student. The college authorities wrote to tell him that the post was still open, and would stay open for him until he decided to come back. Jashan was not tempted by this flattering offer. He had chosen a different path for himself.

Jashan's new-found joy, however, did not last long. In September 1939, Sadhu Vaswani and Jashan returned to Hyderabad. A few days later, a visitor from Karachi, a gentleman by the name of Shamdas Gidwani, arrived. In the course of conversation, he mentioned to Sadhu Vaswani that Jashan's mother had complained to him how she had brought up her beloved son with great love and care, taken pains to educate him and see him grow up into a brilliant scholar, only to see her brother-in-law take him away from her completely.

Sadhu Vaswani grew thoughtful when he heard this. He summoned Jashan and told him, 'I want you to go back home. Your duty is to be with your beloved mother.'

Jashan was broken-hearted. But he did not utter a word of protest. Silently, he packed his bag and returned home to his mother. It was then that Krishnadevi realized, once and for all, that Jashan had a destiny to fulfil.

11

CLARITY AT LAST

*Life's greatest achievement is to establish a living link with
God. Let everything else be taken away from us, but let
the link be maintained. For this, it is necessary to develop
awakened consciousness.*

J. P. Vaswani

Jashan returned to his Master in Hyderabad with the
blessings of his mother. Little did he know that his joy
would be short-lived and that he would be back in Karachi
a few days later. This was due to misplaced generosity on his
part.

A demonstrator in the laboratory of the Department of
Physics, where Jashan had carried out his research, a certain
Mr Belani approached Jashan for a favour. He knew about
Jashan's brilliant research for his master's thesis and of
his subsequent loss of interest in the body of work. So he
requested Jashan to give him all the data so that he could
submit it as his own and acquire a master's degree without
any effort on his part.

Jashan readily agreed and handed over the matter to
the delighted Mr Belani. The latter, who attended Sadhu
Vaswani's *Gita's* classes, immediately went and narrated the
entire incident to Sadhu Vaswani, complimenting him on
the generosity of his disciple.

In the evening, when Jashan came to Sadhu Vaswani, he found displeasure writ large on his face. The Master chided him, 'You have not done the right thing in giving away your thesis. Not only are you cheating yourself, but you are also being a party to untruth and falsehood. Only after you have submitted your thesis can you return to me.'

This time Jashan rushed home and applied himself to the task as though his very life depended on it. Working day and night, he completed his thesis, personally typed it out, and submitted it, all within fifteen days. It was assessed by none other than the future Nobel Laureate, Sir C. V. Raman.

When Jashan first heard that Sir C. V. Raman would be his examiner, he was sure that he would not pass his MSc, because what he had formulated was exactly the opposite of the Raman Effect. His misgivings, however, turned out to be unnecessary. Sir C. V. Raman, in true scientific spirit, appreciated and encouraged Jashan's scientific bent of mind and ensured that he qualified for the MSc degree. The degree was to prove extremely useful some years later when the St Mira's college was founded in Pune. They needed a principal who had a master's degree and Jashan was able to take on the responsibility.

Academics and research were intrinsic to Jashan's personality. His spiritual journey was also, in some way, linked to his scientific research. Had he gone in for a PhD, Jashan would have liked to work on the topic of light. Light, in its physical form, is always associated with heat. Yet whenever Jashan sat in silence and beheld the light within, it was always cool and refreshing. He wanted to understand the correlation between the light within and the light without. He would jokingly speak about 'light heat' and 'light without heat'.

As he was to later describe:

This quest for light without heat took me inwards. Outside of us there can be no light without heat. If we want light without heat, we have to go within. This quest was something beyond metaphysics. It was the quest for *vidya* and vidya is science. It has its rules, its disciplines, whereas metaphysics is mere knowledge. Vidya is wisdom. It is to be lived, to be experienced. Metaphysics is knowledge, something to be known. Vidya transcends the brain, whereas metaphysics has to do with the brain. For me, this quest was to bring science and spirituality together. Nothing else can do that. And the two together can bring about transformation.

Another thing I was interested in at that time was to find out a substance that tasted like meat but which was not a food of violence. I was interested in that because that, I thought, would induce at least 70-80 per cent of people to eschew meat; and slaughter would be considerably reduced.

Jashan returned to Sadhu Vaswani for the second time to begin life as a disciple. During the fifteen days that he had spent at home working on his thesis, Krishnadevi had used every spare moment she had to teach him basic life skills such as cooking, cleaning, and spinning. She recognized that a disciple needed to be equipped with multiple abilities, especially those that pertained to everyday life.

Despite her years of struggle after becoming a widow, Krishnadevi had ensured that her children, boys and girls alike, received whatever education they wanted. In dress, diet, and daily living, the family lived extremely simply. That was what built character, for all Krishnadevi's children grew up to be quite different from their peers. Hari Vaswani, after completing her BSc in 1935 from D. J. Sind College, took over as first assistant of the P. P. C. M. Girls School in Sukkur. The following year she moved to Hyderabad as headmistress of St Mira's School founded by Sadhu Vaswani. She passed away in 2009. Her last words were, 'Kanha kay ghar jana hai (I have to go to Sri Krishna's abode).'

Jashan's younger sister, Sundri, stood first in the MSc examination of the University of Mumbai, and was consequently awarded a scholarship to pursue studies for a PhD in London. There she secured a doctorate in mathematical statistics in 1946 – the first Indian woman of the University of London to be awarded a PhD in this subject. She returned to India and became a consultant for quality control to several industrial companies. Subsequently, she joined the Society for Servants of God based in Delhi. She served them for the rest of her relatively short life.

Jashan's brother, Ram, was the only one of Krishnadevi's children who married and had a family – wife Gopi and children, Kumar and Sheela. He settled in the US. Another brother, Hiro, ran a magazine subscription agency and started a journal India Digest. The youngest, Harkrishen, completed his higher education in Sweden, and then worked as an engineer at Larsen and Toubro. He died in an accident at the construction site of a huge project that he was in charge of.

Jashan Vaswani was a seeker from his most tender years. The grace of the Master was upon him from the time of his birth. Unseen, at a subtle level, the Master had guided the destiny of his future disciple, unfolding the plan for which the Divine will had brought the infant to the Earth plane. Jashan's entire life, until then, had been a preparation for the role of disciple. Every talent, every degree, every experience was to serve the role to which he was now committed.

The shift from pure science to spirituality was but a natural evolution. *Atma vidya* is the science of the spirit. Since ancient times, the great rishis of India have had a scientific approach to matters of the spirit. For them there was never any contradiction between science and spirituality. Both are interconnected. While science seeks to explain the outside world, spirituality is the search for answers in the inner world. Applied science improves the standard of living while applied spirituality improves the standard of life. Moreover, the rishis never made a distinction between secular knowledge and spiritual knowledge. Knowledge *per se* was considered important; secular knowledge, ideally, culminated in spiritual knowledge.

Jashan Vaswani stood poised to walk the straight and narrow path that leads to the highest knowledge – the knowledge of the Self or Self-realization.

THE DISCIPLE

The way to peace and joy is the way of letting go.
Let go of people and things: let God take over!

J. P. Vaswani

12

The Lesson of Humility

'We are proud of our power and inventions; yet what are we?' asked Sadhu Vaswani of Jashan one day, out of the blue.

He then proceeded to answer the question himself, 'We are grass that floats on a stream! For infinite are the worlds, and the universe is a river: ever full, ever flowing!'

'In such a world how must one be?' asked Jashan in a soft voice.

'The world was built in beauty and man was meant to live as a songbird: unfettered, free. But alas, he has become a bird in a cage. It is the cage of self-centredness. Not until self-centredness goes may man become truly free and full of the joy of life. And the prison of self-centredness opens to the key of humility.'

'What is the mark of him who has attained to true humility?'

Taking a pencil, Sadhu Vaswani drew a zero and said, 'This is the mark of him who has attained; he becomes a zero!'

Sadhu Vaswani paused for a while, and Jashan held his breath. 'Blessed be thou, if thou bend until thou break, becoming nothing: a zero. In the yoga (union) of two zeroes is the One Infinite!' he said.

In his own life, Sadhu Vaswani revealed what it was to become a zero. Over and over again he would repeat 'naham naham, tuho tuho' (I am nothing, it is you alone). Humility was demonstrated in every gesture and in every word he spoke. Jashan observed and absorbed.

The very first lesson Jashan received from his Guru was the lesson of humility. Breaking the ego of the disciple is one of the tasks of the Guru. The ego is like a cataract that blocks the disciple's inner vision. The Guru is the specialist who must perform the surgery to remove this cataract and restore the vision.

The ego is the sense of 'I' attached to youth, looks, intellectual power, career, relationships, position, abilities, and so on. These attachments and identifications keep the seeker bound to this worldly plain. They are the source of a continuous flood of varied emotions that toss the seeker about on the high seas of life. They blot out the light which the Guru alone can enable the disciple to see and become one with.

Jashan had been outstanding throughout school. He had been a topper in college. He had been applauded and feted. All this, however, was irrelevant from the spiritual perspective. Here the only thing that mattered was the ardour of aspiration for something beyond these material accomplishments.

Once, the Master was sitting with some fellow devotees at a fellowship meeting. When the meeting was over and he got up to leave, someone ran and brought the Master's sandals and placed them before him. Slipping his feet into the sandals while expressing gratitude to the brother who had brought them to him, Sadhu Vaswani then went out and brought the brother's shoes and placed them before him saying, 'I am a servant of all.'

Tears of love and reverence welled up in Jashan's eyes. There were no words to describe Sadhu Vaswani's humility. The Master taught by precept as well as practice. He was a living, walking scripture. His every word and every action was the manifestation of a teaching from the sacred texts.

On another occasion, Jashan and his fellow disciples were assigning various duties to themselves and other volunteers for a *langar* to mark the festival of *Janmashtami*. Sadhu Vaswani happened to pass by and inquired what the meeting was all about.

'We are allotting duties to each one for the langar, Dada,' replied Jashan.

'What duty are you giving me?' the Master wanted to know.

'Dada, we will be truly blessed if you join us for the langar. If you insist on it, we will give you the 'duty' to remain seated at the entrance to the hall, and to bless each one who enters to take her/his place in the langar. That would really make our day!' said one of the group.

'No, that's not a proper duty,' said the Master. 'I shall take on a different task; I shall sweep and clean the floor of the hall after each batch, so that the place is clean and ready for the next one.'

Sadhu Vaswani continuously reiterated the importance of humility. He spoke of it in his public talks, wrote about it, urged his followers to cultivate it, and, most importantly, demonstrated it in his own life. The two dangers for the one seeking to be truly humble are ostentation and pretension. Sadhu Vaswani shunned both. 'God asks not for great things,' he said. In an age intoxicated with ambition and the mad rush for 'bigness', Sadhu Vaswani's life rang with the message 'Sow little seeds of love and you will reap a rich destiny'. It was his humility that prompted him to refuse even the title of Guru. 'I am a Guru of no one,' he would say. 'I am everyone's disciple.'

Jashan saw these teachings demonstrated over and over again in his Guru's words, gestures, and attitudes. Recalling this period with his Guru several years later he writes:

> He would not permit us to touch his feet. Before we could bow low to take the sacred dust of his feet, his hands were already on our feet. It was only at night, when he went to sleep, that I had an opportunity of kissing his holy feet.

There were times when Jashan would feel that he was specially loved and was important in his Guru's life. And then would come a harsh lesson bringing with it immense pain and anguish.

Once, Sadhu Vaswani had to attend an important meeting. For days on end, prior to the meeting, he would say, 'If it be God's will, none except Jashan will accompany me to the meeting.' Jashan was filled with a sense of self-importance. It has been repeated so many times that everyone concerned believed that only Jashan would accompany the Master. Then came the appointed day. The Master asked everyone to get ready for the meeting but he did not take Jashan's name at all. He was ignored. Jashan kept hoping that he would be asked, but the Master paid no attention to him at all. Finally, everyone, except Jashan, left for the meeting. Jashan was shocked and heartbroken. How had that happened? Why had the Master treated him so? How could he have been so cruel and unjust? Feeling mortified, Jashan decided that he was not going to live with Sadhu Vaswani any more.

When the party returned at night, Jashan could hear everyone happily chatting and discussing the event. When the Master called for him, he refused to go. He did not see any justification for being treated in such a callous manner. For three days, he could not eat, sleep, or do anything. He avoided the Master completely. On the third evening Sadhu Vaswani entered his room and said, 'My child! Until you become nothing, you will gain nothing! You may stay here for years, but you will gain nothing, until you have become nothing.'

Jashan broke into sobs as the Master lovingly embraced him. How loved he felt when the Master talked to him in that tone. How much he had suffered and how little he had understood his Master.

'Make me nothing, Dada, but never leave me,' he implored between sobs. Henceforth, he resolved that every time he felt such anguish he would say to himself, 'My Master knows everything. He knows what is good for me!'

Despite this profound lesson, the occasions to feel hurt, despondent, and lonely were many. One day, Jashan noticed that the Master was ignoring him completely. Every time he entered and left the room, there was no acknowledgement of his presence, no response to his greeting. It was as though he simply wasn't there. He felt such an absence of warmth and sympathy. One night, after having been subjected to this treatment for several days in a row, Jashan felt that he just could not bear it any more. He decided to run away. Leaving the ashram he took refuge in a nearby garden. Because he had left in a highly emotional state, he had forgotten to take a blanket or woolen along, and so spent the night shivering in the bitter cold. His mind was overactive in imagining how he was never going to go back to the Master. Bitter tears coursed down his cheeks.

With the break of dawn Jashan got up, stiff and exhausted, and, without quite understanding why, he walked back to the ashram and knocked at the door. The Master himself opened the door. His face shone with divine light and his eyes were filled with love and joy. Flinging himself at the feet of the Master, Jashan shed copious tears of pain at having being away from the Master, and from joy at having found refuge at his feet once again. All seemed perfect in the world at this moment.

'Do you think you can run away from me?' Sadhu Vaswani's words, expressed in his mellifluous voice, seemed to come from another plane. Jashan could only ask for forgiveness, over and over again, for his lack of faith and surrender to his Guru's will.

'The God that rules millions is the Ego,' said Sadhu Vaswani. 'Enthrone on your heart the God of Love, if you, my child, will cease to wander!'

'How do I enthrone the God of Love on my heart?' asked Jashan.

'Be humble as ashes and dust.'

'How may the ego be annihilated?'

'As the seeker makes progress on the path, he finds that sometimes he prides himself on his efforts. Sometimes he loses the joy of existence. "It is so difficult," he says, "to be spiritual." Then comes to him a realization that his efforts and endeavours are not pure, but tainted and spotted. The darkest spot, he finds, is the little self, the ego, the 'I'. And he begins to realize that, of his own accord, he can do nothing. Then he learns to accept whatever comes – abasement, criticism, and disgrace – as the will of God. The love of God gradually fills him. His egoism dies. A higher stage is still to come when he realizes that God loves him and hath awakened love in his heart. Then he realizes that Divine Love and Divine Grace encompass life from beginning to end. Then all desires, appetites, and attachments depart. He is free, he is calm.'

'Tell me of some who demonstrated this in their life, O beloved Master,' begged Jashan, loathe at having this conversation draw to a close.

'When the Sikh Temple, now known as the Golden Temple, was being built in Amritsar, his disciples said to Guru Arjan Dev, "Master, let the temple building be the loftiest in the land!" But Guru Arjan Dev quietly answered, "Let the temple be built lower than all buildings. What is humble shall be exalted. The branches of a fruit-laden tree bend low to the Earth."'

Sadhu Vaswani would also quote Jesus Christ who said, 'Blessed are the meek for they shall inherit the Earth.' This message, he would emphasize, was not intellectually credible, it could only be spiritually discerned. Had not Jesus Christ washed the feet of his own disciples before they sat down for the last supper with him? No task was too low and no service too humble for Jesus.

It is easy to intellectually understand the unhappiness and bondage that the ego brings about. It is easy to talk about it and to write about it. Alas, living it is something altogether different. The Guru must repeat the same thing over and over again, for the ego rises up in a million different subtle ways. And unless it is eradicated like a life-threatening disease, humility and true freedom cannot be born.

During a visit to Karachi, once, the Master wrote a letter and informed Jashan that it needed to reach Hyderabad that very day. In those days, if one needed to get a letter delivered urgently, the quickest way was to go to the station and find someone travelling to Hyderabad, and ask him or her to personally deliver it. So both the Master and disciple decided to take a trip to the station.

Jashan jogged down the platform looking into the compartments to see if he could find any familiar face in the train. Sadhu Vaswani, along with a couple of his disciples, waited at one end of the platform. On the spur of the moment, the Master decided that he would go to Hyderabad himself to deliver the letter. He was spontaneous like a child. As the train began to move, he quickly stepped into a compartment along with his group. Imagine Jashan's surprise when he saw the train moving out of the station and Sadhu Vaswani and his fellow disciples waving to him from the moving train. Jashan was left shocked and all alone.

He returned to the ashram, wondering at how unpredictable the Master could be. For a moment he felt a trace of annoyance and hurt. Why had the Master not warned him that he would climb on to the train? Why did he always leave him out and take the others along with him? He, too, would have loved to go with the Master on this impromptu visit. Then he remembered what he had told himself, 'My Master knows what is good for me.' And with that he calmed down.

Maintaining that line of thought at all times, however, proved to be a challenge. Jashan thought of all the efforts he had made to read biographies of saints, to read and recite the scriptures, to attend satsang on a daily basis. Yet he felt that the goal of total surrender and equanimity seemed so far away. He wondered whether he was progressing or regressing.

With a heavy heart and eyes glistening with tears, he approached his Master. Sadhu Vaswani, with infinite patience and love, responded:

'It is true you have read many books. But to the pilgrim on the path, books are a burden. And you say you have studied the lives of saints; your daily life does not bear witness to it. To study is not to turn over the pages of a book. To study is to ponder well, is to meditate, is to assimilate the teaching in one's life. And every morning you read from the scriptures. Are you any better than the parrot who recites, again and again, the name of God? And every evening you go to the satsang at the right time. Are you better than the temple bell, which at the exact hour, calls the worshippers to the shrine?'

The Master's words made Jashan more aware of himself at all times. From then on, a part of him would observe himself when talking and working with fellow disciples. It made him also observe the nature of his own thoughts when sitting alone.

The path of the disciple is one of aspiration, of constant battle with appetite and desire. Copious tears are part of this effort, for numerous are the trials and difficulties. But, at every step, faith keeps the disciple going. As Sadhu Vaswani said, 'The path is often thorny, and as you will tread it, your feet will bleed but in your heart will bloom flowers of beauty, and your face will shine as the lily or the lotus in the lake!'

One evening when the Master and disciple were seated in the garden, Sadhu Vaswani asked Jashan, 'Are you anxious to find God?'

'Yes, more than anything else!'

'Then you must be prepared to lose yourself.'

'How must I lose myself?'

'Give, give, give, until it hurts to give. This will release you from bondage to the ego, and to things.'

'But what is God?' asked Jashan.

'The deepest Self of man is God! Man never knows himself until he sees the God in himself.'

'If we be, indeed, of God, how is it that we retain no recollection?' inquired the disciple.

'The greased mirror cannot reflect aright. So the mind, clouded by desires and passions, obscures reflection of the great memory lying within the soul.'

'What is it that stands between man and God?' continued Jashan.

'Man, under the influence of his gross physical environment is blind to the beauty of God and runs after the vanities of the world. Veils have fallen on man; he remains sunk in ignorance and apathy,' explained the Master.

'How may these veils of ignorance and apathy be lifted?'

'By His grace and mercy, alone, may we see Him as light.'

'What may I do,' asked Jashan with fervour, 'to grow wings and fly to the realm of radiance and light?'

'Realize, first, that you live in a state of banishment from the Beloved. Then know that you must die to 'selfhood' in order to live in the Beloved.'

'Tell me the path that leads to the Beloved?' asked Jashan.

'Annihilate the ego. It is the one great source of impurities of the heart. When the ego dies, the heart becomes pure and you will see the face of the Beloved shining in the mirror of the heart.'

By temperament, Jashan Vaswani was argumentative. With his scientific bent of mind, analytical abilities and gift of repartee, he was always able to win an argument. At the same time, his logical mind made it difficult for him to accept things easily. He was inclined to question everything that did not make sense to him. Blind belief was foreign to his nature. As a result, for several years, he argued with the Master on many things. In the initial period these arguments would often go on for hours. While Jashan, out of habit, would not want to relent, Sadhu Vaswani would continue,

unmoved, simply to enable Jashan to understand the futility
of endless debate.

This proclivity to argument led to Jashan being called
'Gauro' by the Master. In Sindhi, 'Gauro' means heavy,
implying the one who gets into futile discussions for no
rhyme or reason, or one who is quickly irritated. At the
same time, Jashan was extremely sensitive and, so, after an
argument he would brood over the matter for extended
periods of time and become unapproachable.

'If you continue to remain 'Gauro' in the company of
saints then you will never imbibe anything,' said Sadhu
Vaswani to him one day. 'You have to let go of things and
become light.'

Looking back on those years, J. P. Vaswani was to later
write:

> The Guru was ignoring my ego, not me. At the time,
> I was a young man, fresh from college. I had just
> graduated with high honours and I thought I had the
> world in the palms of my hands. I did not fully realize
> his worth and value then, and I used to argue with
> him.

One day, a former student of Sadhu Vaswani, who had
risen to the important government post of the Director
of Public Instruction (DPI) in Bihar, arrived to meet the
Master. Sadhu Vaswani was busy with some work in his
room. So the visitor and Jashan sat down together outside
the room to wait. The visitor said something to Jashan,
which led to a discussion. And the discussion turned into an
argument. It continued for a while, when suddenly the door
opened and Sadhu Vaswani came out.

The visitor complained to the Master that his young

disciple was extremely argumentative, that he argued over small, futile things. After his departure, Sadhu Vaswani turned to Jashan, and in a quiet voice, asked, 'How long will you continue to waste all your life's energy in such discussions and debates?'

For the first time, something seemed to sink deep into Jashan's consciousness. Looking back on that day, J. P. Vaswani wrote:

> His words passed into my heart and soul; and even then, his Grace flowed into me, and I felt transformed. To what avail were arguments and heated debates? The lion within me seemed to turn into a gentle lamb. I realized at that moment that I *was* nothing. I *had* nothing. I *knew* nothing; and all that I had to do was to seek the lowest place in life.

Jashan had overcome one major obstacle on the seeker's path. But there were yet many more mountains to scale. And the Master ensured that the pace never slackened. Jashan was growing rapidly in inner purity and peace. Gradually, he grew more silent. He only spoke to ask legitimate questions and have his doubts cleared by the Guru. He grew more intuitive, seeking to lose himself in his Guru. This transformation was evident in the new nickname the Master now gave him – 'Jyotish' or the child of light.

13

THE LESSON OF OBEDIENCE

When will the day come when, out of the very depths of a
yearning heart, will come forth the cry: 'I need nothing,
neither pleasures or possessions nor power do I need.
I need Thee and Thee alone!'

J. P. Vaswani

In 1944 Jashan and some other devotees accompanied the Master for a short visit to the holy city of Varanasi. To the delight of all, the house in which they were lodged was right on the banks of the sacred Ganga. For Jashan, it was a dream come true, to be able to meditate on the banks of the Ganga every day and to bathe in her sacred waters.

Every morning, Jashan would get ready to walk down for his bath in the river, when the Master would call him and give him some work. At any point in the day when he was ready to go to the river, something or the other would come up urgently, and he would not be able to make it. The days sped by and finally it was time to leave Varanasi. The train was to leave at noon, and Jashan was determined that he would, one way or another, have his dip before they left for the station. Moreover, many friends and relatives had requested him to take their name and offer a special prayer for them when he dipped into the holy river.

Grabbing a towel and making his way out of the main door, he headed briskly towards the Ganga when, suddenly, he heard his name been called out by one of the disciples. She informed him that Sadhu Vaswani was looking for him. Promptly retracing his steps, Jashan went to the Master's room. He was needed to draft a letter that needed to be dispatched immediately. Attending to this with full attention, Jashan forgot about the Ganga. Thereafter, it was time to leave for the station.

As the train chugged out of the Varanasi station, Jashan felt sad. It seemed so ironical to have been right there on the banks of the Ganga and yet, not to have been able to even touch her waters. It was as if he was simply not meant to do so. Unlike the past, however, this time Jashan felt no resentment, no anger and no hurt. He accepted that his Master knew what was best for him.

That night, curled up on his hard berth, Jashan had an unforgettable dream. Lord Shiva appeared before him. He looked resplendent with the holy ash on his forehead, the crescent moon as an ornament in his hair, a tiger skin draped around him and a trident in one hand. The other hand was held up as though to bless Jashan. On his face was the most beautiful smile. Then, to Jashan's utter surprise, he noticed that the Ganga, which is always depicted as emerging from the matted locks of Shiva in five gentle streams, was not there. Jashan was shocked to notice this.

'Dear Lord!' he gasped, with folded hands, 'Where is the Ganga? Why is she not flowing from your locks?'

'Don't be so shocked, dear Jashan,' said the Lord, smiling. 'You are right. The Ganga used to flow from my head, but now, she has changed direction.'

'Changed direction?' Jashan repeated, astonished. 'But Lord, how can the Ganga flow in Kashi, if not from your sacred locks?'

'I will tell you,' Shiva replied. 'The Ganga flows at the sacred feet of the saints and mahatmas of this sacred land. You need not be so sad and restless. Were you not at the feet of your beloved Gurudev these last few days in Kashi? The Ganga was flowing right there, at his feet. Why are you sad then?'

The train braked and came to an abrupt halt, and Jashan woke up with a jerk. He was filled with a tremendous sense of peace and joy. Recalling that incident, J. P. Vaswani writes:

> A light seemed to illumine my soul, spilling over to light up the holy feet of Sadhu Vaswani who slept, as always, with a beautiful smile on his angelic face. Instinctively, I touched his feet and bowed my head in devotion. 'Foolish, foolish me!' I chided myself. 'I spend my days and nights at the feet of a saint, how can I long for Ganga *jal*? Are not Kaaba and Kashi, Mecca and Mathura, Ganga and Jamuna, at the feet of the Guru?'

In the subtlest of ways, the Guru had given him the most important teaching that Guru-bhakti or devotion to the Master, and selfless service to him, grow with complete obedience. As the ego diminishes, passions die down, and the mind becomes purer and more serene. In that stillness the Divine Light is perceived, even as in the clear waters of a lake the reflection of the sun is seen, unbroken and bright.

The Indian scriptures repeatedly emphasize the sanctity of the Guru's feet. According to the *Guru Gita*, the water that touches the Guru's feet is considered holier than the water of the Ganga. The text goes on to say that even if the Guru is not physically present, one can sprinkle water on one's head while remembering his holy feet. The water of the Guru's feet has the greatest power: it can dry up one's sins, destroy ignorance, and end karmas, all of which are the cause of death and rebirth. Most important, water of the Guru's feet can lead the disciple to the realm of light and wisdom.

The disciple, in obeying his Guru, obeys God. God does not appear to us directly, nor does he guide our lives openly. He acts through His chosen messengers who live and work amongst us, and who impart to us His timeless teachings. The Guru alone can take the disciple to the ultimate goal, with his grace, for he, himself, has reached that goal and lives ever established in that state. The disciple is a novice and cannot judge the wisdom of the Guru. He must trust and accept whatever he is told to do or not do.

One night, out of the blue, the Master told Jashan, 'Go away from here!' His tone was angry and harsh and caught Jashan unawares completely. 'If you dare to come here again, you will be turned out!' Jashan felt his legs trembling and his throat go dry. What grave mistake had he committed? And where was he to go?

One or two other disciples intervened on his behalf, only to be told that they could leave as well. In obedience to his Master, Jashan went out of the premises of the ashram and sat down outside the gate, completely numb with pain. His heart ached as never before. Life suddenly seemed bleak and empty, devoid of sense. Kneeling down, he prayed fervently to his beloved Guru. 'Where should I go, O Beloved One? To whom should I turn? I can't live without you, for *you* alone are my whole life!'

In sheer despair he fell into a dull stupor only to awaken suddenly in the dawn to find his Master standing before him. 'How are you?' asked the Master in the most normal of tones, a sweet smile playing on his lips. Jashan could not believe it. He looked up at the Master, standing tall and magnificent, aglow with the divine radiance of one who communes with the Eternal. His heart ached so much with joy at the sight of that familiar expression filled with love, and of the blissful presence before him. He noticed how in his hand Sadhu Vaswani held a cup of tea, lovingly brought for his disciple.

Jashan's frame was wracked with sobs. This time, however, he kept repeating, 'Thy will be done, thy will be done, each and every time.' The 'why' and the 'how' had become irrelevant in his life. He accepted everything that the Master sent his way – the joyful and the painful, the simple and the complex, the suffering and the praise. From the depth of his heart came the words, 'I accept anything you mete out to me, anything at all, howsoever hard and cruel it may appear on the surface. I accept anything that will mould me and shape me into what you will me to be! My body, and my mind, all that I have, I offer unto thee. Do with me what thou wilt!'

One of the most severe tests that the disciple is put through is the pain of separation. The Guru sometimes asks the disciple to be far away from him. In J. P. Vaswani's own words:

> For a teacher knows that a raw fruit requires both sunshine and shadow, in order to ripen in maturity. So, too, the disciple must have the double experience of fellowship and separation; for in separation, too, there is union. Spiritual obedience to the teacher, not mere physical nearness to him, is the mark of a true disciple.

The sudden departure of Krishna from Vrindavan for Mathura is the perfect example of a Guru giving his disciples the taste of separation. The Gopis were devoted to Krishna, but in their devotion was an element of *moha* or delusion; they loved him but did not understand him and his world mission. The shell had to be broken – the shell of moha – so that an understanding of Krishna might come to their loving hearts. And when they learnt of his departure, they wailed. They wept. And in weeping they understood a little of him and his mystery; of his work in the world, his mission to the world!

On another occasion, Sadhu Vaswani wanted his disciples to build the Gita Mandir at the Mission's campus in Pune. All the volunteers had been allotted different duties related to the construction of this building. Jashan was assigned the task of raising ten thousand rupees to cover the cost of construction. Looking back at that incident, J. P. Vaswani writes:

> I cringed at the thought of going to friends, begging for donations. But I had promised to myself to walk the way of obedience.
> Next morning I presented myself at the house of Dr Boolchand. The family welcomed me warmly, and, as they were just about to sit down to breakfast, earnestly requested me to share the meal with them.
> I picked at the delicious food placed before me, for I had lost all appetite, just thinking of the ordeal ahead. The meal was over. The children of the house left for school. Dr Boolchand's sons left to attend their business and Dr Boolchand invited me to his library.
> 'Thank you, God,' I thought to myself. 'You have given the privacy of a one-to-one meeting with the gentleman. Now, I hope you will give me the courage to broach the matter of the donation, and also bless my effort with success.'

I cleared my throat, preparatory to making my request. I saw that my host was busy at his desk, and waited for him to be free.

He looked up from his desk and said to me, 'Dear Jashan, it is God's grace that has brought you here today. Last night, the thought came to me that I must make a small contribution to the Gita Mandir that is being built at our Mission. I have written out a cheque, and I request you to hand it over to Gurudev Sadhu Vaswani as my humble offering.'

So saying, he placed the cheque before me. I could not believe my eyes when I read the figure on the cheque – it was ten thousand rupees!'

Through many such experiences Jashan understood that no matter how difficult, unpleasant, complicated, or even embarrassing the task before one, if there is the will to obey, God takes care of the rest. That is the secret behind the seemingly impossible tasks that spiritual leaders are able to accomplish.

Sadhu Vaswani would tell his disciples, 'You may wear out dozens of pairs of shoes, walking to the temple or the satsang, day after day. But you will achieve nothing, till you walk the way of obedience to a saint.'

Jashan walked the way of obedience, and the following incident reveals, in his own words, to what extent the Master's word and the Master's will had become his guiding force:

One morning, Sadhu Vaswani said, 'I want to go down to the hall.' So we brought a chair. He used to be carried in a chair (after the fall that left him with a broken hip) and we brought him to the hall. He sat there for some time and then he dozed off. When he got up he asked, 'What is the time?' I told him, 'It is 12 o'clock.' He said, '12 o'clock during the day or during the night?' I said, '12 o'clock during the day.' He said, 'No it's 12 o'clock at night, it is midnight.' I said, 'Must be; if the Master says it, then it is night.' He said, 'Go and see; go and see outside and then come and report to me.'

Now this is something which you may not believe but when I actually went and saw, the sky was dark, the stars were shining and I came and reported it to him. I said, 'It is 12 o'clock at night.' Then, after a little while, the inquisitive person that I am, I said, 'How did this happen at all?' So, I once again went out and saw that it was, in fact, day. But his saying had such an effect on me, or whatever it is, that I actually, I'm telling you, I actually saw stars. That was a great day in my life when I realized that whatever the Master says, he is right.

Jashan understood that when the surrender to the Guru is total, miracles happen. He had, finally understood the true significance of the dictum 'Thy will be done'. Later, in his writings, he described the quality of obedience in the following words:

Obedience to the Guru is a great virtue, for it negates self-will, egoism, and indiscipline, and inculcates the divine qualities of humility, self-surrender, and devotion. Obedience must come from within, and it is born out of three important attributes: faith, respect and devotion. These are the foundation of obedience.

14

THE LESSON OF SEVA AND LOVE

Which is the best exercise for the heart?
Reach down and lift up as many as you can.

J. P. Vaswani

The Upanishads, the *Bhagavad Gita*, and many other scriptures are in the form of a dialogue between the teacher and the disciple. They show how direct interaction facilitates easy assimilation, and the understanding of the most subtle and complex truths. The Guru also teaches through his silence, for his vibrations are powerful catalysts for awakening the dormant shakti or spiritual force in the heart of the sincere and alert aspirant. All this was manifested in the relationship between Sadhu Vaswani and his disciple, Jashan Vaswani.

'What is service, Dada?' asked Jashan of his Guru one morning when the two were seated face to face.

'Service is doing the will of God. There is nothing beyond it. The world has many doers. But in this period of social disorder and chaotic decay, the tortured soul of humanity cries for will-doers – those who do the will of God. Our politicians have been doing, doing, doing; they have been doing mischief. Our social workers have been doing, doing, doing; they have been doing disorder. Their doing has been the undoing of God's plan. Strive to be a will-doer, my child.

Then will your action, blended with bhakti, be radiant with knowledge.'

'How should one be a will-doer, Dada?'

'Be a little child! Practice surrender to the Lord in the little things, the insignificant things of everyday life.'

'If life gives me the freedom to choose, tell me what my choice should be.'

'Choose not, my child! But acknowledge and adore His will. Accept the burden His wisdom lays on you. And believe that every burden is a blessing.'

And so Jashan did whatever came each day. He would accompany the Master on his travels, take dictation of letters or draft letters himself. He would type them out and also type out the Master's lectures and articles. He would edit the *East and West* monthly journal, kindle the sacred *havan* fire, attend to fundraising and the numerous other tasks associated with the Master's work.

The monthly journal, *Excelsior*, launched in 1939, was handled by Jashan alone. It was devoted to carrying the message of the rishis to the youth. Distinguished writers such as Aldous Huxley, A. J. Edmunds, Leon Bruel, and Raoul Lecoq contributed to it. Thanks to Jashan's considerable dedication and effort, the circulation of the *Excelsior* went beyond that of the leading daily newspaper, *Sindh Observer*. There were thousands of subscribers because the subscription had been kept very nominal. The journal ran for seven years and came to an end only with the partition of India.

Sadhu Vaswani was a prolific writer in both English and the Sindhi language. By typing and proofreading his Master's works, Jashan not only improved his own spoken and written Sindhi but also grew in knowledge of the great Hindu scriptures, as also the scriptures of other faiths. Sadhu Vaswani translated many prayers from other traditions into

Sindhi such as 'Our Father' of the Christians and some of the beatitudes of the *Bible*, prayers from the *Guru Granth Sahib* and the *Dhamapada*.

Sadhu Vaswani explained how seva had many forms. He would say:

> 'I know not much. I only know that there is suffering in the world. And men and women wander in darkness. In such a world, let me go about giving love and compassion to all. Let me serve the poor and the broken ones, serve my brothers and sisters, serve birds and beasts and all creatures in whom is the breath of life. Let me not waste energy in questions or controversies. Let me light a few candles at the altar of suffering creation.'

> 'If I meet a hungry man, let me not ask why he is hungry, when so many others feast at their banquet tables. Let me give him food to eat. If I meet a naked man, let me not ask why he shivers in the cold of wintry nights, when so many have their wardrobes filled to overflowing. Let me give him garments to wear. And if I meet a man lost in sin, let me not ask why he is lost, but with a look of compassion, with a song or a syllable of love, let me draw the sinner to the Spirit.'

> 'Let me draw by awakening the longing that lies latent in all. Let me lead some out of darkness into light!'

The Master's every act was a seva. He was a saint who did not aspire to moksha or liberation from the cycle of birth and death. Repeatedly he said to his numerous disciples, 'I will keep on taking birth again and again, till the last human being has been liberated.' And pointing to a street dog he said, 'I would not mind being reborn as a dog if thereby I can give relief to someone in suffering and in pain.'

One particular incident Jashan would recall over and over again:

One day, as Sadhu Vaswani took a walk on the roadside, he saw a beggar lying underneath a tree. His clothes were tattered and torn; his feet were caked with mud. Sadhu Vaswani asked me to bring a bucket of water. As soon as the bucket was brought Sadhu Vaswani, the uncrowned king of our hearts, who had but to lift up a finger and hundreds of us would rush to find out what his wish was, with his own hands, washed the body of the beggar and gave him his own shirt to wear. The beggar pointed to the cap on Sadhu Vaswani's head. Without the least hesitation, Beloved Dada passed on to the beggar his cap.

On that occasion Sadhu Vaswani spoke words, which I can never forget. He said. 'This shirt and this cap and every thing I have, is a loan given to me to be passed on to those whose need is greater than mine.'

In those words is enshrined a teaching which, if put into practice, can change the face of the world. Everything we have – our time and talents, our knowledge and experience and wisdom, our money and possessions, our energy and enthusiasm, our influence and authority, our life itself – is a loan given to us to be passed on to those whose need is greater than ours.

The true Guru wants nothing for himself. He has come to the earth only to give. The disciple must strive for liberation through service, for this entire world is a training ground. As the *Gita* says, the world is a *yajna*, a cosmic sacrifice. Every aspect of nature lives in sacrifice. The sun shines and the trees bear fruit for others; the rivers offer themselves without questioning and judgment. Each one of us, too, must live in the rhythm of nature and give ourselves to the world, selflessly.

Speaking to his disciples of the way of service, Sadhu Vaswani, one day, said:

> 'There was a poor old man shivering in the cold. Someone passed by, searched for a coin in his pocket, found he had none. He lifted up his heart to God and sighed, "I have not a pie to give, but do Thou bless him! Bless this poor, old man shivering in the cold!"'
>
> 'Was not that prayer, too, a service? And could it be that the universe heard it not?'

Right karma is not only good action but includes good thoughts, and aspirations, good words, and kindly dreams. Giving sympathy and love to a fellow pilgrim on the path is an important aspect of seva.

Another incident that was etched in the mind of Jashan, was later described by him in his writings:

> I returned from an errand on which Beloved Dadaji had sent me. On the way I saw several of my brothers and sisters absorbed in speaking to each other. I paused to listen. I gathered that they were discussing, in the severest language, a sister who had been 'caught' in sin. And a voice within me whispered, 'Move on! This is not the place for you!'

When I met Sadhu Vaswani, I spoke to him of what I had seen and heard on the way. And Sadhu Vaswani said, 'My child, remember, there is no sin greater than the sin of separateness. When you sit in judgment upon a brother or a sister, whose sin has been exposed, you indulge in a worse sin, an inexcusable crime. And in judging another, you but condemn yourself. Is it not true, that if you strip yourself of all 'coverings' you will find that within you lurk all the sins man is capable of committing? Alas! The shadow of your passions darkens your eyes!'

'If I am not to condemn a brother who has sinned, how shall I help him to change his ways?'

'Let the sin of your brother teach you to turn the searchlight on yourself. It will reveal to you your own sin. And as you endeavour to cleanse yourself and to extirpate the sin, you will know how deep are the roots thereof and how oppressive it is to keep up the good fight. And through your experience you will know how great is your need of sympathy and love in your struggle against sin, how when this sympathy and love flow to you, you are strengthened in your efforts to find a lasting cure. The best way to help an erring brother is the way of sympathy, example, love!'

After a brief pause, Sadhu Vaswani continued, 'As you sit in your morning meditations and your evening prayers, and as you move about during the day, send out loving thoughts to all who have fallen into the dark abyss of sin but would fain climb out of it to greet the light of the morning sun. And pray for them who lie fettered in prison houses and for all who are on beds of illness groaning in the agony of pain. For the sinner, too, is a sick man; he needs the

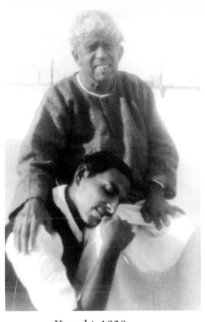

Karachi, 1938
Guru and Disciple.

Karachi, 1938
Author - secretary - typist
in the service of the Master.

Karachi, 1944
Beloved of the Master.

The Guru's household
From left: Hari Vaswani (Jashan's elder sister,
seated), Jashan, Sadhu Vaswani, Shanti and Sati
Thadani (seated).

Pune, 1962
St Mira's School
Enthusiastic participant in all school events.

Pune, St. Mira's College,
Principal and Professor with a
difference.

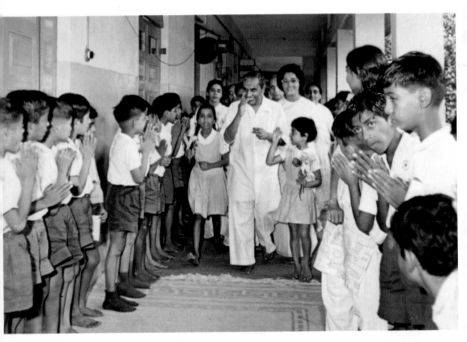

Pune, 1966
St Mira's School
The beloved of teachers and students alike.

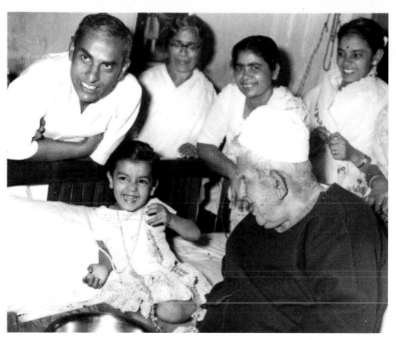

Pune, 1962
Sadhu Vaswani with Jashan on extreme left and Baby Krishna,
(the youngest member of the Guru's household) in between them.

Pune, 1965
Elaborating on THOUGHT OF THE DAY of the Master.

Pune, 1964
Celebrating the Master's Birthday.

Pune, 1965
The disciples become the legs of the Master.
Taking the Master for the evening satsang.

loving treatment of a great Mother Heart. Nothing
else will cure him, nothing else.'

Through his own life, Sadhu Vaswani enabled Jashan to
understand that 'The highest stage of happiness is reached
when you feel that you are unable to live without striving to
make some others happy'.

Through the Master, Jashan also understood the miracles
that love could bring about in the lives of individuals. He
saw, time and time again, the truth of the Chinese dictum
that love is the strongest weapon. It can conquer all.

Jashan recalled how a certain devotee of Sadhu Vaswani
had once been a complete profligate. His wife, to derive a
little comfort and solace, would come to Sadhu Vaswani's
satsang every evening. Her husband did not approve of
it. One day, drunk, he came and met Sadhu Vaswani, and
showing a fist at him, he said, 'If only you knew how much
I hate you.' Sadhu Vaswani, the gentle being that he was,
quietly looked into his eyes and said, 'Brother, if only you
knew how much I love you.' And the words resulted in a
miracle. The man, who only a few moments earlier had said
that he hated him, fell down at his feet crying, 'Forgive me.'
And from that day onwards, his life was changed. He started
accompanying his wife and children to the satsang. And
Jashan learnt, through this and numerous such instances,
the most important lesson in life: that he could build bridges
with all creatures, big and small, with all beings through love
and compassion.

Sadhu Vaswani summed up this teaching in three short
lines:

> The wisdom of the Ages,
> The wisdom of the Sages,
> Is in one word – Love!

Another time, while sitting with the Master in the garden, watching the setting sun, Sadhu Vaswani asked Jashan, 'What is the highest aspiration of your life?'

'I want to enter samadhi and become one with the Lord.'

'I don't want you to get a vision of God with closed eyes,' Sadhu Vaswani said to him. 'I would rather have you see God with open eyes in all that is around you, in all men and creatures, in every atom of an atom and in the Atman within.'

Sometimes, Jashan would feel impatient. He longed to have that ultimate experience that the saints and Rishis talk of in the scriptures and which the poets of Sindh extol in ecstasy. In one such impatient mood, he one day approached his Master and asked, 'Is there a shortcut to God?'

'Yes, there is. Create a longing within yourself. Create love within your heart. Create a vacuum in your heart. That vacuum will be filled in by the Beloved whom the Vedas call the unknown and the unknowable.

'And how do you create that longing within?'

'Every day go into silence and meditate on the words and deeds of Krishna or Chaitanya, of Jesus or Buddha, of Nanak or Kabir. Let your longing reflect itself in tears. Call out to the Lord continuously with full and unbroken longing. Ramakrishna Paramahamsa used to say, "How many weep for God? Weep for the Divine Mother and She will not leave Her child. Weep for Her and She will come and greet you and lift you in Her lap."'

After a pause, seeing the longing in his beloved disciple's eyes, the Guru reiterated, 'Aspire! Aspire! And aspiration, like the smoke of fire, always rises upward. So let the fires burn within you continually.'

Jashan looked deep into his Master's eyes. He felt he was gazing into eternity, into endless oceans of love and bliss. And Jashan could only whisper in awe.

'Who art Thou, O beloved?'

'You want to know? Then love me, love me, and you will know me. The more you will love me the more you will know me.'

Jashan Vaswani, who had always been a natural leader among his peer group, linked his life with one whose will was superior to his own. As the most beloved disciple, he was also the one who was the most severely tested. Yet the constant presence of his Master worked wonders. Jashan watched Sadhu Vaswani waking, eating, working, dreaming, sleeping, serving, chanting, meditating, ever-loving, denying himself to none! The constant close proximity of the Guru ensured that his thoughts, his attitude, and, above all, his sacred vibrations were continuously imbibed by the disciple. Through this process of osmosis, the gap between the disciple and Guru was slowly reduced, until came that final blessed and beatific state, when the Guru and disciple became one, functioning, as it were, through two different bodies.

Living in that divine atmosphere, Jashan was often transported into the highest realms of bliss. And the words poured out of his heart:

In all the world,
There is scarce another
Like unto Thee!
Thou art the mountain peak:
I am a frail climber!
Thou art the ever-loving mother:
I am a child lost
In the fair of this world!
And yet, this have I learnt of thee,
That I am thy yesterday,

Thou art my tomorrow.
I am a tiny stream:
Thou art the rushing torrent.
And, if only I flow into thee,
Together we shall move on
And become one in Him
Who is the end
And fulfilment of life

15

THE GURU'S VISION

*More than developed brains, we need
enlightened hearts!*

J. P. Vaswani

Sadhu Vaswani used to keep in touch with world events
by reading a variety of journals and papers. He even
wrote a series of articles under the heading 'European
Spectrum' which were published regularly in the monthly
journal *Excelsior*. As a historian and philosopher, he had
a vast vision and a deep understanding of world politics.
Commenting on the world situation of the 1930s and early
40s, when the impulse of narrow nationalism was wrecking
havoc in a great part of the world, Sadhu Vaswani pleaded
for a loftier vision of life, one which went beyond patriotism
to embrace all humanity in an attitude of reverence. Such a
vision had been upheld by heroes such as Rama, Krishna,
and the Buddha. It was a vision inspired by the force of love,
which was regenerative and constructive. It was opposed to
the existing vision, inspired by the force of hate, which led to
division and destruction.

Sadhu Vaswani spoke out on the various platforms to
which he was invited, of the need for leaders who lived by
the ideal of renunciation. Raja Janaka, he would say, was

the perfect example of such a leader. True renunciation is detachment from things, forms, and one's own self. And only those who renounced could really serve. He who does not renounce cannot grow in the life of the spirit. For attachments are bondages and lead one to constant compromise.

Sadhu Vaswani himself had renounced all desires and possessions. Never did he aspire to the fruit of any action. He was rich only in dreams and aspirations for India and her silent millions who suffered under the grinding yoke of poverty, ill health, and deprivation. To lift this huge segment of humanity to a life of dignity required leadership of a different kind. Such leadership, he believed, was best exemplified by rishis such as Vishwamitra and Vasishta. They had guided Raja Dasaratha and Prince Rama to live up to the great ideal that kings and princes should be servants of the people. Moreover, effective leaders were men who blended both action and meditation in their lives. Krishna, Rama, and the Buddha were all examples of leaders who were awake within and active on the outer plane.

The Master's love for books and great appetite for learning led him to visit bookshops whenever the opportunity presented itself. There, he would sometimes spend hours browsing through new publications. He would also purchase a number of books and leave the bookshop feeling relaxed and refreshed. In his company, Jashan's knowledge of world affairs became deeper. His own natural inclination for reading and learning, were further developed. He understood that to live in and serve the world, knowledge of the outside world was important. So while he explored the inner universe, he also gained a deep insight into the world affairs.

Jashan sometimes had doubts about the combination of

action and meditation in one's daily life. One day he asked his Guru. 'But so many men of God live alone, in their own bliss,' he commented.

'History is a procession,' came the quick reply. 'Do not stand aloof but mingle with others and walk in the procession. Perchance, you will find the avatara walking beside you!'

'Yet, how can one be with others who do not think like you and don't want to walk your way?' persisted Jashan.

'Be self-sustained but not isolated. Contact humanity and, in this contact, meet your God. Life is fellowship; it is mingling of the individual with the great life. The great God is not shut up in temples. He is in the procession of life. You will find him in the sweat of life, in the tears and tragedies of the poor. To Him you belong; not to a sect, not to an ism, not to a geographical area or a political party.'

Sadhu Vaswani would repeatedly hold up the ideal of the great gurus, saints, and sages of India who lived in this world amongst men, and still remained uncontaminated by worldliness. And while doing so, they had demonstrated in their lives the virtues of love, forgiveness, and compassion. And Sadhu Vaswani would constantly tell Jashan, that at all times, even while attending to his daily work, he must keep his mind on God. Jashan reflected on this for long, and then enquired, 'How can I do both things together: attend to my work and at the same time keep my mind on God?'

Sadhu Vaswani did not reply but, later in the day, gave Jashan an unforgettable lesson which he later described thus:

There were times when he didn't answer when I asked him something. This time, after two hours, he said, 'Take me out. I want to go to the town.' So I took out the car and he sat by my side. While I was driving he kept on talking to me and I kept on answering. He said, 'Did you get your answer?' I said. 'What answer?' He said, 'You remember that question that you had put to me?' I said, 'Yes, yes, yes.' He said, 'Now you are driving the car, your attention is fixed on the road, you are careful to see that you don't have an accident. At the same time you are also talking to me. When you can do these two things together, why can't you work and keep your attention fixed on God? And now turn the car, take it back to the garage. I don't have to go to the town.'

In his life with his Master and through his travels with him, Jashan imbibed much that widened his horizon and unfolded before him a greater canvas of life. With his Master he visited Calcutta where the Master had lived while he was a professor at the Metropolitan College, Calcutta, and where he had met his own Guru, Sri Promotholal Sen (affectionately known as Naluda). He visited Nadia, the birthplace of Nimai, later known as Sri Chaitanya Mahaprabhu, the Krishna-intoxicated. He visited Varanasi, where he met Pandit Madan Mohan Malviya, the founder of Benaras Hindu University (BHU) who had invited Sadhu Vaswani to address the faculty and students of the BHU once every year. Pandit Madan Mohan Malviya had earlier invited Sadhu Vaswani to become a member of the faculty of the university. But Sadhu Vaswani was then working as the principal of Mahendra College, Patiala, and had declined the invitation. Jashan visited the Mulagandhakuti Vihara at Sarnath, where Sadhu Vaswani delivered a lecture on the Buddha's message to the nations. Wherever Sadhu Vaswani went, he met the elite, but, at the same time, he also made it a point to commune with the poor and suffering, offering them food and coins.

Through the Master, Jashan came in touch with a number of great luminaries, sometimes in person and, at other times, through letters: Swami Sivananda, Sri Meher Baba, Dr S. Radhakrishnan, Dr Albert Schweitzer, to name just a few.

Jashan learned to adjust and adapt to a variety of situations, while travelling with his Master. Once Sadhu Vaswani was on a lecture tour of Karachi. He was invited to stay with a humble devotee whose lodging consisted of just two rooms. The family occupied one room, while the other was offered to Sadhu Vaswani for the night. Jashan laid a wooden plank on the fireplace and curling up on it went to sleep like a baby. Serving his Guru and knowing that he was comfortable was all that the disciple wanted. His own comforts never counted.

Sadhu Vaswani was singular also in his reverence for all religions and scriptures. He not only read widely the scriptures of all religions, but was also a prolific writer of the biographies of saints and men of God from around the world. In fact, he is one person in the hagiology of the world who has written on saints belonging to all races and religions, communities and countries, with a spirit of understanding. In his writings there is no criticism, but pure appreciation. Jashan who had grown up with an open mind, now found the opportunity to take appreciation and love for different religious figures to the level of real knowledge.

The most notable thing that Jashan learnt from his Master was the freedom given to each one to evolve according to his or her own ability and inclination. Sadhu Vaswani never imposed any study or any specific text on any one of his disciples. Later, Jashan was to write on how they were always free to do what they wanted. He describes it as:

When we had doubts or any difficulty, any question, we would go to him. He would say, 'Go and sit in silence, you will get the answer.' 'Silence is your teacher,' he would say again and again. He wanted everyone to be self-reliant. Sadhu Vaswani never exercised authority over the lives of his disciples but sought a way into their hearts through love and understanding.

Identification with each and every individual was sometimes more easily understood than practiced. The Master was fond of fruit, and a fruit vendor would visit regularly bringing with him the fruits of the season. He would carry them in a huge basket on his head and go from door to door slowly lightening his burden as the day wore on. One day, Jashan was with the Master while he selected some fruit. To Jashan's surprise, before even picking up any fruit, the Master first passed on a ten-rupee note to the vendor, which, at that time, represented a lot of money. Having done that, he helped himself to the fruit he needed and accepted from the fruit vendor the change he was offered back. He did not bargain or question the man for the price of the fruit.

Jashan was convinced that his Master had been short-changed, and he ticked off the man. Sadhu Vaswani was silent. Later that day, he refused his lunch. Thinking perhaps that the Master would eat later than usual, Jashan again asked him about lunch after an hour. Again the Master refused. By late afternoon Jashan realized that he had done something that had greatly displeased the Master. He had an inkling that it was because of the way he had spoken to the fruit vendor. Feeling very distressed, he went to Sadhu Vaswani with folded hands and begged to be forgiven.

Sadhu Vaswani looked at Jashan with pained eyes and asked, 'Did you not see Krishna, my beloved, in the fruit seller?'

Jashan was forgiven and the Master took his meal. Thereafter, whenever Jashan or any of the other disciples said or did something wrong, the Master would punish himself. He would not punish the person who had done wrong. And that would cause so much anguish to the disciples that they would do their best to abstain from anything that would cause pain to the Master.

Sadhu Vaswani identified so completely with the other. In Jashan's words:

We entered a bus one day. There was only one vacant seat. He made room for me and asked me to sit by his side. I said to him, 'Dada, if I sit, there will be very little room left for you.' Beloved Dada answered, 'We will love each other more and there will be plenty of room.' In Beloved Dada's mind there was no feeling of separation, between his own body and the body of another. Both were tabernacles of the One Spirit. This is what gave him a sense of identification with the sufferings of the poor and broken ones. He did not merely have compassion for the poor. He actually felt that their sorrows were his sorrows. Not unoften, he wept, seeing another in grief.

To live by his Master's teachings, Jashan needed to live in constant self-awareness. Even one moment of forgetfulness would lead to a slip and the Master would notice it instantly.

One day, after having been rudely treated by a brother, Jashan entered the Master's room on gentle tiptoe, to find him seated in a corner. He was the very picture of serenity, his face alight with an unearthly glow. His hands were folded in prayer. And out of his lips flowed words, which Jashan could barely catch.

'Why this war of 'thee' and 'me'?' asked Sadhu Vaswani. 'There is but One and, in the One, thou and I are one! One heart beats in all. One soul sustains us all. This is knowledge: to meditate on the mystery of at-one-ment. This is life: to know Thee, O spirit, as the One-in-all.'

As Jashan listened to these words, his agitated mind was set at rest. His doubts were dispelled. Suddenly, he found love and peace filling his heart and he sent out these feelings to the brother who had been harsh with him. In his heart he spoke to him, 'Let us be at peace, brother, with each other. For One heart doth beat in us both. And One soul doth sustain us still!'

16

THE GURU'S HOUSEHOLD

*The hands that help are holier than those that
turn the beads of the rosary.*

J. P. Vaswani

The household of the Master consisted of five people:
Sadhu Vaswani, Jashan, Shanti Vaswani (the spiritual
daughter of Sadhu Vaswani), Sati Thadani, and Jashan's
elder sister, Hari Vaswani.

Shanti had come to Sadhu Vaswani when she was ten
years old. He had saved her from the jaws of death during
a severe illness, when all doctors had given up on her.
Thereafter, she refused to leave Sadhu Vaswani. Moving
out of her parents' home she became a member of the
Guru's household. Sadhu Vaswani formally adopted her
as his daughter. Her purity, gentleness, complete single-
minded dedication to Sadhu Vaswani, and her immense
compassion for all beings, were deeply moving. While
Jashan was intellectual, highly perceptive with a logical
bent of mind, Shanti was deeply devotional, mystical and
the embodiment of love. For her there was absolutely
nothing beyond Sadhu Vaswani.

Jashan had a very special bond with Shanti who was close
to him in age. Of her he wrote many years later:

She used to take care of me. She had a mother's heart. As a student of the intermediate class she had to take a subject called Logic. Logic as you know is of two types: inductive and deductive. While deductive knowledge is easy to understand, inductive is a little more difficult. She had difficulty with that. So Sadhu Vaswani asked me to spend some time with her everyday teaching her inductive logic. But she would not listen to anything. She would say, 'First tell me the story of some holy man, some saint of God, and then you come to your inductive logic.' She was just like that.

She did not complete her BA because she was simply not interested in studies. She loved little ones. She would tell them stories, give them toys and sweets. She also loved animals. Once a cat passed away leaving a litter of helpless kittens. Shanti would take milk, dip cotton in it and feed them. It came so naturally to her. And she was so immersed in two scriptures, the *Bhagavad Gita* and the *Sukhmani Sahib*. I don't know how many times she must have gone through the *Sukhmani Sahib* paath. Every moment that she got was spent in prayer.

Jashan referred to Shanti as his upa-Guru. In trying times when the Master would be annoyed with him, it would be Shanti who would soothe him and gently emphasize that his unwavering faith in the Guru would help overcome everything. She would say, 'Whatever happens, don't look left or right. Just look straight at your Guru. Ultimately, victory will be yours.'

Sati Thadani was one of the first members of the Sakhi Satsang, the Fellowship of Women, established by Sadhu Vaswani in Hyderabad in 1931. She looked after the cooking and other domestic chores of the household assisted by Shanti and, sometimes, Hari. There was no outside domestic help. Sati also edited the Sindhi magazine, *Shyam*, taught in the St Mira's Primary School, and attended to myriad other tasks as and when required. Hari Vaswani was the principal of St Mira's School in Hyderabad, and an ardent disciple of Sadhu Vaswani.

Before Sadhu Vaswani left his physical body, a new member joined his household, a little girl called Sita Thadani. That the Master accepted her in his home is significant. Little Sita represented the third generation, the future. Equally significant was the fact that she was a girl child; for in the girl child did the Master place his faith and hope.

Sita's mother, Gulshan Thadani, attended Sadhu Vaswani's satsang regularly. When she was expecting Sita, she, one day, tripped on the steps of the satsang hall and fell. Although everything seemed all right, she remained concerned about the long-term health of her baby. Sadhu Vaswani blessed her and assured her that all would be well with the child. Little did Gulshan realize that this child would, of her own, choose to leave her parents' home to live with the Master.

Sita was the first child of Kishore and Gulshan Thadani, and the elder of their two daughters. One evening, after visiting the Mission along with her parents, the little toddler refused to go back home. No amount of coaxing would persuade her to leave the Mission. Hearing the wails of the child, who was being forcibly removed from the Mission, Sadhu Vaswani enquired as to what the matter was. When informed about Sita's refusal to go home, he said, 'Let her be here.' And so Sita spent the night with her aunt Sati Thadani, a member of the Master's household. However, this was not to be just a one-off episode. Sita, thereafter, never went back to her parents' home. She took to her new home as a duck to water. It was as though she recognized Sadhu Vaswani's household as her own and its members as her own real family. She wanted to be nowhere else.

Sadhu Vaswani changed Sita's name to Krishna, which means 'attractive', saying that people would be attracted to Krishna. The choice of name, too, was highly significant. To begin with, Krishna was the Master's *ishta devata*. Several of his poems in the *Nuri Granth*, speak of his love and longing for Sri Krishna. Krishna was also the name of Dada Jashan's mother.

Looking back on her early childhood Krishna recalls:

I looked upon all three of them – Sati Thadani, Hari Vaswani, and Shanti Vaswani – as my aunts, but Dadi Sati took personal care of me, especially when I fell sick. Dadi Shanti was in charge of the fruit, which is something I loved. I used to steal fruits and eat them. The household budget was very limited, so everything was bought in small quantities. We lived very frugally. On days when there was less fruit Dadi Shanti would decide that everyone would get only half a banana. But I used to be very hungry and so when I found that they were all sleeping, or when I saw that nobody was around, I would help myself to a fruit. Of course, Dadi Shanti would find out. And she would say, 'Krishna, never do something untruthful. If you are hungry or you want to eat a fruit, come and tell me. I will never say no.' That is how she would teach me, in her gentle, loving way.

Little Krishna became a builder of destiny at the tender age of two-and-a-half years for it was she who chose her new home and future Guru. Sadhu Vaswani had had to wait till the age of forty before he could renounce his family and career and fulfil his lifelong desire of becoming a fakir. Jashan was twenty-one years of age when he was finally permitted to join his Guru, becoming both a disciple and a member of the Guru's spiritual family and household. Krishna, therefore, was greatly blessed, for she virtually started life in the Master's lap.

Thus began what, in many ways, was an unusual childhood. Krishna lived, ate, slept, and breathed the very air of the Master and his closest disciples every day of her life. At each stage, she received guidance of the highest order.

Life in the Sadhu Vaswani household was exceedingly frugal and simple. Everything had been lost during Partition and whatever little remained was constantly shared with the needy. There was just one cycle on campus and anyone who had work outside the Mission used it by rotation. Jashan would go about town from morning till evening, regardless of the weather, to meet publishers, get the Master's books printed, run errands for Sadhu Vaswani and attend to other Mission-related work.

Food was eaten seated on the ground, with Sati Thadani serving the members. Sadhu Vaswani always ate separately. The family lived from day to day, practicing complete trust in Guru and God. As Krishna recalls:

Sadhu Vaswani would say, 'At night do not keep water filled in your containers. Tomorrow morning, God will provide us water. That is the faith you must have in God.' That was quite something in those days when we did not have a 24-hour water supply. We would get water only for two hours from the municipal corporation. During that period we would fill the *matkas* for the *sangat* who would always drink water after the prasad distributed at the end of the satsang. At night, Bade Dada (Sadhu Vaswani) would insist that all the pots be emptied in the flowerbeds. Members of the sangat who knew about this would fill their flasks and take the water home, treating it like prasad. And, believe it or not, whatever Bade Dada said, actually happened. We never ran short of water. We never had to worry about anything. All that was required just came to us.

When Krishna became a part of the ashram family, Sadhu Vaswani was already bedridden. He inculcated in little Krishna the habit of practicing silence. He would coax and encourage her by telling her that if she sat still for five minutes, he would give her a chocolate. Sometimes she would sit on the bed next to him, at other times on the ground beside the bed. When he was in excruciating pain, her little heart would feel anguish, and with her tiny fingers, she would rub his neck. Little did she realize what a towering personality her spiritual father was. In her child's eyes, he was just a loving presence in whose company she felt supremely happy and loved.

The little girl's parents visited her every evening when they came for the satsang. Sometimes she would also be sent to visit them and her little sister in their home. Sadhu Vaswani would ensure that a member of the Mission would drop her and pick her up. Never did she spend the night in her parents' home: because Krishna's family members were non-vegetarian, and alcohol was also consumed in the home.

Sadhu Vaswani was very concerned that Krishna should not consume any food of violence even by accident.

Before he left his physical body, Sadhu Vaswani entrusted Shanti to Jashan's special care, saying, 'Now you must take care of her because she will not be able to bear my separation.'

Jashan did everything to fulfil the promise to his Master. Whatever Shanti said became a divine law for him. Because she had a heart problem, she could not accompany Jashan anywhere. So he would take her permission before stepping out of the Mission whether it was for a daily walk, a satsang, or some errand. Nothing was ever done without her permission and blessings. Just as Sharada Ma came to be looked upon as the mother to all after the *mahasamadhi* of Ramakrishna Paramahamsa, so also did Shanti acquire that stature because of Jashan's love and reverence for her.

As the Master had predicted, Shanti never recovered from the grief of Sadhu Vaswani's passing on. She survived him by just four years, giving up her body on May 16th, 1970. Her ashes rest by the side of the Master at his sacred Samadhi. Every year, May 15th and 16th are observed as Shanti Mahayagna in remembrance and honour of this great soul. The occasion is marked with the recitation of the sacred scriptures, havan, and seva. Every month, on the bright *ekadashi* day, as well, a Shanti yajna is performed. Thus does this spiritual daughter of Sadhu Vaswani continue to live on in the lives of devotees and disciples, pouring on them blessings from the beyond.

Sati Thadani remained a part of the Master's household but, as she became increasingly frail, the duty of cooking was taken over by her young niece Krishna who was trained under her careful supervision. Dadi Hari lived until 2009.

Little Krishna was just four years old when Sadhu Vaswani left his physical body, but he had touched her life for always. The seeds planted by him in her deep unconscious mind would slowly grow and bear fruit when the time was ripe. She, too, was left in the care of Jashan who was to guide and shape her through her growing years, grooming her for a role that she was destined to fill.

17

THE REBIRTH

He who loses himself in his teacher
is the true disciple.

J. P. Vaswani

One of the greatest lessons imbibed through constant association with the Master was reverence for all life. For him everything, sentient or insentient, was sacred and required to be treated with reverence.

Once, while out walking with the Master, Jashan suddenly saw a stone along the path that they were walking on. Without interrupting the speed of his walk, he just stepped ahead and kicked it aside to ensure that the Master did not trip over it. He did not notice Sadhu Vaswani cringing at his action. Hence, he was surprised and dismayed when he saw a look of displeasure on the Master's face. He began wondering what he had done wrong. When he could not pinpoint anything, he timidly asked his Guru, 'What has gone wrong, Master? Why are you displeased? Have I made any error? Please tell me.'

To this Sadhu Vaswani replied, 'If God dwells in the scriptures, does He not dwell in the stone? Seeing you kick the stone gave me a lot of pain. Always remember, God does not exist in the holy scriptures only. The same God is in this stone, in the trees, the leaves, the flowers, and the rocks. God is omniscient. He is in everything and everywhere. Hence, treat everything with kindness and gentleness.'

Jashan, who thought that he had grown in self-awareness, realized that developing total self-awareness was an incredibly long journey. He understood that he should have picked up the stone and gently put it aside. Later he was to tell his fellow devotees, 'Sadhu Vaswani taught me, not merely in words but in deeds of daily life, that we must revere and respect everything, everyone we see around us.' And J. P. Vaswani would teach his fellow devotees the prayer: 'O Lord, teach me to regard all life as sacred. There is but One Life that flows into all – men and birds and animals, living and non-living things. May I touch everything with love, treat everyone and everything with respect!'

To people who were plunged in grief, Sadhu Vaswani would say, 'Feed the birds every day and you will be abundantly blessed.' He turned the spacious terrace of his residence, Krishta Kunj, in Karachi into a place for feeding birds. Grain in large quantity, along with water, was kept in readiness every morning and noon on the terrace. Birds, especially doves, would flock there in hundreds to have their fill.

At the World Animal Day celebrations, once, Sadhu Vaswani enquired of the organizers who the chief guest was of the meeting.

'Who but you, Dada, could be our chief guest,' said the organizers.

'It is but meat,' Sadhu Vaswani replied, 'to have an animal, as the chief guest on the World Animal Day.'

Pointing to a pet dog in the front row, Dada requested its owners to place him on the chief guests' chair. This received an uproarious applause from the children. By strange coincidence (if there is, indeed, such a thing as coincidence) the same evening, as Sadhu Vaswani was taking a walk in the park, who should the disciples find walking behind the Master? The same dog that had been placed in the chief guest's chair!

Satsang or fellowship meetings formed an important part of Sadhu Vaswani's daily program. Even during his travels, daily fellowship meetings were held in the house of his hosts.

The *Gita* declares that the mind is one's greatest friend but also one's greatest enemy. Therefore, the greatest self-discipline is required in purifying and uplifting the mind. For that, the senses must be kept pure, because the mind rushes out into the world through the sense organs. When the senses are either overfed or starved, the result is weakness, disease, and hallucinations. The speech, too, must be pure. The scriptures, Sadhu Vaswani would emphasize, teach us that we should speak only what is necessary, in a sweet tone, and only when it is beneficial to the listener.

Jashan would remember how the spoken word goes forth like an arrow, blessing or wounding some human heart. Once uttered, the word does not come back! At the same time, Sadhu Vaswani would say that one must not be afraid to mention what one believes to be true. He said, 'Stifle not the utterance, the sound of your soul, by conventions, customs, and fossilized traditions. Speak out the truth; but not in bitterness.'

Jashan understood how communication is not just by words, expressions, and gestures, but also by vibrations. Negative vibrations result in bad dreams, which are nothing but an expression of one's subconscious life. Hence the importance of exposing the mind and the senses, at all times, to all that is pure, and noble. There must be purity of motive, thought, and impulse. Then alone can our will, thoughts, and imagination be pure and undefiled. Then alone will the practice of self-discipline bear fruit.

Sadhu Vaswani would repeatedly urge his disciples to be careful of their thoughts. He would say, 'A man becomes what he thinks of.' And also, 'Never forget that every thought you think, every word you utter, every action you perform, every feeling, every emotion that wakes up within you, is recorded in the memory of nature.'

The three greatest enemies of the mind are lust, anger, and greed (*kama*, *krodha*, and *lobha*). In the *Bhagavad Gita*, they are described as the gateways to hell. Self-mastery implies conquering these three dangerous enemies. And unless the disciple learns to master himself, he can be a master of nothing and no one.

Purity of mind is reflected in the countenance and in the radiance of the eyes. Sadhu Vaswani noticed how his beloved disciple's eyes had a divine glow, how his voice had grown even gentler, and how his face radiated devotion and love for his Master. His silent presence and single-pointed attention to every need of the Master were all noticed. The Master was happy.

Jashan asked him, one day, for a map of daily life. And he said, 'Aspire each day to live a holy life. Therefore, never speak untruth. Always avoid slander. Heal divisions. Strive for harmony. Be compassionate to all creatures. Shun luxuries, shows, idle talk, and vain arguments. Spend some time in silence and meditation. Abandon incontinence. Live in perfect charity. Sing the Holy Name and breathe out peace to all beings.'

Another time, in Karachi, Sadhu Vaswani came into Jashan's room and said, 'Jashan, I am feeling hungry.'

'You and hungry?' asked Jashan, quite taken aback. 'This is the first time that I've heard you say that you are hungry! How is that possible? Tell me what you want. I will go and bring it for you.'

'Are you sure?' asked Sadhu Vaswani.

'Of course, Dada.'

'I want to eat *pharoo-aan* (a seasonal fruit that grows in Sindh),' repeated Sadhu Vaswani.

'Is that all you want? I will go and bring it right away,' and Jashan got up to leave.

Climbing on to his bicycle, Jashan rode into the town. He went from shop to shop asking for pharoo-aan but nobody had any. The fruit merchants all said that it was not the season. Jashan was determined to get it and offered to give the fruit merchants a hundred rupees if they would procure the fruit from somewhere. It was the very first time that his Guru had asked him for anything and he wanted to be able to give him that.

Despite his best efforts, Jashan was not able to find any pharoo-aan. So, finally, he returned to find the Master busy at his table. Jashan ruefully informed him about his unsuccessful mission.

'I did not need pharoo-aan,' smiled Sadhu Vaswani. 'I only wanted to teach you a lesson, that everything has a season. Out of season you cannot get it. The season that you are in now is the season for you to be united with God, with the Guru. Don't waste this time!'

Whenever the Master felt the slightest trace of complacency in the disciple, he would inject a sense of urgency into him. 'The human birth is the only gateway to God. You cannot get there through the body of an animal. This is a golden opportunity that each one of us has been given.'

Living in the physical proximity of the Guru, whatever little trace of negativity remained in Jashan was drawn out. The Master drew him closer and closer to the Light. Jashan had renounced his body, his youth, his mind, his intellect, his future, all at the feet of his Guru. His surrender was total. Over a period of seven to eight years, he had become as malleable as clay in the hands of the potter, to be shaped as his Master willed. The divine spark that had been within him as a child, which had been kindled to grow a little brighter through the meetings with fakirs and holy men in his teenage years, steadily grew into a roaring flame in the continued presence of the Master. Love consumed him totally. Then, one day, did Jashan experience the highest grace of his Master and his heart sang out in pure rapture:

O Friend!
My joy is boundless,
For the Beloved hath chosen me!

My garments are dipped
In colours of the sunset
And my heart is dyed deep
In the colours of love!
I am become a beloved of the Beloved!

Unworthy I,
Yet, he hath chosen me.
He hath looked on me in compassion.
And calling me to himself,
He said, 'Thou art not a stranger:
Thou art my own, my very own!'

I am become, O friend,
A beloved of the Beloved!

Out of the mire of worldliness,
He lifted me up!
And he gave me to drink
The living waters of grace.
My heart is cleansed:
And within me a fire burns.

I am become, O friend,
A beloved of the Beloved!

The affairs and activities of the world
No longer please me.
I do but yearn to bask
In the sunshine of the Beloved's gaze.
Wounded in my heart with the wound of love.
I am become, O friend,
A beloved of the Beloved!

I know not what hath come over me.
In my heart is yearning
For him, alone for him.
I love him more than life.
To him do I belong,
Birth after birth.

I am become, O friend,
A beloved of the Beloved!

18

THE CHOSEN ONE

May my face be always turned to Light! May
my footsteps always lead me to the right:
And even if I stumble, may I be granted the
strength to rise and get back to the Path.

J. P. Vaswani

In 1947, India was partitioned, and Sind, with its majority Muslim population, became a part of Pakistan. A mass exodus of the Hindu population began. While most migrated to India into cramped and overcrowded refugee camps, others spread around the world where relatives and friends were already settled. Although the partition affected the provinces of Punjab and Bengal as well, these were split into two, one part going to Pakistan and the other remaining with India. That way, even though Punjabi and Bengali refugees from the newly-formed Pakistan were uprooted and dispersed, they still had a homeland in India where their language and culture continued unchanged. For the Sindhi Hindus, however, there was no longer any geographical, cultural, and linguistic space of their own. Sind went entirely to Pakistan.

Sadhu Vaswani and a small group of his followers remained in Sind for a little over a year after the partition, until prevailing circumstances compelled them to leave. With a grieving heart, Sadhu Vaswani bid a tearful goodbye to his beloved sun-lit Sind; the Sind of the Sufis and their soulful songs; the land of his forefathers. He landed in Mumbai on 10th November, 1948, accompanied by Jashan and a few close disciples. Three months later, he moved to Pune and made it his base. Thus began a new phase in the Master's life, one that he would later refer to with sadness as 'the years of exile'.

In the first few years following the partition, Jashan spent much of his time accompanying his Master on visits to refugee camps. They were appalled at the scale of poverty and suffering of the refugees. In one stroke they had lost homes, lands, employment, material goods and, for many, even loved ones. Devotees were urged to do whatever they could to serve these unfortunate people who lacked virtually everything. Sadhu Vaswani would spend hours listening to the tales of woe of an unending number of Sindhi visitors. He would instil courage and hope in them so that they could find their feet and become, once more, the prosperous and philanthropic community they had traditionally been. Whatever offerings Sadhu Vaswani himself received were passed on to those he considered needier than himself. Above all, he poured out love and benedictions on them. Jashan was both a witness to and a participant in the healing process. So totally was he a part of his Master's ministrations to one and all, that he absorbed the same demeanour, tone of voice, and words.

One of the first things that Sadhu Vaswani established, after moving to Pune, was the daily evening satsang. Steadily, the numbers attending it grew. In 1949, a Welfare Department was set up by Sadhu Vaswani to help needy Sindhi families. Then followed a charitable dispensary and St Mira's School, especially established for Sindhi children. In 1958, however, an English Medium St Mira's High School was opened to all the children of Pune. All these institutions functioned from the Jeejeebhoy Castle and its vast estate, where the Sadhu Vaswani Mission is located today. Eventually, Sadhu Vaswani and his household, too, moved into a section of that building. The estate was eventually purchased thanks to the generous donations raised by numerous devotees and admirers of Sadhu Vaswani.

Over the years, the Master also began to travel to other cities in India, to visit his numerous followers scattered across the country. He was also invited by a variety of organizations to give talks and preside over functions. Sadhu Vaswani would always travel by third class, accompanied by Jashan and a group of disciples. Along the way they would hold *bhajan* and *kirtan* sessions making the journey one long, joyful satsang.

In 1954, Jashan started the *East and West* series, a monthly periodical where he published the writings of Sadhu Vaswani so that they could reach a wider audience. The *Excelsior* that he had so successfully edited and circulated in Sind had ceased to get published after the hasty departure for India. Shortly, thereafter, the construction of the Gita Bhavan also got underway. In 1962, St Mira's College for girls was started and affiliated to the University of Pune. Jashan became the principal, a post that he was to retain for sixteen years.

The post-Partition period was one of intense seva for Brother Jashan, as he now came to be called. Between 1953 and 1958, Sadhu Vaswani's health deteriorated, and on August 29, 1959, he had a fall, which was to keep him bedridden for the rest of his life. Years of excruciating pain and restless nights followed. His weak state of health made it impossible for him to personally meet the hundreds of people who flocked to see him everyday. And so, Brother Jashan began shouldering some of the Master's responsibility. Very soon he endeared himself to the devotees, many of who would collect around him at night for talks and discussions. These soon became regular informal fellowship meetings.

The task of principal and professor of St Mira's College took up considerable time, as did the editing of the *East and West*. Through it all, Jashan offered personal seva to his Master, day and night. He would take dictation from the Master, attend to his correspondence, represent him at various meetings, and attend to all his personal needs. The Master would be carried outside on a chair by four disciples. When visitors came to meet the Master, he wrote out beautiful thoughts for them on cards. Brother Jashan would be asked to read these out and interpret them. Slowly, Sadhu Vaswani withdrew more and more from outer activities, devoting a greater amount of his time to the interior life. The tenderness, reverence, and deep devotion with which Brother Jashan served his Master are summed up in the comment that Sadhu Vaswani made to him, 'I am reminded of my father when I see you looking after my needs with such tender concern!'

The spiritual path is not easy. There are continuous obstacles to be overcome. Even when a disciple has scaled the heights, there is always a danger of falling off the peak. To remain safe and secure in spiritual attainment, he (or she) needs the protection of the Guru and God. Brother Jashan had many challenging years in independent India, building up his Master's work and taking care of his Master's failing health. The following incident is just one example of the kind of situations that he had to deal with.

One day, a young man who had resolved to travel across the country on bicycle, came to get Sadhu Vaswani's blessings before embarking on his journey. Full of ambition and excitement, he was met by Brother Jashan outside the Master's apartment. Brother Jashan showed him the closed door of Sadhu Vaswani's room and informed him that when the Master was ready to receive visitors, he would open the door himself.

The impatient young man was incensed and said, 'Who do you think you are? How dare you come in the way of my meeting Sadhu Vaswani? I am on a cycle tour. I don't have the time to wait.'

'But my friend, Sadhu Vaswani's door is closed and we cannot disturb him now,' replied Brother Jashan in a calm but firm voice.

In frustrated rage, the man slapped Brother Jashan on his face. Completely unperturbed, Jashan remembered the words of Jesus Christ that his Master so often quoted to him, 'If someone strikes thee on the right cheek, offer him the left.' And so, Jashan offered him the other cheek. The man, even more enraged, thinking that Jashan was being extremely cheeky, slapped him even harder. Jashan remained unperturbed and silent.

Shortly thereafter, the door opened and Brother Jashan invited the angry young man into Sadhu Vaswani's room. The Master received the visitor in his usual warm and loving way, giving him generous gifts as prasad.

A devotee who was present when this incident took place reported the matter to Sadhu Vaswani when the visitor left. The Master was moved to tears and silently embraced Jashan very warmly. He felt fulfilled at having a disciple who was a man of true humility, for only such a one can be a man of forgiveness. The man of humility never thinks of avenging himself. He forgives the wrongs that have been done to him and prays for the wrongdoers, in the immortal words of Blessed Jesus, 'Father! Forgive them, for they know not what they do!'

The long years of selfless, devoted service, and of gruelling work, reaped rich spiritual dividends. In 1958, Sadhu Vaswani expressed the desire that the occasion of Brother Jashan's 40th birthday (2nd August) be celebrated in a fitting manner. This was the first public acknowledgement that Brother Jashan was being groomed to continue the Master's work. It was also the Master's way of establishing a tradition, whereby Jashan's birthday celebration would become an annual feature of the sangat.

A year later, on his 41st birthday, Sadhu Vaswani read out to the sangat the message that he had written for Jashan:

> How blessed are we to have one such as him in our midst! And on this auspicious day, I breathe out an aspiration that my dear Jashan may go from heart to heart, home to home, nation to nation, carrying with himself the message of the rishis and sages of India!
>
> And today, I have been saying to myself, 'My reverential salutations to those who seek the Beloved in the temple of the heart!' Most of us are busy running after wealth and possessions, hankering after name and fame. Only a fortunate few seek the Beloved. Only a blessed few seek to enter the shrine of the heart. To this category belongs my dear child, Jashan! He has sought to find the Beloved in the cave of his heart. In quest of the Beloved has he undertaken the journey within!

Once again, the Master was affirming before the entire sangat that Jashan was the chosen one. It was a clear indication that the mantle of the Master would one day rest on his young shoulders. He had been the exemplary disciple who, in the flower of his youth, when he had talent, success, personality, acclaim, and a brilliant future before him, had chosen, instead, to walk the straight and narrow path to the temple of the Beloved. Uncompromising in his quest, and steadfast in his devotion and service to the Guru, he had reached his destination. Having attained that, he continued to serve the Master with utmost humility and love. He retained his discipleship. Therefore, he was worthy of becoming, eventually, a Master in his own right.

In 1960, on his 42nd birthday, Sadhu Vaswani wrote the following message for Jashan:

Child of my tears and prayers; Child of destiny!

This day I give thanks to Him, the builder of Destiny, that I have seen your face again and touched your feet and been blessed once more. I know I soon must quit this scene and rise from flame to flame and seek the stars. India, alas, is broken and the world is sad and lonely. A prayer rises in my heart, today, that you may still trust the rishis, the Seers of the Secret of Life; that you may have always a heart of sympathy and love; that you may always seek your joy in communion with the common life and in the songs of children; and that, in the tumult and noise of modern life, you may still bear witness to the City of Saints and Sages.

Rich is your spiritual inheritance from your revered father. Compassion is the crowning aspiration of your life. Is not compassion the Ganga, which flows on, gently pouring in the heart the water of healing that the sad world needs? Is not compassion the key to that freedom which we find in the hearts of the noblest and the purest among mankind? Far from my home am I today. Blessed be the name of the Lord that, in my exile here, I have been blessed by you and taught by you the great lessons of compassion and sympathy. To Him I bow down with a prayerful heart. May He grant you strength and illumination to fulfil your mission in life.

Last night I went afar from you: I know not where I wandered in homeless space. Methinks I saw God lonely standing in a corner, and dreaming His dreams and saying, 'Dreamers I need!' You are one of His dreamers! May your life be richly blessed in the holy service of sympathy and love! And may you bear witness, wherever you be, to the tree beneath which the Buddha sat to receive Enlightenment – the Bodhi Tree of brotherhood and love, of fellowship between all nations, all races, all religions, all countries, all communities, fellowship between the East and West!

This time the mandate of Brother Jashan was clearly spelt out. 'Child of tears' and 'Child of prayers' refers to the great tapas that the Master did to be worthy of such a disciple. It is an expression of deep gratitude and joy, for, as Jesus Christ said, 'Many are called, few are chosen.' For the sake of these fortunate few, saints take interest in several seekers after Truth, but only a few chosen ones will rise to the pinnacle of glory. For the sake of these few select ones, saints draw innumerable souls in the hope that the former will fling asunder their worldly fetters and devote themselves solely to God.

'Child of tears' also refers to all that the Master invested of himself in nurturing the one who came to him as a tender sapling, raising it into a powerful, majestic tree that could now give shade and shelter to many. Tears, according to Sadhu Vaswani, are of great significance in the spiritual journey. 'For without tears,' he says, 'there is no real yearning.' He believed that it is when you shed tears of longing, the tears of yearning for the Lord, that you draw close to Him. 'Radha,' he said, 'shed tears, and only then did she get Shyam.' Hence, Radha became Radha only because of her tears.

In this message are also spelt out the concerns of Sadhu Vaswani, which he was directing his disciple to address. The first was the state in which India found herself. She had gained independence, but had yet to attain true freedom: freedom from want. Innumerable were the poor and suffering in India. Men of sacrifice and service were needed to lead India out of poverty, injustice, and divisiveness into an era of glory and greatness that had been hers in the past. Jashan would have to awaken young leaders to the timeless wisdom of the rishis; to the understanding that only through sympathy and love, through mixing with the common people could India be served and uplifted.

For Sadhu Vaswani, dreamers were of utmost importance. Only those who had a dream, an ideal, he stressed, would be able to transcend their limitations and make a difference in the world. He would say, 'BELIEVE AND ACHIEVE.' A dreamer is one whose life is dedicated to selfless service as a means of realizing his or her dream. And this service is inspired by the vision of the oneness of all life. Sadhu Vaswani loved to quote Emerson who said, 'Hitch your wagon to the star!' In other words, the dreamer is the one who has a great and powerful vision, and for which he strives with faith and fearlessness, undaunted by the obstacles and setbacks along the way.

Thus did the Guru publicly anoint Jashan. The disciple had become an instrument, tuned to perfection. It was now fit to render any melody composed by the Master from the Earth plane or from beyond the stars. Jashan was to travel around the world building bonds of brotherhood between all people and also between humanity and other creatures: birds, animals, fish, rivers, mountains, and so on. Great strength and blessings were required to fulfil such a mandate, for the world does not heed to such wisdom easily. Many and complex are the problems that beset the world. But the answer to all these problems is to be found only at the spiritual level, through love and compassion, and through service of the poor and suffering. Jashan, through personal effort and example, was to pave the way for a new world order, the great dream of his Master.

That this message was understood by one and all, is clear from a poem that Brother Jashan's sister, Hari Devi Vaswani, wrote several years later, long after Sadhu Vaswani's departure from Earthly plane.

> And he 'pon whom the Master's mantel
> Was to fall, when he was about
> To enter forty-second year,
> These be the words the Master wrote,
> This be the message he did give,
> Not merely to him, his beloved child,
> But through him to all aspirants,
> To all pilgrims, to all seekers,
> Wending their way to the City
> Of rishis and saints and sages ...

Hari Vaswani quotes several lines from the Master's letter and then goes on to say:

> Thus did the Master bequeath treasures,

Of the spirit, richer than wealth
Of the world, to his chosen one,
The child of Destiny, the Child
Favoured by gods and goddesses.
And now in the Master's footsteps
The Child of Destiny doth walk,
Moving about from place to place,
Spreading the teachings of the saints
And sages of the East and West.

From Sadhu Vaswani's message it is also clear that the two most defining characteristics of his disciple were compassion and sympathy. Compassion begins in awareness. As J. P. Vaswani in his writings describes:

The first step on the path of compassion is to be aware that the One Life flows in all. The second step of compassion is the acknowledgement that all creation is one family; all beings of the world including birds and animals are my younger brothers and sisters in the one family of creation. The Buddhist scriptures tell us the story of Ananda, asking the Master, 'Would it be true to say that the cultivation of loving kindness and compassion is a part of our practice?' To which the Buddha replied, 'No, it would not be true to say that the cultivation of loving kindness and compassion is part of our practice. It would be true to say that the cultivation of loving kindness and compassion is all of our practice.'

A Jewish teacher tell us, 'Kindness gives to another. Compassion knows no 'others'. Compassion binds the world together. The man of true compassion gives without judgment. He never ever asks if the others deserve his charity or compassion.'

On the night of 15th January, 1966, Sadhu Vaswani said to his beloved disciple, 'Jashan, my child, I would like you to be by me tonight.' And Jashan – ever obedient, ever loving, and attentive – was beside his Master through that fateful and memorable night. At 8:20 a.m. on the 16th of January, Sadhu Vaswani left his physical body.

Despite his own deep sense of personal loss at this poignant and sacred juncture, Jashan recognized that to grieve was selfish. Although he would sorely miss the radiant and loving physical presence of his most revered and beloved Master, he would henceforth be in touch with him on a subtler plane. And he would always remain the surrendered, sincere, and devoted disciple of Sadhu Vaswani.

As hundreds of people started streaming into the Mission to bid goodbye to Sadhu Vaswani, Jashan's peaceful countenance and gentle voice instilled hope and comfort into the hearts of thousands who felt bereft. It was Brother Jashan who set the funeral pyre alight, at the very spot at which Sadhu Vaswani had sat many a time under the canopy of trees. On that spot today stands his sacred samadhi.

Jashan looked back on a time when he had asked his Master one day, 'What is the happiest moment in the life of a Guru?'

'When he loses his disciple,' came the prompt reply.

'How is that?' had asked Jashan in wonder.

'The Guru works, day in and day out, so that the disciple may be led to the *sadguru* within his heart. And when this happens, the disciple himself becomes a guru. The Guru loses a disciple. It is to him a day of great rejoicing. His work is over! His task is fulfilled!'

This process had slowly but visibly manifested. The disciple had steadily been completely transformed. The fire of the Spirit had transmuted him into the very substance of the Guru, until, like his Master, he too, began to shine with the light of the Life Divine. Many years later, when writing about the Guru-shishya relationship, J. P. Vaswani described:

> The Guru and the shishya do not live apart: the twain is one in consciousness, in function, and transmission of the Spirit. A shishya, indeed, cannot live apart from his Guru, for a disciple to be torn from his roots in the Guru is suicide.

The greatest legacy that Sadhu Vaswani bequeathed to his people was his perfected disciple, J. P. Vaswani.

THE MASTER

The call of life is: Onward! Forward! Upward!
Inward! Godward!

J. P. Vaswani

19

THE SACRED MANDATE

*The Guru loves all: but he who loves the Guru and
surrenders himself to Him, serving Him day and night,
will attain the Highest!*

J. P. Vaswani

The initial period after the departure of his Guru was one
of immense pain and grief. The songs of separation that
poured out of Brother Jashan's lips during this period are
heart-wrenching. He invokes his Master as a magician who
dyed him with his magic and then simply went away. He
laments the fact that it took the Master just one moment to
withdraw, leaving his loved ones bereft and alone. Nothing
and no one had been able to bind him. He simply slipped
away, breaking thousands of hearts in the process. The
disciple describes how his eyes can now only rain tears for
his Beloved.

Verse after verse, the anguish pours out. 'O Beloved,' says
he, 'you were like a swan bird that has left behind imprints
for us to follow. Fragrant was your life, full of beauty, as the
lila of the Lord. You captured every heart with your lila
and, then, you flew away. Your earthly span was like one
brief night. How could I know that it would be so brief?
The times we spent with you were sheer ecstasy. Now the

thought of your departure plunges me in sorrow. What can poor hapless Anjali (nom de plume) do? She can merely go from pillar to post asking where she may find you again.'

Brother Jashan came to be addressed as 'Dada Jashan', 'Dada J. P. Vaswani', or simply 'Dada'. To those that flocked to him, he would reiterate that, 'Sadhu Vaswani can have no successor; for he lives and will continue to live, age after age. He has no need of a successor.' Dada Jashan also declared to all the followers of Sadhu Vaswani that when the Master was about to pass away, he had said to his disciples, 'I can do greater things through you than I have done through this body.' And that was exactly what the disciples, led by Dada Jashan, resolved to do.

The numerous activities and service programmes of the sangat that Dada Jashan introduced after the physical departure of his Guru, bore the sacred name of his Master. They were all consecrated to him and continue to be so. Repeatedly, Dada urged the sangat to practice the presence of the Guru, to carry his name on their lips, his image in their hearts, and his message in their deeds of daily living. He himself, would, every day, after his early morning meditation, come into the *kutiya* of his Guru to seek his blessings and receive his guidance. His evenings would also conclude with some moments of silent communion with the Master, in his kutiya.

A ten-foot high bronze statue of the Master was installed in the roundabout near St Mira's English Medium School and the place was renamed as the Sadhu Vaswani Chowk. The Brotherhood Association, established by Sadhu Vaswani in Sind and further developed in India, was renamed the Sadhu Vaswani Mission. Everything, henceforth, would be in the name of Sadhu Vaswani.

One of the first things Dada Jashan laid emphasis on

was *kaar seva*. He wanted all devotees to do seva with their own hands, and he personally joined in the collective effort: of cooking for and serving the poor, conceptualizing and carrying out projects for social welfare and rural development, and so on. On the sangat's insistence, Dada Jashan also began to give regular talks during the satsang. Initially, these were restricted to Sundays, when he spoke on the thought of the day. This would be drawn from the book of 365 thoughts written by Sadhu Vaswani in Sindhi. Gradually, a pattern developed: on Thursdays and Sundays he would discourse in Sindhi, while on every fourth Thursday of the month, he would speak in English. The last Saturday of every month was especially devoted to addressing the youth.

For six years after the departure of his Master, Dada Jashan made it a point never to stay out of Pune overnight. His travels were restricted to visiting devotees in Mumbai or the surrounding areas of Pune, which he could do in a day. This was because the urns containing the Master's sacred ashes were temporarily placed in the kutiya (Sadhu Vaswani's room) and for Dada they represented the physical presence of his Guru. The urns awaited their final resting place at the samadhi. The challenge was in getting a life size statue in pure white marble of Sadhu Vaswani. Dada Jashan would not be satisfied with anything except the very best, and that took time.

It was only in 1972 that Dada started travelling for a few days at a time. As a result of these travels across India, numerous Sadhu Vaswani Centres and satsangs were established in different parts of the country by members of the Sindhi community. Dada would then be invited regularly to visit these centres to give talks; perform *bhoomi puja* of new buildings of the Mission; preside over havans, ceremonies for newborn babies, meditations in memory of dear departed ones, engagement ceremonies and weddings. He would be requested to inaugurate new factories, open new shops, restaurants, bank branches, and so on. The number of people drawn to him grew in leaps and bounds.

In 1980, Dada Jashan began his travels outside India. The first such visit was to Colombo, in 1982, where he was invited to address the World Hindu Conference. Admirers around the world, then, insisted that he visit them in the different countries where they were settled. And, since Sindhis are settled in virtually every country of the world, the invitations were, indeed, numerous. At the same time, he was also invited to participate in international symposia, conferences, and meetings.

Thus, after long years of apprenticeship, Dada Jashan began to fulfil the mandate he had received from Sadhu Vaswani: to carry his Master's teachings around the world, build bridges between people of different faiths and communities, and inspire people to spiritualize their daily lives. Everywhere he went, he would emphasize that in the love of God and the service of man is the secret of true life.

Gradually, centres were opened in many countries by a small group of inspired and dedicated individuals. Dada urged those in charge of the centres to organize a satsang every day. The Sanatana Dharma, he stressed, was not a once-a-week affair. It was a vital part of daily life. However, for many, this daily meeting proved difficult for they were too busy with their shops and businesses. In some places, however, it did take off, thanks to the dedication of the women of the community. Over the years, programmes have developed for all age groups: the Gurukul for children (weekly classes on culture and spirituality), Bridge-Builders for the youth, and a range of activities for adults. As a result, Dada has been able to reach out to entire families and communities.

Today, the Mission has more than thirty-six centres around the world: in India, the USA, Canada, Panama, West Indies, Trinidad, the Virgin Islands, UK, Spain, Japan, Morocco, Dubai, Indonesia, Malaysia, Singapore, Manila, and Hong Kong. Followers, however, are present in all the continents.

Once the centres were established, a regular pattern of annual trips abroad, to every continent in the world, became a part of Dada's life. The programmes soon took on a fixed pattern, which continues until today. They include *rooh-rihan* satsangs or informal fellowship meetings, held early in the morning, in the home where Dada stays. Everyone is free to talk to Dada and ask questions, both personal and practical. Then, there are the more formal question-answer sessions held in public halls. Sometimes, these are organized specifically for the youth. A third type of programme includes recitations from the scriptures and kirtans followed by a talk by Dada. The fourth programme, where Dada talks in English, normally draws larger crowds. In Puerto Rico, for example, 90 per cent of the audience at such talks consists of Puerto Ricans. Arrangements are made for simultaneous interpretation of the talk into Spanish. In London and several other cities, the audience at Dada's talks swells to thousands.

Programmes abroad also include discourses at Buddhist monasteries, churches, temples, universities, schools, symposia, and world conventions. Dada's eloquence, erudition, and spiritual force have drawn ministers, ambassadors, industrialists, high-level government officials, and others to his talks. Whenever he is asked about the purpose of his visit to the West, his reply is, 'In my mind there are no distinctions of the West or the East. Both belong to the one heavenly Father's home. I love to think of the whole Earth as my country, and to do good as my religion. I am a pilgrim. In the spirit of a pilgrim, I move on, from place to place. I go wherever the will of God takes me. I go in quest of fellow pilgrims, in whose hearts there may be love for spiritual things, longing for the unseen.'

A pilgrim, he emphasizes, is one who has no attachments. He knows that nothing and no one belongs to him. He belongs to the Lord alone. The pilgrim moves on, without hurry and without resting, towards his goal. When asked if he has followers around the world, Dada says, 'I have no followers. I am a follower myself. They are all followers of the Master.' Such is the humility of this man of God who conquers hearts by suffusing them with the sweet fragrance of love, purity, and goodness.

Over the years, a three-day Sadhana Camp has also been introduced. This offers a break from the daily routine and permits a complete immersion in spiritual living. The camp includes prayers, guided meditation, talks, kirtans, havans, walks with Dada, questions and answers around a bonfire, and some form of social service. During his travels, as per the tradition of his Master, Dada Jashan always makes it a point to visit orphanages, homes for mentally retarded children, old-age homes, refuges for the poor and the suffering to offer a treat, bless the inmates, and shower his love upon them.

During a press interview, he was once asked, 'What is your ambition?' Prompt came his reply, 'I have no ambition. Every ambition is a chain that binds us to this Earth. I, but, aspire to be a servant of my Master, whose name my lips are not worthy to lisp.'

Dada Jashan does not plan his programmes. Invitations come, requests are made and, on their basis, programmes are organized. He strongly believes that whatever the Master wants done will happen. As a disciple, he continues to lead a surrendered life.

In the initial years after the partition, Dada Jashan's mandate was to serve the Sindhis in particular. As an uprooted and dispersed community, many were in great need of spiritual guidance to face their multiple challenges. They also suffered from the angst of losing their language and culture. That is why, wherever he travels, Dada urges Sindhis to keep up their language, which is fast losing ground with the young generation. This is because Sindhi is no longer of political and administrative use, since there is no state in India where it is the main language. And language, according to Dada, is the great marker of cultural identity. In every town or city that he visits, he makes it a point to have some satsangs in Sindhi. Even if there are just five people who can speak the language, Dada will ensure that they have a satsang together. In Mission centres around the world, he encourages members to teach Sindhi to children in the Gurukul. In addition, he also advises parents in the West to inculcate in their children, a love for Indian culture and tradition.

Sadhu Vaswani firmly believed that Sindhi literature has a message to give to the world. Dada hopes that by keeping the language alive, this literature will, some day, be translated into other languages. It is for this reason also that the Sadhu Vaswani Mission continues to do most of its work in the Sindhi language. The organization could have had a much wider reach and a far bigger audience had it used Hindi and/or English. But the idea was always to keep the Sindhi language from dying out.

Keeping the focus on the Sindhi language is also a way of holding the community together. Without a land to call their own, Sindhi Hindus today have multiple homelands, and nationalities. There is no land that they collectively identify with; hence, the importance of the Sindhi language and a common spiritual focus. The latter, based on certain simple but universal teachings, is relevant to all spiritual seekers and is not restricted to a narrow religious base.

Dada also urges Sindhis to learn about the many great heroes and holy men, martyrs and mystics who contributed to the rich culture of Sind. There is a general impression among people, including the Sindhis themselves, that Sindhi Hindus have always been only businessmen. This is not true. Therefore, the Sindhi community needs to become aware of its own cultural heritage, teach it in its schools and, in this way, make a meaningful contribution to the cultural life of India and humanity.

Dada goes out of his way to render assistance to anyone even remotely interested in studying the language. Once, en route to Miami, he stopped at St Louis for a brief halt. Among the many admirers and friends that had gathered to meet him, one young man requested Dada to teach him to read and write Sindhi. Instantly, Dada gave him his first lesson in the language. He also presented him with a primer on learning Sindhi. As an experienced teacher, Dada was able to ensure that the first lesson was thoroughly grasped. He left the learner considerably motivated.

Another teaching that Dada Jashan seeks to give his community is that of vegetarianism. Sind came under the influence of Islamic culture two centuries earlier than the rest of India. Because it was a feudal society, when the feudal lords embraced Islam the peasantry promptly followed suit. Therefore, Islam became the dominant religion. As a result, eating meat became a part of the Sindhi way of life. One result of this was that when, after 1947, Sindhi Hindus migrated to India, those in Gujarat found it hard to rent houses. Gujaratis, who are often vegetarian, did not want tenants who ate meat.

Dada Jashan, in his travels around the world, has constantly sought to awaken Sindhis to the importance of vegetarianism. As a result, his followers recognize that the best offering that they can make to him – more important than money or seva – is a pledge to turn vegetarian. For many Sindhis this poses a real challenge, and giving up meat becomes for them a major turning point in life; one that begins a journey of self-discipline and self-restraint. It implies living life with conviction and daring to be different from others in the community even though this may sometimes invite scorn and ridicule.

Sucheta and Kumar Chugani of Casablanca describe how when Dada accepted to visit their city, they went vegetarian two weeks prior to his visit. They cleaned out their kitchen of all non-vegetarian food and got rid of their stock of liquor. They purchased new kitchen utensils, crockery, cutlery, and plastic storage containers, so that they would not have to offer Dada anything that had ever been in contact with 'food of violence'. Dada stayed with them for three days and three nights. His presence had such an impact on Sucheta that she has remained a vegetarian since that visit several years ago. A year later Kumar also gave up eating meat.

The second step in Dada's effort to promote vegetarianism is to advise Sindhis against engaging in business that involves cruelty to animals. For instance, there was one follower of Dada who had trawlers to catch fish by the thousands. The fish would be left to multiply in a particular area and then they would be harvested in huge numbers. When he proudly explained how he had built up his business, Dada asked him gently whether he was aware of the terrible karmas that he was gathering. Dada's words somehow touched the man's heart and he resolved to change his business.

When people consult Dada on whether to open restaurants as a possible business, he urges them to open vegetarian restaurants because having non-vegetarian food would, once again, accrue bad karma. Or, he suggests that they start a business to introduce mock meat in the market to offer people an option. There are some who heed what he says and others who do not. Dada also asks businessmen to reflect on how much they want to multiply their fortunes and for what purpose exactly. He points out how large fortunes left behind are not necessarily beneficial for the young. Easy money often leads to the formation of wrong habits. Moreover, it is good for young people to face challenges and to have to struggle, for that brings out the best in them.

Another piece of advice that Sindhi businessmen receive from Dada, when they invite him to inaugurate new factories or showrooms, is that they must live by the three great laws of prosperity. An industry, says Dada, grows in prosperity when,

1. It satisfies some need of the people and is service-oriented,
2. Honesty is regarded as the best policy, and,
3. God is made the senior partner. For this, it is necessary to offer Him 10 per cent of the profits to be used as the Lord directs in the service of good causes.

Dada has brought into being what his followers refer to as an international 'Dada family'. Members of the community, flung across the world, have forged new bonds in their common love for and devotion to Dada. He has instilled pride in them for the Sindhi identity and kindled interest in some hearts to study the beautiful and lyrical Sindhi language. He has given them new ideals, beyond business and material well-being, and taught them to open their hearts generously and share their prosperity with the less fortunate. In short, he has brought back many traditional values of the Sindhi way of life, among members of the Sindhi diaspora.

Over the years, as the second and third generations of Sindhis born outside Sind were growing up, Dada started reaching out to the wider Indian and international audience. He uses the analogy of the family. While one will always have duties towards one's own family, the *svadharma*, one must also fulfil duties towards the wider community, the *lokasangraha*. Both are necessary in an individual's life. In Dada's case, the *lokasangraha* aspect of his work started on its own when invitations from Indian institutions and international organizations around the world started pouring in from 1982 onwards.

Among the many forums where Dada has been invited to speak are the World Hindu Conference at Colombo; talk on 'World Peace' at the Dag Hammarskjold Auditorium of the UNO; the 10th Hindu Conference in New York organized by the Vishva Hindu Parishad of America; a talk entitled 'World Without War' at the House of Commons, London; the Global Forum of Spiritual Leaders and Parliamentarians on Human Survival at Oxford; Parliament of World Religions, Chicago, Cape Town (South Africa) and Australia; the International Seminar on 'Vedanta and Sufism' at Mumbai, to mention just a few.

The lokasangraha aspect of Dada's life received a further

impetus when, at the age of eight-three, he undertook to study Hindi. Soon he began giving regular talks over various television channels in Hindi. Thereafter, he was invited to address many forums around the country in Hindi. This decision to speak in Hindi was prompted by persistent requests from admirers around India who had heard his talks in English and wanted more, in their own mother tongue.

In the final analysis, Dada's work for humanity is greater in scope than his work for the Sindhi community. Even though Sindhis constitute 95 per cent of the donors and patrons of the Sadhu Vaswani Mission, they represent only 15-20 per cent of those who benefit from the educational, medical, and social welfare programmes of the Missions. These are meant for everyone. Moreover, the spiritual discourses aired over the television reach countless non-Sindhi homes across India. Similarly, Sadhu Vaswani and Dada Jashan's talks in world forums and their publications continue to reach an ever-widening circle of people around the world. They are slowly but surely changing hearts, opening up minds, and taking sincere seekers a step closer towards a more humane and peaceful world.

20

REACHING OUT TO THE SANGAT

*Without God we can do nothing. With God
there is nothing that we cannot do!*

J. P. Vaswani

In the 1970s, when he did not travel much, Dada was accessible to his many followers in Pune. His innovative ideas and gestures drew an ever-growing number of people to his Master's teachings. He brought joy, creativity and abundance into numerous lives and created what became life-long bonds with his followers.

In order to spare a thought for the poor and the hungry, Dada started a practice of missing dinner every Friday evening. Several joined him with enthusiasm. Dada would advise them to have the meal prepared, nevertheless, and, instead of eating it, pack it up and arrive at the Mission. A large group of people would then accompany Dada on a long walk through the streets of Pune, distributing the packed dinners to the homeless. On an average, a group of forty to fifty people would participate. The joyful surprise on the faces of the homeless, each time in a different locality of the city, was touching.

Every Sunday morning, Dada would hold a satsang and, thereafter, he would go for a long walk. Of course, a large number of people would join in. Often the whole group would leave the Mission only to return in the late evening. Dada would not plan the route of the walk. It would be spontaneous and he would go wherever the whim took him. At that time the streets of Pune were not as busy and congested as they are today. If, on the way, he happened to pass by a devotee's house, he would drop in for an impromptu visit. Sometimes, he would stop for a cup of tea; and this implied serving tea to the hundred odd people who accompanied him. The housewife would rush around, generously assisted by members of the walking group. With joy and laughter tea would be produced, served, and relished.

At other times, Dada would announce that he had come for lunch. First, he would hold a satsang in the home, thereby divinizing the atmosphere of the house. This would be followed either by a thought for the day, or a brief question and answer session. At other times, he would interact with the children in the family. While this was going on, several women, with great excitement and with a flurry of activity, would be briskly working to turn out an impromptu meal for so many. Food never ran short and the hosts would later marvel at the ease with which a huge task had got done in such a short time and with so much of laughter, creativity, and joy.

Dada would walk briskly on these excursions and those who could not keep pace with him would follow by cycle rickshaw. Often he would stop at different homes for breakfast, tea, and lunch. But there was one condition to these visits. If anyone, along the way, invited Dada to their home, he would not come. Therefore, it became an unwritten law that, while one could pray for Dada's presence in the home, it was something that was never to be vocalized.

Dada also visited many small towns and villages throughout Saurashtra, Gujarat and Maharashtra, where many Sindhis were settled. Often during these travels there would be a total lack of basic facilities. This never daunted Dada who would, nevertheless, halt for one night and do a programme with the local communities. Sometimes people set up makeshift toilets. At other times bathing was done in the open with two devotees holding a piece of cloth as a curtain. No effort was too great for Dada for spreading the word of his Master.

Devotees celebrating their birthdays in Pune would often receive the blissful surprise of Dada's unexpected visit. If that was not possible, Dada would personally write a card. But what touched people the most was his presence at the time of the death of a loved one. Grieving parents, children, spouses, or siblings would inform Dada when doctors had given up hope on a patient and when it was just a matter of time. He would immediately arrive in the hospital or the home with a group of people. They would charge the atmosphere with the continual singing of God's name. This would continue until the soul left the ailing body. So many were helped to cross over by Dada in this manner. He would advise his followers on the importance of continuous chanting for a loved one who was unconscious. 'To you all he is unconscious,' he would say, 'but the subconscious will receive those vibrations. So whenever a person goes into a coma, let the person sitting with him or her go on singing loudly. If you cannot do that near his ear, then keep a recording instead.'

Even though Dada is outgoing and loves meeting people, initially he shunned any activity where he was the sole focus of attention. Once, on his birthday, while he was the principal of St Mira's College, the faculty and students decided to have a big celebration. Dada was not in favour of it, but knowing that no one would listen to him on this issue, he decided to play truant and disappear for the day.

Through one of the devotees he arranged for a gown and a car. At 5:00 a.m., on his birthday, he concealed himself in the folds of the gown, bowed down at the Samadhi, and surreptitiously got into the car. The watchman had gone for his ablutions; the gate was unlocked as it was an auspicious day and people were expected to come early and pray. Dada was, thus, able to drive away undetected and unhindered.

He picked up his helpful devotee on the way, and proceeded towards Alandi, where he had decided to spend the day in solitude and prayer at Sant Tukaram's shrine. But fate had other plans in store for him. After being on the road for a while, a cyclist suddenly shot out from nowhere, on to the road. In order to avoid him, Dada swerved hard and the car went off the road, sliding and tumbling down the slope.

The car was a wreck, but Dada and his devotee survived. Dada asked the devotee to arrange for the car to be salvaged, and to bring another car for them, without informing anyone at the Mission about the incident.

After seeing Dada safely ensconced in a small *dharamsala*, the devotee left to do Dada's bidding. Without any food or water, Dada spent the whole day in ecstasy, singing one song after another. When he spoke of the experience later, he said that one by one, all the sages and saints, avatars and incarnations came to meet him. They shared a lot with him, but the one common message they all conveyed was, 'Always bow down before love.'

In the meantime, at the Mission, Dada's absence created pandemonium and panic. Dada's mother, Krishnadevi, organized five search parties to go in different directions and visit all of Dada's favorite haunts, but to no avail. They returned after several hours, disconsolate. Dada simply could not be found.

Later in the evening, to everyone's relief, Dada returned to the Mission and narrated his experience. By then there was searing pain in his ribs from the impact of the steering wheel. It required immediate medical attention. Three weeks passed before the pain subsided. Thereafter, he bowed down before the love of the sangat and agreed to be part of the annual birthday celebrations done in his honour, out of love and devotion.

21

DEVOTEES AND DISCIPLES

*There are many ways to God. But the surest
and shortest is the way of love.*

J. P. Vaswani

A disciple, according to Dada, is one who has sold his mind to the Guru. In other words, he surrenders totally to the Guru and retains, thereby, no identity of his own. In return, he gets the protection of the Guru. Disciples, therefore, are very rare. There is a saying that you can get hundreds of Gurus but you cannot get a *chela* or disciple. For, how many today are willing to offer the body, mind, and soul to the Master?

A devotee is one, who loves the Guru and pays attention to his teachings, but he or she has not sold his or her mind to the Guru, i.e. he or she does not surrender totally to the Guru. Therefore, devotees give monetary offerings to the Guru. Since they cannot give of themselves completely, they offer whatever they can by way of wealth and time for voluntary work, so that the Guru's work may spread and so that more people may benefit from it. It is their way of expressing gratitude for the many blessings received from the Guru.

Since Dada does not consider himself to be a Guru, he claims not to have any disciples. A journalist once asked him,

'Tell us Dada, who is your favourite disciple?' Pat came the answer, 'I am my own disciple. I have many things to learn yet.' The questioner persisted, 'Dada who is your second most favourite disciple?' Pat came the reply, 'I seek to be a disciple myself.' For Dada there is only one Guru and he is Sadhu T. L. Vaswani.

Devotees have remarked how Dada does not encourage people to touch his feet. In fact, he expressly requests people not to do so. When he was younger and people touched his feet, he would promptly bend down and touch their feet in turn. Today he cannot do that. There are two reasons for his discouraging people from touching his feet. First, it is because of his complete humility. The other reason is because, for most people, touching the feet is nothing more than a ceremony, a tradition. The real significance of the gesture is neither understood nor appreciated. Hence, it remains an empty gesture, a mere formality.

The feet represent the ideals for which the holy man stands. When we touch the feet of such a person, it implies that we, too, seek to live by the same ideals. So touching the feet is like making a promise that we will abide by the teachings and ideals of that particular holy one. Hence, only when we have understood his ideals and have resolved to live by them, should we touch the feet of a man of God. Without such an understanding, all that the devotee gains, is a sense of satisfaction at having done what he or she deems appropriate.

Sadhu Vaswani never initiated anyone in the formal way. His initiation was silent and subtle. No words were exchanged and no formulas were repeated. He simply touched hearts and transformed them, and, gradually or all at once, the individual began to grow.

The question may well be asked – if Sadhu Vaswani did

'A day when I have not learned
anything new is a wasted day.'

'Books are my first love.'

The joy of sport.

Cooking and sharing is so much fun.

Pune, 1970.
The humble sevak.

Devoted son and fulfilled mother.
With Krishnadevi Vaswani during her
last days.

Always time and a loving word
for the poor and neglected.

Fellowship with feathered friends.

Every child must be treated with reverence.

'I see the presence of God in every aspect of His creation.'

Pune, Yerawada Jail.
Satsang with the prisoners.

Beloved Master and Guide
of innumerable followers around the world.

not believe in any formal initiation, and if he did not accept anyone as a disciple, how did one know that he or she had been accepted by him? Dada Jashan explains that the initiation came, sometimes, through his loving eyes, sometimes through his touch, sometimes through a powerful, life-transforming thought. But whenever it came, no assurance in words was given! It was to be *understood*. There were some who failed to understand it. Having eyes, they did not see; having ears, they did not hear. Dada emphasizes that even now the Master's inspiration continues to flow. It is, as it was then, to be *understood*. His grace continues to flow, and it may be received by all sincere souls who turn to him for help and guidance.

Today, many people ask Dada for *naam* or initiation with a mantra. They see friends and family members, who are members of other spiritual organizations, receiving *mantra diksha* from their gurus and they feel that they are missing out on something. So they insist that they, too, must get naam. There is a perception that by doing so, they will be formally accepted as devotees of Dada.

The real significance of naam, however, is more profound. In its real sense, naam is given only after a *disciple* has been tried and tested over quite a long period of time. Then he or she receives naam from the Guru and it goes right into the heart and completely transforms the disciple. And how does that happen? There are three layers of personality – the Atman, the mind, and the body. Most common problems, diseases, sorrows, and personality problems arise at the level of the body or the mind. Now the mind itself has several levels – the conscious mind, the subconscious, and the deep unconscious mind or the causal body, the *vasanas*. It is at this level that the seeds of the personality and the seeds of many problems, mental and physical, exist. Doctors and psychiatrists work on the physical and part of the mental level respectively: the conscious and the sub-conscious mind. However, the psychiatrist is not able to reach to the level of the causal body, which is the deepest layer of the mind. Therefore, she/he is not always able to strike at the root of the problem.

Only the Guru can work at the deepest level of the personality. Guru Nanak in his *bani* says, 'Sarb rogh ka aukhad Naam.' That is to say that every disease, *sarb rogh*, whether it is of the body, of the mind, or of the soul, can be cured by the holy name of God. That is because the naam is a vibration. Every one vibrates to a particular frequency, and this vibration is the deepest level of the being. Disease, physical or mental, implies that the vibration of the individual has been disturbed. The vibration of the naam penetrates the entire being of a person and sets right his or her vibration, which has been disturbed. Once that happens, the problems disappear and total health is gained. That is the power of the naam.

Merely doing japa is not enough. It is the spiritual Master who has to fine-tune the vibration of the disciple, and heal or transform him or her. That is how Jesus Christ was able to transform Mary Magdalene. That is how Valmiki, who was a highway robber, could transform himself through the mantra given to him by Narada Muni. Naam is, therefore, that which the Guru gives when he is sure that the person to whom he is giving it is receptive. Otherwise, it does not serve its real purpose. In most cases the heart is not ready to receive it.

There are many gurus, however, who manipulate the vibration of the disciple through other means. Dada Jashan, for instance, never received naam from his Guru. Even some of his own closest disciples have never received naam from him. As Dada explains, in olden days, rishis gave initiation only through eyes, not through touch or through the mantra. The vibrations of a holy man are received mainly through his eyes. Therefore, is it important to look into the eyes of a holy one.

Men of God also transfer spiritual energy through the touch of their hands. The best way of becoming worthy of receiving their blessings, and for making progress on the spiritual path, is to serve them. A holy man, explains Dada, is a man of deep gratitude. For little, ordinary things, he feels grateful to us. If such a man has accepted a glass of water from your hands, says Dada, you are blessed. For the holy one will not forget your service to him.

Today when Dada gives naam to his devotees, it is because they have demanded it for many years. Since they insist upon it, Dada has adopted the practice, as a way of encouraging them on the path, to give them comfort and a sense of belonging, because they feel the need for it.

Another aspiration of Dada's numerous followers is to mark special occasions in his sacred presence. Dada is generous with his time. However, there are certain conditions that devotees must fulfil in order to have the blessing of his presence.

Engagement ceremonies are often held at the mission with the prior consent of Dada. Before agreeing to such a request, however, the young couple and their families are given to understand, among other things, that there will be no dowry accepted by the boy's family. In addition, both families will abstain from serving non-vegetarian food and liquor during any of the celebrations associated with the engagement and wedding.

Only if these terms are agreeable to all concerned, will Dada commit himself. During the ceremony itself, Dada asks the groom and bride-to-be in turn, whether they are ready, willing, and eager to take the other as a life partner. He advises them to treat the parents-in-law as 'parents-in-love'; and, to do their best to be true to each other because, these days, he says, to be 'absolutely true' is extremely difficult. He also stresses that whatever has happened in the past is a closed book and must be forgotten, but that from this moment onwards, their lives should be like an open book for one another. The young man is advised to remember birthdays and anniversaries because much of the grievance of young wives is that these occasions are forgotten or overlooked. The importance of discussion and dialogue in the case of misunderstandings is highlighted and, finally, Dada recommends that if one partner wishes to move on the spiritual path, the other should be of help, rather than a hindrance.

The prospective bridegroom must declare before the whole sangat that he will not accept dowry and, most important, that he will never raise his hand against his wife. Parents-in-law-to-be of the bride must publicly declare that they will treat their prospective daughter-in-law as a daughter.

Agreeing to a wedding without non-vegetarian food and liquor is not something that most Sindhis find easy. For most, a large wedding is a question of prestige. Dada's feelings about many Sindhi weddings are summed up in the following words:

I am deeply pained when I see the ostentatious and lavish wedding functions that are now becoming a habit with some of our families. Expensive buffets are laid out, and much of the food heartlessly wasted or thrown away in a country where millions of people can't get even one square meal a day. Loud, blaring music and crass display of wealth distract our attention from the deep and profound significance of the wedding rituals.

Dada seeks to explain to his followers that one must not focus on pleasing others. When we do so, we build up expectations; we imagine the rewards, the advantages, and the appreciation that would accrue to us through our efforts; and when this is not forthcoming, we end up blaming ourselves and others. Nothing we ever do can please everyone. Therefore, instead of trying to please people, we should try to please God. 'Do whatever you have to do in the ever-radiant presence of the Lord,' he says. At the time, he also gives people a slogan to repeat to themselves when they are troubled by the opinions of others: 'They say. What do they say? Let them say!'

The demanding of dowry is something that Dada has repeatedly condemned as a curse on the community. The woman, he emphasizes, represents Lakshmi, the goddess of wealth and prosperity. That is how she must be treated, instead of being bartered away in marriage. He also recognizes that women must be educated and empowered so that they take the initiative in refusing dowry for their sons. It is the women who must take the lead in cultivating simplicity.

Another important ceremony over which Dada is invited to preside is the sacred thread ceremony for young boys. Before accepting such an invitation, however, Dada insists that the boy turn vegetarian. Since this is not easy for everyone, the young boy is asked to try it out for a period of six months. If he is able to abstain from 'food of violence' then he qualifies to have the ceremony performed by Dada. While putting the sacred thread on the boy, Dada explains its significance. The three strands represent truth, compassion, and purity – the triple strand of true life. The boy must take the pledge to live these qualities. Numerous girls, subsequently, requested Dada to not deny them the opportunity of wearing a similar thread. Therefore, Dada also performs the ceremony on women who are ready to take the triple pledge.

Devotees have learnt over the years how much Dada dislikes show and ostentation of any kind. Once, on a visit to Saurashtra, Dada was received at the entrance to a town by a large crowd of devotees dancing to a merry tune played by a band of musicians. Dada got down from the car and met them very lovingly and humbly. Then, to the astonishment of all those present, he briskly walked through the crowd, overtook the band and procession, and reached the house of his hosts in record time before the procession of band players.

Dada does not enjoy receiving awards either, for, as he says, 'Awards and titles are chains. What has a seeker after God got to do with them?' However, since most awards and citations are announced as a fait accompli at public functions, there is little he can do to refuse them. On such occasions, he accepts such tributes in a spirit of humility, with the words, 'All glory to the Master!'

Many are the distinctions, honours, and citations that have been conferred on him – 'Ajata Shatru' (friend of all) from the Bharatiya Vidya Bhavan, London; the U Thant Peace Award in the US; the Prani Mitra Award from the Animal Welfare Board of India; Honorary Citizenship of the state of Georgia, USA; the proclamation of a Dada J. P. Vaswani Week by the Mayor of Chicago, to mention just a few.

Simplicity is what Dada seeks and what he is most content with.

22

Touching Multiple Lives

Fulfil all your obligations, attend to your daily duties,
be attached to nothing, no one – and be ever ready
to depart when the call comes!

J. P. Vaswani

Every single moment of Dada's life bears witness to his words, 'If you want to be happy, make others happy.' His mission is to reach out to the poorest of the poor, to the hungry, the hopeless, the suffering and the forlorn, bringing them love, comfort, and hope. It is for this reason that the Sadhu Vaswani Mission today has branched out into a variety of activities touching multiple lives in numerous domains.

Besides a free Homeopathic Dispensary, a diagnostic centre, and a clinic located on campus, the Mission today has developed a sophisticated and state-of-the-art medical complex located in Koregaon Park, Pune. The inspiration for this came through a personal experience of Dada Jashan, which left him deeply distressed.

Once, while he was on a visit to Mumbai, Dada witnessed a terrible accident. An old man had been knocked down by a vehicle on a busy road. He lay unconscious but no one stopped to help. Numerous pedestrians and vehicles passed by, all completely indifferent to the dying man.

Dada stopped his car and rushed to the man's side. With the help of friends he had him carried into the car. Then began the most harrowing search for a humane hospital, clinic, or nursing home that would agree to give treatment that was urgently required to save the man's life. Hospital after hospital, clinic after clinic refused to attend to the man simply because he did not have a name and an address. These were needed for their records, explained the personnel at the hospitals. Finally, it was a little-known hospital in the suburbs that accepted to treat the patient. The old man remained in the hospital for three days and then passed away.

Deeply distressed and anguished by the careless attitude of the hospitals, Dada resolved that, by God's grace and the blessings of his Master, he would build a hospital where no sick or injured person would ever be turned away; where even the poorest of the poor would be offered treatment with love and respect; where no patient would be reduced to a mere number.

On January 9, 1989, that dream came true when the Nobel Laureate, Mother Teresa, inaugurated the Inlaks and Budhrani Hospital, a multi-specialty general hospital. Today, the Sadhu Vaswani Medical Complex also includes the M. N. Budhrani Cancer Institute, the K. K. Eye Institute, and the Fabiani and Budhrani Heart Institute. The ideal placed before these institutions by Dada is: 'Every patient is a picture of God. To serve him is to worship God.' The hospitals serve only vegetarian food and no distinction is made in the treatment of patients who pay and for those who cannot afford to.

The Eye Institute serves villages that lie within a radius of about 225 kilometres from Pune, in four districts of Maharashtra – Ahmednagar, Satara, Raigarh, and Pune. In the initial years 95 per cent of the institute's work was charity work and only 5 per cent was for paying patients. Today, the paying patients account of 15-20 per cent of hospital care and they subsidize about 50 per cent of the charity work.

The work is funded by devotees and well-wishers around the globe. A total team of about 125 members, of which eight are located full time in the rural areas, work for this cause. Twenty-eight eye check-up camps are held every month in the villages. Patients who require surgery are brought to the hospital in Pune. Every morning, batches of about sixty villagers are dropped back to their villages and the same evening a fresh batch checks in. This happens throughout the year except for three days during Diwali.

The heart institute is the newest one in the medical complex. It, too, has a community outreach programme. In this case, however, it is not a daily activity given the nature of treatment and the costs involved. Besides four to five camps a year in the rural areas, a similar number of camps are organized at the institute itself. These are publicized extensively through local newspapers in the whole of Maharashtra and the response is overwhelming. The camps in the village are one-day affairs.

A prayer room with the scriptures of the various faiths lies on one side of the reception of the general hospital. Quotes by Sadhu Vaswani and Dada Jashan line the walls and are a constant reminder to staff and patients alike that God is ever present and working through them. Dr Shiv Gupta, the Head of the Department of Cardiology, talks of the attitude of some patients:

About three or four years ago, I was operating on a patient. He had an infection in his heart that had spread and I was sure that we were going to lose him. We did what he had to do and I spoke to the relatives.

They, surprisingly, did not lose heart. They said, 'We have come to Dada's hospital. You give the treatment but we have His blessings.'

The patient is alive until today. This is one of the medical miracles that I have seen. Several patients show extraordinary faith and resilience in the face of tremendous suffering because, as they say, '*Hum Dada ke hospital pe aiya hai. Dua to bahut hai idar* (We have come to Dada's hospital. There are many blessings here).'

The General Hospital, among other things, provides artificial limbs free of cost and this cost is borne by the Sadhu Vaswani Mission. Such patients also receive a walking stick, a walker in the case of the elderly, or a crutch where required. In cases where, for one reason or another, an artificial limb is not suitable, the individual is presented with a tricycle. One devotee from Morocco was so moved that he invited the manufacturer of these limbs, Salil Jain, to Casa Blanca in Morocco. Jain returned with an order for 102 limbs, which he then went back to fit personally.

The practice of distributing free limbs was launched on Dada's 90th birthday. On that occasion, 90 free limbs were offered to those in need. Steadily the numbers have increased. Today the hospital offers 2,000 limbs annually. The Sadhu Vaswani Mission is the only NGO that is based in Maharashtra and which travels across the whole state, offering this service. Every three years patients are contacted again to tell them that they need to replace the prosthesis or orthosis.

A few simple daily rituals remind Doctors and other hospital staff of Dada's vision. A morning assembly in different departments brings doctors, nurses, and other staff together. They chant two verses of the beautiful prayer: *Prabhu teri hi kripa se sab kaam ho raha hai* ... (Lord, it is only because of Thy Grace that all this work is happening. And through it you are giving me the credit). As Dr Shiv Gupta says, 'This fact is something that strikes me over and over again; I think that I have done something but then I remember that actually the doer is Dada.'

The Sadhu Vaswani Mission commemorates a few important occasions by organizing special programmes that reach out to the world at large. These programmes are centred on a theme dear to the heart of Sadhu Vaswani and that of his beloved disciple. One such programme was launched in 2012, to commemorate Dada's birthday on 2nd August. Referred to as 'Forgiveness Day' or 'Moment of Calm', this is a global initiative for world peace and brotherhood. Individuals and institutions pledge to observe two minutes of silence at 2:00 p.m. on that day. While doing so they clear the heart of all misgivings, and breathe out an aspiration of peace and harmony. The moment marks the time of birth of Dada Jashan. As Dada says, 'The best giving is forgiving.'

The programme was launched from Chicago while Dada was away in the US on his annual visit. Speaking to his followers around the world over YouTube he said:

Most of us have no peace because we hold grudges against others, we have negative thoughts. At least once let us forget all these thoughts by forgiving everyone who has in any way wronged us. I do not have the time today, otherwise I would have explained to you and to myself that whatever is happening to me, to you, is according to the law of karma. Perhaps in the past, near or remote, I have done something to somebody. Whatever I have done must return to me otherwise the balance cannot be returned in the Universe. This Moment of Calm takes you all beyond those things that keep us captive. Just experience this Moment of Calm, by forgiving all wrongs that have been done to you. It was Jesus who came and taught this lesson. He said, 'If a brother smites you on the right cheek, give him the left also.' The person who builds his life on this ideal, he has the experience of this peace that passeth, that surpasseth all understanding. I would wish every one of you to have this experience.

In 2013, Dada was in New Jersey when the Moment of Calm was observed. His message this time was the following prayer, which is relevant for every one, every single day:

So bless me lord that I may learn to return good for evil, a blessing for a blow, may my heart be so filled with love that there is no empty nook or corner in it for resentment against anyone. Thou art seated in the hearts of all, therefore, let me meet everyone with respect, and treat everyone with love. Let me not remember any wrong that has been done to me, any hurt that has been inflicted on me. I forgive all. I love all. I forgive all. I love all. I forgive all. I love all.

The programme is steadily increasing its reach, particularly among school children and the youth in college. One million seventy thousand pledges were received in 2014, when the participating schools were asked to take part in a contest of creating a Forgiveness Tree. The tree is considered the ideal symbol for forgiveness. You throw a stone at it and it gives you fruit in return. Children were asked to make a model of a tree and hang on its branches little hearts with messages of forgiveness on it. Schools all over the world participated, for the theme of forgiveness cuts across all religious and racial boundaries. Some schools made a permanent installation of a Forgiveness Tree so that parents, teachers, students, and support staff could constantly reflect on the need for forgiveness beneath it. Children had the opportunity to exteriorize grudges against parents, peers, teachers, and friends. In India, the programme was conducted in various regional languages. Muslim, Christian, and Hindu teachers looked up their various scriptures to come up with appropriate quotes on forgiveness. And the students found the universality of this profound message in their various traditions.

One young woman, who volunteered to help with the programme, described how, as a single mother of an only child, she was always irritable and impatient. At the least provocation she would smack her son. But when she went into silence, it suddenly struck her that she was being very harsh with her child. Instead, she needed to forgive him for his mistakes and mischief and also treat him with love. With tear-filled eyes she made a new resolve. That evening she went down on her knees, hugged her son and said, 'Please forgive me, I have been so hard on you. I realize now how wrong that was of me.'

A rich businessman from Mumbai had fired an employee because of a major oversight. The family of the fired worker had come and pleaded with him. Without an income they would be in terrible distress. But the businessman did not relent. That afternoon he took part in the Moment of Calm and had a sudden change of heart. He contacted the employee and called him back. After a long chat with him, he agreed to give him one more chance. The employee was relieved, his family was delighted, and the businessman felt a burden lift from his heart.

Another message the organizers received was from a man who had divorced his wife ten years ago. Being from a middle-class background he had married a wealthy girl. Over the years, both he and his family grew tired of her because she had never done any housework prior to her marriage and seemed quite incapable of doing so thereafter. They had two children before parting ways. Over the years, as he had seen his children grow, the man had often wondered whether the reasons for his divorce were sound enough. When he observed the Moment of Calm, he claims that he had complete clarity for the first time. He wrote to say that if this campaign had taken place ten years earlier, he probably would not have divorced his wife.

Since 1998, the Mission celebrates Thanksgiving Week from February 18-24. This week marks Dada's recovery from a series of heart operations that all took place within a few days of each other – angiography, a quadruple by-pass surgery, and the installation of a pacemaker in the heart. As a special mark of gratitude the Mission offers, during this week, free artificial limbs to the limbless, free angioplasty, by-pass surgery, pacemaker implants, valve replacement, cancer treatment, kidney transplants, and other major medical interventions to poor and needy patients at its own medical complex.

In the course of the week, a variety of programmes are organized in the evening, each with a different theme. And each evening, the special invitees are a specific group of society that needs love and care. Recently the invitees were the senior citizens from all around Pune. Arrangements were made for their transport and they were treated like royalty for the day. There were may be as many as 2,000 such guests on one evening. They also had the privilege of being specially addressed by Dada himself.

Animal Rights Day is the third important occasion celebrated on 25th November, Sadhu Vaswani's birthday. Celebrated as the World Meatless Day, this is a well-known programme today. Millions of pledges pour in from around the world as people resolve to go meatless on that day. There are even some who turn vegetarian for life on that occasion. Today, through talks over YouTube and through a growing number of short films, Dada Jashan is spreading awareness of the need for compassion towards animals and other creatures.

The Mission offers food, clothing, and other necessities to those segments of society that are not able to earn their livelihood – the infirm, the aged, and the handicapped. Such assistance is offered not just to individuals but also to institutions for the underprivileged. The ashram prepares and offers two meals to such people every day, in addition to morning and afternoon tea with snacks.

Dada has also launched several initiatives to empower people. For those who are able but disadvantaged socially and economically, the Mission offers free vocational training. Typing and sewing are taught to women and sewing machines offered to them at the conclusion of the course, thereby flagging them off on a life of financial self-reliance. Handcarts for selling fruit or vegetables are offered to those who would work as peddlers, and so on. In the earlier years, women were also encouraged to knit sweaters, make pickles, and *papads,* and the Mission would find a market for these. Today, the younger generation prefers other forms of occupation.

Considerable developmental work is under way in forty villages adopted by the Mission. Some of these are in the backward areas of Kutch, Saurashtra and Maharashtra, where many villagers live below the poverty line. Seva here includes the provision of drinking water, digging of irrigation wells, tree plantation and conservation, health camps and vocational training, education of children, rehabilitation of poor families, and provision of rations.

Intensive work has also been done in the Sindhi settlements of Pimpri and Ulhas Nagar. Over the years, every household in these settlements has been given a bathroom and a fan. The provision of bathrooms was out of special consideration that Dada had for women who would otherwise have to go out at all hours of the day and night to use common facilities and, in the bargain, often face harassment. Proper plumbing and draining facilities were also developed in these areas. The Mission has provided thousands of gas and electricity connections to such homes over the years.

Assistance is also offered in times of natural and man-made disasters such as earthquakes, floods, fires, and communal riots. In 1993, for instance, there was a devastating earthquake in Latur, Maharashtra, where thousands of poor villagers lost their lives and many more were rendered homeless. Devotees of Dada Jashan from around the world heeded his plea for assistance, and donations poured in for relief operations in the quake-hit areas. While immediate help in the form of cash and food rations were distributed to the victims, the Mission also undertook some long-term rehabilitation measures. A year and a half later, the Mission had completed a housing project comprising of a school, a temple, and 91 homes.

Like his Master before him, Dada Jashan believes that no celebration is complete until the poor and the sick have been served. So seva is an intrinsic part of every Sadhu Vaswani Mission programme. In such instances, inmates of charitable institutions of the town are invited to lunch and offered useful gifts such as blankets, utensils, clothing, and cash. They are also welcomed to participate in the programmes organized for the occasion. Dada urges all his followers to keep aside a share of their earnings for the service of the less fortunate ones.

Seva is popular with all the Sadhu Vaswani Centres around India and the globe. In centres abroad, Sindhi devotees generously serve the needy and the suffering of their host societies. In Jakarta, a devotee manufactures artificial limbs and offers them free of cost to the needy. Another runs a school for the homeless. Everyday 200 people are offered three meals. In Casablanca, a devotee who has a knitting business offers knitting machines and expertise to rural folk living in backward, mountainous villages, providing them with an alternative occupation. In London, volunteers regularly feed the homeless and, on special occasions, offer them warm clothes and blankets. In Hong Kong, food is offered to street sleepers and to inmates of old age homes.

Seva is not limited to human beings alone, for the Jiv Daya programme of the Mission undertakes the daily feeding of birds and stray animals twice a day. A veterinary mobile van goes to different villages around Pune taking care of cattle and donkeys that are used in construction work.

The youth are encouraged to grow in selflessness. The Bridge Builders, as they are called, are an action-oriented group with the motto 'Hope, Help, Heal'. They meet with

Dada once a month but create their own programmes and take their own initiatives to do acts of kindness and service. These include taking a group of girls (aged between eight to sixteen years) from underprivileged backgrounds for a day out. They help them prepare small cultural programmes which they then help them present. They treat children from the orphanages to a picnic and play games with them.

At other times, the activities are simple acts of kindness to ignite the desire to do likewise in other hearts. Once a group of Bridge Builders went to the mall and invited all those cleaning the mall to sit down and have a McDonald's burger while they themselves cleaned. Another time, they went to a parking lot and cleaned the cars of people, leaving a nice little note for the owners. Or they went to the railway station and helped people carry their luggage. Or they bought raincoats during the monsoon and distributed them to the people and children near the railway station. They remind each other of what Dada says, 'If you want to be happy, make others happy.'

The youth have monthly sessions with Dada when they put up a skit and follow that up with a Q&A session with Dada. The skits are on themes relevant in the lives of the young such as 'Thank You', highlighting the necessity of thanking the many people, particularly family, who are so important in our lives but who we also take for granted. Another time the theme was 'Stay Connected', important in an era when people are texting each other all the time, or are hooked to WhatsApp or Facebook. After these events, the youth put forth questions pertaining to their concerns and Dada answers.

Dada epitomizes the ideal of Khwaja Moinuddin Chishti who urged his followers to develop river-like generosity, sun-like affection, and Earth-like hospitality. According to this Sufi saint, the highest form of devotion was to redress the misery of those in distress, to fulfil the needs of the helpless, and to feed the hungry. Through the Sadhu Vaswani Mission's myriad projects and programmes, Dada Jashan's life has been a perennial source of nourishment, hope, and healing to countless heads and hearts.

23

A Story for Every Occasion

*Great thoughts are nourishment for our soul. If you do not
have such thoughts of your own, you can always borrow
them from some of the great ones of humanity.*

J. P. Vaswani

Dada Jashan has a story or an anecdote to illustrate every
teaching. As he says, 'Stories are speaking pictures and
they help all of us relate to the universal predicaments and
the common human values that characters and situations
in the story depict for us.' He highlights the importance of
story telling in the following words:

Children of my generation were privileged to
listen to stories directly from the loving words of
grandmothers, mothers, aunts, and uncles. Teachers
in colleges and schools too, were adept at storytelling
to reinforce whatever they taught. These were all
replaced, subsequently, by the *Amar Chitra Katha*
comics, and then by televised scriptures and epics.
But it is a pity that the age-old mode of 'connectivity'
in the family that storytelling represents, is a tradition
that is dying.

Dada points out that, in India, the Vedas have always been accessible to only a select few. The Puranas, however, offer the wisdom of the Vedas in story form. They are, therefore, accessible to every level of society, from the highly learned pundits down to the illiterate peasants. They are the vehicles through which the great religious truths and precepts enter the homes and hearts of the masses. Spiritual masters, throughout the centuries, have used stories, examples from nature and from every day life to clarify their teachings and to bring home the essential truths. Dada has written numerous books on the lives and the stories of great men from all faiths and periods of history. In addition, his talks are rich in anecdotes from his Master's life, or from his own life, in addition to the pertinent examples from every day life or from different spiritual traditions. These make his teachings easier to remember and more interesting to listen to.

'The very first quality of a human being,' says Dada, 'is self-control. Not many have self-control. Therefore, we have not yet become human. Most of us are still animals.' Dada illustrates this point with a story:

> There was a holy man. They put to him this question: 'How did you attain such a height?' He replied, 'All I did was, when the mind prompted me to speak, I remained silent.' And that was what the Buddha also taught his disciples. He told them that in one incarnation, he had been born a prince who did not speak a single word. Year after year passed, and he did not speak. So every one thought that he was dumb.
>
> Once, the king announced that he would offer

a rich reward to the person who either heard the prince speak or who made him speak. Now, one day, the prince went to a forest. Sitting beneath a tree, he heard two birds chattering with each other. A hunter happened to pass by. By the sound of their voices, he was able to shoot one of the birds. As it fell down dead, the other bird started crying. So the prince said to it, 'Why did you speak?' And the hunter heard that. Dropping his prey, he ran to the palace and said to the king, 'I heard the prince speak.'

An enquiry was made but the king was not satisfied.   He felt the hunter was lying. So the poor hunter was sent to the gallows. Everything was made ready for his execution and the people gathered at the public square. Just then the prince happened to come riding by. When he saw the condition of the hunter, he again repeated those same words, 'Why did you speak?'

So all the people now heard the prince speak. The hunter was let off but, the question, 'Why did you speak?' is one that comes to us down the centuries.

Why do we speak? There are so many words that we don't need. It is said that, on an average, a person speaks thirty thousand words in a day. All that energy should be turned inwards.

Talking about the importance of truth in the course of a workshop for educators, Dada described an anecdote from the life of Sadhu Vaswani to illustrate his point:

One day Sadhu Vaswani was not keeping well. Usually he took lunch at one o'clock. That day he said he did not feel like eating. We asked him again at 2:00 p.m., only to receive the same answer. We were feeling hungry but we could not eat until he had eaten first. Finally, at 4:00 p.m. he said, 'Okay if you want me to eat, I will eat only some vegetable but no bread or chapatti.' When the vegetable was brought to him, he started eating and said, 'I find that I am hungry after all.' We felt happy. So we said, 'Let us bring you a chapatti.' He said, 'No, I will not take chapatti because these lips have uttered the words, "I will not take any chapatti or bread."'

Today, says Dada, there is no emphasis on truth. 'How many of our graduates speak the truth?' he asks.

One teacher got up and asked, 'Dada I am often confused between tact and untruth.'

Dada explains the difference with a little anecdote:

I think tact is a good thing. It is good to have tact, not untruth. Benjamin Franklin was once America's ambassador to France. In those days the French were anti-American. If they saw an American, they liked to punish him. So Benjamin Franklin was once caught in such a crowd. Just to save himself on that occasion, he said to the French who had captured him, 'Is it not enough misfortune that I was born in America and not in France? And now you want to punish me?' So instead of punishing him, they carried him on their shoulders. That is tact.

Another teacher asks Dada how to handle teenagers who today, want a lot of freedom which parents are unwilling to give. Dada replies that it is parents who are taking too many liberties. It is mothers who are not playing their roles, for motherhood is a twenty-four-hour job. That is why children are reacting. He explains how the *Gita* urges each one to do his or her *svadharma* or duty, for that is the role we have been given to play in the great unfolding cosmic drama of life. If we play our part well there will be no chaos and unhappiness in the world. He then illustrates the point with an incident from his youth:

> I remember when we were scouts, we used to have a variety entertainment show every year. Now in this variety entertainment play I was given the part of Napoleon in one of the scenes. There I stood in my imperial majesty. I had to lift my finger and my soldiers would come and ask what my command was. The curtain fell. In the following scene I became the servant of a rich landlord. He ordered me to bring him a glass of water. In that moment I felt tempted to tell him, 'Five minutes ago I was Napoleon and you were a soldier. Is this the way to speak to an emperor?' I'm happy I did not yield to the temptation otherwise the whole drama would have been spoilt.
>
> So, each one has been given his or her duty. It may be a major one – the President of India. It may be an ordinary one, that of a sweeper. Yet, if each one of us does not do his duty faithfully, sincerely, honestly, the whole drama will get spoilt. Each one of us is an actor and once you understand this you will have respect for each other; because the Napoleon of today becomes the servant of tomorrow.

At the conclusion of a special meeting of teachers of the St Mira's Schools and College in Pune, Dada tells them the following story:

There was once a holy man but he looked as though he was mad. Sometimes holy men deliberately look like that because they don't want to show that they are holy. So that particular holy man was walking towards a tree and some children, assuming that he was mad, started pelting him with stones. A villager intervened and said, 'Little boys what are you doing? You should not pelt stones at a holy man.' The holy man immediately stopped the villager from scolding the children. But the villager was determined that the children should be punished and asked the holy man, 'How shall we punish them?' And the holy man answered, 'Look at the tree! You pelt stones at it, and it gives you fruit in return. Should I be worse than the tree? Of course not. In fact, I should become better than the tree. If the tree gives fruits, I should give them something better.' And he embraced every one of those students.

On another occasion, that of Republic Day celebrations at a school, Dada tells the following story to the children:

Mahatma Gandhi once visited a school. He was almost naked, wearing just a dhoti and *chaddar*. A child told him, 'Gandhiji why don't you wear clothes? If you have difficulty procuring them, I can tell my mother to prepare a shirt and pant for you.' Gandhiji smiled and said, 'My child, you will have to tell your mother to prepare 33 crores of shirts and pants (that was the population of India then) only then I will be able to wear clothes.' He was completely identified with the people of India.

A teacher asks, 'Dada how can we learn to be always serene, to overcome the tossing of the mind?' Dada gives an anecdote to explain what the mind is and how it may be transcended:

Many years ago, I had a strange dream. I dreamt that I had vomited and from that vomit, a creature arose. It was a chameleon and it kept changing colours – white, black, and then yellow. Since I was wearing shoes that had thick soles with spikes, I took off one shoe and hit the chameleon with it. It remained unaffected and continued to change colours. I hit it again, but it remained unaffected. I continued to hit it, but, despite all my efforts, nothing happened to it and it simply continued changing colours.

In my dream itself I got the answer to this enigma. The chameleon is the mind. It has innumerable forms. Until there is *Gurukripa*, it will continue to exist, and continually keep changing. Only with Gurukripa does the mind perish; and then we receive the gift of a new or transformed mind. This mind with its nine colours continually deceives us and troubles us. But with Gurukripa it dies, making room for a renewed mind. Then we realize that we are not the mind. We are a form of light.

24

The Embodiment of Love

I seek to tread the path of humility and love. The wisdom
of the ages, the wisdom of the sages, is in this one world –
Love. Love everyone; not only those that are good but those
whom the world regards as evil. Love not only men but all
creatures who breathe the breath of life. Love every ray of
sunshine, every drop of water, every grain of sand. And I
ask you to bless me that I may try, in my daily life, to bear
witness to this teaching.

J. P. Vaswani

Dada's life does, indeed, bear witness to these words of his. His daily gestures, his concern for others, for the lesser creatures, and for nature around him, all demonstrate how his life is nothing but an unending stream of love. Connected as he is with the Supreme source of love, he pours it out like a perennial spring where those who drink are revived, revitalized, and born anew.

During an interview, once, Dada was asked the following questions:

Q – *Dada what is the way to God?*
Dada – Love is the way. Intellectual ratiocination will not take you to Him. Roll up your intellect and place it at His

lotus feet. Love Him with all your heart and soul and you will attain Him.

Q – Do you mean to say that mind and intellect are useless? Why, then, did God create them?

Dada – The mind helps us in doing our daily work, in carrying out our respective businesses and professions. The intellect helps us in discriminating between the real and the unreal, between the true and the false. Once you know that God alone is real, all else is unreal (*Brahman satyam, jagat mithyam*), the intellect has done its work. You then make God the goal of your life. The intellect is no longer necessary. And then, as I said, roll up your intellect and lay it at His lotus feet.

Do not try to understand God with the help of the intellect. God is unfathomable. He is the Unknown and the Unknowable. Even the Vedas cannot fathom Him. Do not seek to understand God and His ways. But love Him. Let your love for Him grow from more to more. Let your love for Him be undivided. And you will attain Him!

'Love, love, love even thine enemy,' said Gurudev Sadhu Vaswani, 'and though he hate thee as a thorn, thou wilt blossom as a rose.'

Gurudev Sadhu Vaswani always returned love for hate. 'Why do you do so?' he was asked. Quietly, he answered, 'Each man gives what he has. God has given me nothing but love!'

Dada's love expresses in every gesture, however mundane it may be. It is visible in the way he cuts his vegetables with precision, focus, and perfection. It is visible in the way he eats with full attention and gratitude. Perhaps that is the key to his steady good health. Never is there any haste or worry in any of his actions.

His love flows out to include every sentient being and even insentient objects. Every object is treated with gentleness and respect. In the ashram, when winter sets in, his immediate concern is about the well-being of the various helpers on the campus: whether they have enough bedding and warm clothes. When it pours, particularly at night, he is concerned about the guard on duty outside. On one such occasion, when Dada happened to wake up in the dead of night because of the pounding rain, he asked Krishna Kumari, his disciple, to call the guard and inform him that he should remain in his cabin until the rain stopped. The guard was so overwhelmed to receive the message. He never imagined that he was so much in Dada's thoughts.

When summer brings with it baskets of mangoes offered by devotees, Dada insists that the Class IV employees on the campus first have their fill. There are over a hundred such employees on the large campus. Within his own residential quarters, the helpers are first offered any new fruit of the season. They are encouraged to observe fasts; milk or fruit on those days are readily provided to them. Dada is also always available to listen to their worries, sorrows, and domestic problems. Having unburdened themselves to him, they feel strengthened and empowered to face their challenges.

In the days when a brisk daily walk was a part of his life, Dada would regularly go every morning to Koregaon Park with a few of his disciples. The roads in the area are shady and are flanked, on either side, by large bungalows surrounded by immense gardens. Dada became a familiar figure in the locality to the guards, the sweepers and, above all, to the gardeners who would be, at that time of the day, working in their gardens. They would greet Dada with a big smile and be rewarded with a loving greeting and radiant smile each day.

There was one gardener, in particular, who developed a special affinity to Dada. Everyday he would gather a small bunch of flowers from his garden, make them into a small bouquet and present it to Dada as his daily offering. One day, he did not come. The second and the third day, too, Dada did not see him. He grew concerned. Was the man ill? Had something untoward happened to him? Dada requested one of the devotees to make enquiries with the owner of the house. It turned out that the man had fallen sick. On Dada's request, the address of the man was procured and Dada decided to visit him.

Imagine the man's surprise when one sunny morning he found Dada and his followers before his humble abode! Dada lovingly enquired after his health and offered him any help that he required. Dada had also come with a bag of goodies for him and his family. The gardener was deeply touched. Once he had regained his health, he and his entire family often came on regular visits to the Mission. They had all been transformed by Dada's love and they wanted nothing else.

Strangers who have met Dada for the first time have often exclaimed, how much love they have felt in his presence. Once, a devotee met Dada after a long absence. Seeing the love in the devotee's eyes, Dada held his hands and said, 'You don't know how much I have missed you.' These words made such a deep imprint in the devotee's heart that he says, 'I will do anything just for those words.'

A member of Dada's group describes how once, during his travels, Dada found ants on the washbasin of his washroom. Instantly he declared that the first right was that of the ants and that, therefore, he would not use the washbasin. Instead he willingly washed his hands in the bathing area.

On another occasion, when construction work on the Mission campus was going on, several trees had to be removed. Dada put a stop to all work until he received assurance that the trees were going to be handled with proper care. Either they had to be chopped in a way that the roots would be kept alive, or else they would have to be carefully pulled out from the roots and transplanted elsewhere. Like his Master, Dada does not pluck flowers, for he believes that flowers, too, have families, and they must not be separated from each other. So he does not accept flower garlands.

Dada's love, ultimately, is an expression of his love for God. According to him God's true lovers 'stay awake so others can sleep; they starve so others can be pain-free. Thus is expressed their love for God'.

The remarkable thing is that with all his love, Dada remains ever free and unfettered, for there is no attachment in his love. Seeing the One in all, the Self in all, he knows that there is no such thing as death or separation. He sees the One Life Principle expressing through all things and beings. He identifies with the essence rather than with the name and form. And thus does he only seek to give. The only one for whom he sheds tears is for his Guru; not for his mother, family, or anyone else.

Many are the tributaries of love. Humility, gratitude, generosity, compassion are all the different colours of love.

In Dada's words:

The humility that I am talking about is not false modesty, or pseudo subservience; it is the kind of humility that will add to your strength and power, by making you aware of your true worth as a child of God.

I still persist with my view that the market economy cannot, must not, blind us to the truth about ourselves. Flashiness, aggression, hardselling and arrogance can only get us thus far; beyond a certain level, only self-awareness and humility can stand us in good stead. Therefore, the *Gita* gives us the commandment: *Seek the lowest place.*

Does not Sri Krishna practice what He preaches? He the All-Knowing One, the Supreme Lord, appoints Himself as Arjuna's *sarathi*, charioteer. Even while holding the reins of the horses, he carries out the highest office: that of Gitacharya, as Arjuna's friend, cousin, and mentor.

Humility will not wipe you out; it will only enhance your potential and earn you the respect of those who matter!

Humility frees your intellect from ego, fear, pride, and insecurity. You turn your attention away from the pretty superficialities of life and find your thoughts uplifted. You begin to explore the golden realms of the Spirit; and you begin the journey towards Self-Realization and Salvation.

'Praise no one until he is dead,' says Dada over and over again. For, even at the last moment, a person can change. Formerly, when Mission members would organize a function, they would have to inform the chief guest to make only general comments and to say nothing about Dada. He would be very clear and insistent on the fact that he did not want any praise.

According to Dada, 'Humility is not an attitude or a manner of etiquette; true humility is a way of life, an aspect of one's temperament. Humility cannot be taught. It must be imbibed, inculcated through self-awareness.'

As he says, 'Of what are we proud? Youth, beauty, power, wealth, influence, and position – all, all will pass away, bursting like so many bubbles on the surface of the stream. As for education, knowledge, and high qualifications, they are meaningless without humility.'

Gratitude and generosity are two other defining characteristics of Dada. Never does he forget anyone who has done anything for him, however small. For several years, he would render a monthly visit to a lady who had been a member of the faculty of St Mira's college. After her retirement she had fallen on bad days. Dada was aware of that. So he would visit her regularly on the pretext of offering her a new book. Within the book she would find an envelope with some cash. He did this until she passed away. That is the gratitude that Dada shows for anyone who has ever served him.

In 2008, nine years after his heart surgery in Washington, the doctor who operated on him, Dr Augusto Pichard, and his wife, Nancy, visited Dada in Pune. Welcoming them before the whole sangat, Dada said, 'They, whom I hold in the highest esteem, Mrs Nancy and Dr Augusto Pichard, with love and humility in my heart I greet them both, in the name of our revered and beloved founder Sadhu Vaswani whose portrait is here in front of us ....'

Dada honoured them with a trophy and shawls, a coconut each and numerous books. Both visitors were dressed in Indian attire offered to them earlier by Dada. Dr Pichard, when invited to speak, said, 'I have been waiting for many years to come and spend a little time with you all. Being here I find what I was looking for. I find God in you all. Your smile, your dedication, I can see God in you. I can feel it in this room. Dada has inspired each one of you and I am very honoured and pleased to be here. Thank you very much.'

Nancy Pichard described her feelings thus, 'It is such a privilege for me to be here with all of you, to feel all the love in your heart, to see today all of the miracles that you do on a daily basis, feeding the poor, curing their illnesses, taking care of them. The day that Dada entered our lives was a very blessed day. We humbly thank you for these wonderful gifts and the gift of being able to share this with you tonight. Thank you.'

The following day both attended the daily noon satsang in Sadhu Vaswani's kutiya. It was evident that they were deeply moved by all that they have seen. Dada bent towards them and said, 'My Master was once asked, "Why was the universe created?" He replied, "So that love centres can be multiplied."'

'And you are multiplying them, Dada,' replied Nancy.

'Your love can be felt everywhere,' added Dr Pichard.

The doctor went on to exclaim how, when he had entered the room to meet Dada, the room had been full of gifts. When he returned to the same room later in the day, it was empty. Dada had given everything away. When he commented on the fact, Dada replied, 'Sadhu Vaswani taught us this lesson: To live is to give! Those who do not give are no better than dead souls.'

'There is no dead soul here! It is so full of love here. They reflect your joy, your love,' said Nancy.

'I get it all from them,' said Dada pointing to the sangat. 'They are all pictures of my Master.'

Like all visitors to the Mission, the doctor and his wife were invited to dish out meals to the poor at the ashram.

This is a profound experience and no visitor to the Sadhu Vaswani Mission comes away untouched. The act of offering food to poor, hungry ones and seeing gratitude and blessings in their eyes is a deeply moving experience. In a flash the visitor understands that there is greater pleasure in giving than in receiving; that love costs nothing, yet it enriches both the giver and the receiver binding both in the fabric of life.

Another great characteristic of Dada is his boundless compassion. As he says:

Compassion is indeed the crown of all virtues. It is closely linked to all the cardinal virtues. It arises out of love and charity. It is the basis of seva or service. Truth I regard as one of the gateways to Heaven; and the truth of truths is compassion. Talking about compassion is not what we need today. Compassion must be evident in our thoughts, words, and actions.

Compassion begins in awareness. The first step on the path of compassion is to be aware that the One Life flows in all. The second step is the acknowledgement that all creation is one family. It is not enough to feel compassion or express compassion through speech. It should be expressed in action, in deeds of daily life, in little acts of kindness and love. Selective compassion is selfish compassion. True compassion knows no barriers of caste, creed, race, or faith. It is not giving of your money and your assets; true compassion is giving your love, giving yourself in an endless stream of sympathy that flows out to all. Compassion binds us to our fellow human beings and takes us closer to God Himself.

Dada quotes St Paul's first epistle to the Corinthians. It is part of the New Testament but, as he explains:

To my mind it belongs to the religion of humanity. I regard it as one of the most inspiring passages which outlines the essential virtues for a happy and useful life. Here is a gist of that beautiful letter which the saint wrote to his loyal and devout followers: *Love, compassion, charity, doing things for others: these are the essential qualities. Love never fails. Other things fade and pass away, but love endures. Faith, hope, and love: these three endure. And the greatest of these is love.*

The man of true compassion gives without judgment. He never ever asks if the others deserve his charity or compassion.

25

A TEACHING AT EVERY MOMENT

The true teacher is a lamp-lighter. He keeps on kindling lights in the lamps (students) that come to him. He is not a pump who keeps on filling the brains of students with facts and figures.

J. P. Vaswani

Every day a few people are invited to breakfast with Dada. He talks and jokes with each one. Extremely well informed about politics, agriculture, literature, technology, history, and other topics, he is easy to talk to. On one such morning, Dada talked about the importance of laughter. 'Laughter,' he said, 'is a physical tonic, it is a mental tonic, a spiritual tonic. It should be regular. Then it strengthens the immune system and improves digestion. But it should be regular, daily laughter. The whole body should shake with laughter.'

Dada proceeded to tell a joke with a twinkle in his eyes and a mischievous smile on his lips.

'There were three priests speaking to each other about their collections. The first said, "After collection, I draw a line on the floor and throw the collection in the air. Whatever falls on the right side of the line

263

belongs to God and what falls on the left, to me."
The second priest said, "My method is very similar,
only, instead of a line, I draw a circle. I stand in the
circle and throw money in the air. What falls in the
circle belongs to God, and outside, to me." The third
said, "My method is very simple. I throw the entire
collection to God and I tell him keep what you want
and send the rest to me."'

The audience burst out laughing and Dada shook with
laughter himself.

A lady then asked Dada how much one should rely on
astrology when taking important decisions. Dada responded
at length:

Astrology is indeed an ancient Indian science and
there is truth in it. There is truth in birth charts, which
indicate planetary positions in our horoscopes.
However, I feel that stars can only *indicate*; they
cannot compel. And I believe firmly, that man is the
maker of his own destiny.

A senior professor who had made astrology his
hobby, once said to us, 'An astrologer can tell you
when it is going to rain, but he cannot stop the rain
from falling; all you can do is get your umbrella out,
so that you escape the worst of the shower.'

Suffering and illness come to all of us. If we accept
them as prasad from the spotless hands of God, they
will lose their sting and you will no longer be afraid
to face them! God had made His plans for us; we
must put our faith in His goodness and wisdom and
pursue the path of truth and justice; then, indeed,
man can become the master of his own destiny!

A couple came forward and thanked Dada for something that he had enabled to happen.

The wife – Words cannot express our thanks, Dada.

Dada – Glorify the Master and not the servant. It is the Master who has done it.

The lady who looks after Dada's kitchen approaches with a tray on which are arranged bowls of grain, sugar, vegetables, and lentils. Dada places his hands on the tray, closes his eyes and prays. This is the daily offering from Dada to fellow creatures – dogs, cows, birds, ants, and fish. Offerings to the poor in institutions and who are street dwellers are prepared separately in the ashram kitchen.

A lady leaving for Accra, Ghana, asks for a message. Dada pauses and then says softly:

Whatever belongs to you will come to you. But you will leave all of it behind. Suppose you have got ten times more than what you worked for, that, too, you will leave behind. But there is a treasure that you will not leave behind, that you will carry with you. And the Holy Ones of God, the saints, they enjoin upon us to earn that treasure. They say, 'What will you do with this worldly treasure – table, table covers, silver vessels – all of these you will leave behind. But that treasure is something that you will be able to carry with you and it is for this purpose that you have come.'

Another young woman, knowing Dada's penchant for fountain pens with fine, thin nibs, offers him a beautiful pen. Accepting the gift graciously, he instantly offers the young woman another pen in return. The latter had been gifted to him a few days earlier. Dada uses the gift he receives for a day or two to make the person offering it happy. He then passes it on.

Dada has numerous meetings throughout the day. In the late afternoon, two eminent intellectuals visit him. One is the head of a prestigious professional institute.

Professor – Dada, in the Board meeting we proposed to confer a DLitt for you and we have invited the President of India as the chief guest. He has accepted our invitation in principle. So my request is, kindly accept our invitation.

Dada – What shall I do with such honours?

Professor – You will be honouring all of us at the university.

Second Visitor – On this occasion you will interact with all the students, including international ones.

Dada – For that I will gladly come. Yes. But what will I do with a DLitt? I am on my way out. And I don't deserve it. What have I done to earn an honorary DLitt degree?

Second Visitor – Dada, I can tell you, in this age of Kalyug you have done a tremendous job of awakening people from deep sleep.

Dada – I have not awakened myself yet! *(Chuckling)*

They try to convince him again and again using the same old phrases. They say they have to plan and tie up with so many people. They hope he will not disappoint them.

Dada – My beloved Master Sadhu Vaswani used to tell me that we are mere pilgrims. What has a pilgrim got to do with honours, with titles?

Professor – It will not take up more than 20 minutes of your time, Dada. We will send you an official letter of invitation. Please bless us by accepting. Bless us.

Dada – I received an honorary PhD from an American university, but I don't know what I have done with it. I just threw it away. I am not worth anything.

Professor (suddenly changing the tone of his voice) – If you don't mind, I would request you to tell us the difference between a Guru and a teacher.

Dada – Teacher is an instructor, Guru is an awakener. Guru is one who takes you from darkness to light. 'Gu' signifies darkness and 'Ru' signifies light. We are all in the dark.

Suddenly the professor folds his hands in reverence. For the first time there is an expression of humility and wonder on his face. He is completely blown by that spontaneous explanation and he bows down, his arrogance gone.

Dada – What is the role of teacher then? The teacher instructs. He gives you information. I think the teacher's work has today been taken over by Google.

Again, the professor folds his hands. He is discovering that Dada is not just a simple Godman!

Then Dada asks Krishna to offer books to the two visitors. A generous number are given, all authored by Dada.

Dada – These books come with the prayer: 'Lord may these books glorify Thee and may my name be forgotten!'

Dada takes the professor's hands and places them on his head saying, 'Bless me.' The two visitors looked completely astounded and even more humbled. But they have not received a positive response to their request. They make one final attempt.

Dada (smiling and shaking his head) – If at any time you need somebody to sweep the room, call me. I will come running. That is my work.'

The professor and his companion look shell-shocked. They will have to digest what they have seen and heard. They go out silently.

Later in the evening there is a special meeting with some senior citizens. One elderly lady comes and settles down besides Dada.

Lady – Dada, people call me cantankerous because I complain all the time. Last time I came here on Christmas day in 2011. 2012 was a wasted year for me because I could not meet you. Now 2013 has come and I want to meet you at least once or twice this year.

She hands over an envelope with some offering to Dada.

Dada (in a loving tone) – I feel very, very grateful.
Lady – I should be grateful that *you* are accepting it from me.

Dada pats her on the head. A gentleman by Dada's side says to the lady, 'Come Dadi,' and tries to gently make her move on. She refuses and, kneeling by the side of Dada's chair, she puts her head on the arm of the chair saying, 'No, I want to remain like this for two minutes.'
Dada, stroking her head, tells everyone present, 'She is a wonderful soul. Yes. She is a radiant soul. She is a dedicated

soul, Yes.' He keeps stroking her head. Then turning towards her, he continues, 'I come to Mumbai in the hope that I will have your *darshan*. When I don't have your darshan I say my coming to Mumbai is in vain.'

Lady – At my age, I'm not sure how long I will live.

Dada (laughing) – And what about my age? My age is bigger than yours. *(Everyone laughs)* What is your age?

Lady – Eighty-four.

Dada – Eighty-four is nothing! Mine is ninety-four.

Krishna interjects – No Dada, forty-nine.

Lady (laughing) – Yes, forty-nine. You have the capacity to regenerate. You are extremely alive. We don't have that. At least I don't.

Dada – I am not a saint. I am your servant, your *sevak*. (*He folds his hands before her as she looks at him with so much love.*) The Lord says go and become Maina's sevak. (*She laughs.*) So I say I am ready. (*He chuckles.*) If there is any job to be done, any room to be made clean, any ...

Lady – I have come across so many hurdles right from childhood that I have lost all interest.

Dada – That is *vairagya*. It is a good thing to have no interest at all. Our only interest is God.

Lady – I am living like this only because He wishes.

Dada – Thou and I, thou and I, thou and I, that's all. Nothing else exists. This whole world that you see, they are all puppets. They are being pulled. So they don't exist. You and God. You and God.

Lady – The house can be cleaned but who will clean the mind and soul?

Dada – Yes, but for the mind and soul to be cleansed the house should be clean. You should live in clean surroundings. If we want the Lord to come to us, we should prepare for that. Before a dog sits down, with his tail he sweeps the floor. Then he sits. If God is coming, the house should be made immaculate. It should be clean and pure.

Maina chuckles, feeling very soothed. Krishna hands a gift to Dada for her. She has remained kneeling all this while. Dada once again puts his hand on her head as someone helps her to rise to her feet.

Every morning Dada spends some time on his balcony reading. One morning Krishna Kumari opens the door to the balcony, as usual, only to find that a cat has delivered three kittens on Dada's footrest. She calls out to Dada who immediately instructs her to shut the door. The balcony, he says, is now out of bounds. The cat has chosen that place and it belongs to her until she decides to move her kittens elsewhere. Bowls of milk are discreetly slipped on to the balcony. The cat stays for three days and then takes her kittens away. Once again Dada is able to enjoy his mornings on the balcony.

The next day the maid comes to sweep his room. She quickly and mechanically goes about doing her work. As soon as she is done, she throws the broom in the corner, carelessly. Dada hears that sound while seated at his desk. Calling the lady, he gently tells her that she should keep the broom safely and carefully when the sweeping is over. He explains to her that even the broom is a member of the family. One should treat everything around one with love and affection.

Dada is in New York during his annual visit to the West. An American singer of kirtan, called Krishnadas, sings before and at the conclusion of the Dada's programme. Later, Krishnadas is invited to have dinner with Dada.

Dada – Years ago there appeared a devotee called Rasa Khan. They called him Krishnadas. His songs are still sung in some of the temples in India.

Krishnadas - I would like to find them.

Dada – It is a wonderful name: Krishnadas (a servant of Krishna). There was a Muslim poetess called Taj. She also dedicated her whole life to Krishna and she has sung a number of songs. Do you know the meaning of the word Krishna?

Krishnadas – You tell me.

Dada – One who draws, one who attracts like a magnet. Krishna kept on drawing people to him. Now, tell us how to become a true *dasa*?

Krishnadas – I should tell *you*? (*Laughs*)

Dada – My master told me, 'Don't become a dasa of Krishna. But go and become a dasa of a dasa of Krishna.' Now I have a dasa sitting in front of me. So I shall be your dasa. (*Laughter all around!*)

Dada – Can you play the flute?

Krishnadas – No, I play the harmonium.

Dada – Krishna chose the flute. You are Krishna's flute. Through you he is singing his song. (*Krishnadas's eyes well up with tears.*)

Dada turns to all those present and asks them to do a little kirtan to Krishna. Gulshan begins singing. *Hare Krishna, Hare Rama.* All join in. Dada also joins in with eyes closed.

Later in the day Dada meets Tulsi Gabbard, a Hawaiian senator. Of Samoan origin, Tulsi Gabbard's parents have been members of ISKCON and she is the first American Member of Congress to be sworn in on the *Bhagavad Gita*. Earlier, Tulsi Gabbard had been the chief guest at the installation of a statue of Mahatma Gandhi in the Sadhu Vaswani Meditation Garden. This garden is situated at Secaucus, which overlooks the river Hudson.

Tulsi Gabbard – The wisdom that you shared today and the wisdom of the *Bhagavad Gita* is the greatest gift of India to the world.

Dada – Emerson called the *Gita* 'an empire of thought'. It is said that he and Thoreau both kept a copy of the *Gita*. And yet there are millions of Indians who don't know about the *Gita*.

Tulsi Gabbard – They are missing out.

Dada – I think what the nations need today is a new type of education, an education that makes a man. Yes! Also a woman! (*He laughs.*) Our education is becoming more and more technical. Ah yes! India's one great tragedy is that it is following the path of imitation. All imitation is emasculation. Ah yes!

Tulsi Gabbard – I took my oath of office on the *Bhagavad Gita* in January 2013 and Indians both in the US as well as in India have been very pleasantly surprised at how warmly our country and our government have received the first Hindu in Congress. I am very open, and proud and happy to share who I am with everyone. They told me how they wish more people felt that they could do the same; that they don't have to hide or shy away from their own spiritual practice.

Dada hands over a copy of the *Bhagavad Gita* with

commentary by Sadhu Vaswani to her together with several other books.

The next morning two filmmakers from Chicago, Freddie and Dara, come to meet Dada. Dara had his introduction to Dada when he was asked by a friend to edit some of Dada's video clippings for YouTube. Very quickly he was drawn to Dada's love and wisdom. Subsequently, both Freddie and Dara spent a month in New York with Dada making a film on him. The film is currently being edited.

Freddie – What does it mean to have the mind of Christ?

Dada – It implies total purity of mind. In the case of most of us the mind is soiled, stained. It is a source of desires and it is desire that binds a man to the wheel of birth and death. Because of desire, man is unable to realize who he is in reality. When the mind is purified, man attains self-realization after which comes the next step, that of God-realization. We are unable to see God because our minds are not realized. These eyes cannot see Jesus, these lips cannot converse with him, these ears cannot harken to the voice of Jesus. When the mind is purified, man is thoroughly transformed. Then he becomes a citizen of the kingdom of heaven, the kingdom of Jesus.

Freddie – How do you heal a broken heart?

Dada – When a broken heart comes to me, I can do nothing on my own. I take the broken heart to the Master and I tell him, 'Here is one more broken heart to be healed. Master that is your work.' And it happens.

Freddie – Repeatedly in the past two weeks (during the camp) you have talked of Jesus's 11th commandment: love God with all your heart and soul, and love your neighbor as yourself. When so many people are not happy with themselves, how can they love someone else?

Dada – Jesus came to show people how to walk the way of love. This was perhaps his primary reason to visit this Earth. Left to themselves, people walk the way of selfishness. They want everything for themselves or for their families, or for friends and relatives. But Jesus came to show a new way. He said, 'The way on which you are walking does not lead to happiness. What makes a person happy is love.' And love is essentially selfless. It is the love that we call *agape*: universal love. That is true love. Unless we walk the way of love, we will not be happy, do what we will.

Dara – It has been a pleasure to meet you.

Dada – It has been more than a pleasure. It is the work of God that has brought us together. We shall live for the love of God. We shall love to do the work of God. Now, bless me!

Dara (taken aback) – I don't know if I should bless you! But I appreciate you.

Dada – Jesus is seated in the hearts of all. When we bow down, when we give salutations, we don't give them to the outer form of man, but to the inner Jesus. *(Strokes Dara's hand with one hand while holding it with the other.)* I shall not forget your kindness.

Dara – Nor I yours.

Then prasad of chocolates and nuts is offered to the visitors.

In the late afternoon Dada meets with a group of Westerners who practice meditation and yoga.

Dada – Yoga means that we should come together. Yoga means understanding that each one of us is a child of God.

Some say there was only one child of God, Jesus, and that God sent him to this Earth. Yes, Jesus was a child of God but so are you. Only we don't know it. We are not aware of it. It is this awareness that is needed. But tell me something. Teach me something. So many of you have come. Teach me something. (*Everyone laughs and then falls silent.*)

One member of the group – I can't see all as children of God. It is not natural. It is tiring to try to do so. I don't do that so much. I try to relax and see what I see and relate to them as honestly as I can. But is it better for me to try to see everyone as God, or is that too hard?

Dada explains at length:

'If you live a life of surrender it would be natural for you to behold the One face in every face. All we have to do is to surrender. And if we don't surrender, then howsoever we may try to see the One in everyone around us, it will be a forced seeing and it will not be of any use to us. In surrender what happens is that you belong to someone, and when you belong to someone then life becomes easy. Otherwise it is full of trials and tribulations. But the difficulty is how to surrender? In India we believe that you are not truly free until you are spiritual. Not so here. Here you believe that you are free whether you are spiritual or not. This is the one great message that India has to give to the nations, but not yet, because the people of India don't bear witness to this message.'

'Yoga is life. You may not know the eight steps of Astanga Yoga and yet be a yogi if you live the life of yoga. But you may have written books on Patanjali and not be a yogi yourself. The less we talk of yoga, and the more we live it, the better for us.'

'Today yoga has become gymnastics. We may do a number of exercises, we may sit cross-legged with closed eyes but the door will not open. Within every one of us there is the physical heart and spiritual heart. In the latter is a cave and in the cave burns the light, the light inextinguishable, which not all the storms of this world can extinguish. This light is what we shall see when the grace of God is poured upon us.'

'Therefore, we should put forth effort. You must pass through the stages of *yama* and *niyama* (the first two of the eight-step ladder of Patanjali Yoga) because the foundation is to be built. Without that, the structure cannot stand.'

Dada pauses. Everyone is listening intently and drinking in every word he says. He continues, 'There was a wealthy man who once approached a Guru and said, "I want to be your disciple but please take me to the destination immediately. I cannot wait for more than a week. Tell me whatever is to be done, whatever money is to be spent, I will do it, but take me to the destination." The Guru said, "Won't you invite me to your house?" The Guru was duly invited the next day and the disciple arranged a feast for the holy man.'

'As is the custom, the Guru arrived with a *kamandalu* (a vessel used for begging). It was in a dirty state. The man had prepared dainty dishes for the Guru and placed them all before him. The Guru took a little of everything, piling it in the dirty kamandalu. The man protested, "I have taken pains to prepare such dainty food and you are mixing it all up." The Guru replied, "That is what you want me to do to you. You have not cleansed your heart. It is so dirty and you want me to put the vision of God in that dirty heart." This is what so many people want done.'

Dada asks the leader of the group to teach him something. The latter says, 'I can't teach you anything. I'm sorry.'

Dada offers them more insights into yoga. Then, turning to Krishna, he asks for all present to be offered something. Each person receives prasad of books and chocolates.

The next day, Dada meets with Keidi and Terry who have specially flown to New York from the Midwest to meet him. Both are writers. Terry is working on a book called 'The Call'.

Dada – Blessed are those who hear The Call. Yes. It comes to everyone but very few listen, lost as they are in the world of noise.

Terry – That's the first sentence in my book.

Keidi – You refer to yourself as a pilgrim. What do you mean by that?

Dada – A pilgrim is a seeker.

Keidi – Do you see yourself as a seeker now?

Dada – I'm trying to be a seeker. Yes.

Terry – I bet you are doing more than trying.

Keidi – Sounds like you've got pretty far with being a seeker.

Dada (laughs) – My Master gave me this teaching. He said, 'Be a pilgrim all your life.' He himself was the epitome of humility. He was a very learned man. He worked as principal of three big colleges in India. Then he gave up all. And when they asked him who he was – a poet, a writer, a thinker, an educationist, and so on – he said, 'I am a zero.' Then he paused for a while, 'Not the English zero because that occupies some space, but the Sindhi zero which is only a point. It is only a dot.' Yes! In Sindhi the zero is a dot.

Terry – When he told you to be a seeker did you understand what he was telling you?

Dada – I'm still trying to understand. Yes!

Terry – What have you understood so far?

Dada – So far, one of the greatest lessons I have learnt as a pilgrim is that your love should move out to all, not only human beings, but to all creatures that breathe the breath of life and even to inanimate objects. But your love should be free from all attachments. Nothing belongs to you. You are a pilgrim. You belong to God.

One day a Frenchman came to the town where my Master lived. He had read about my Master in a book and wanted to meet him. He found him sitting in a room where there was no furniture. There was just one mattress on which he sat, a low desk in front of him, a few books by his side. So the Frenchman asked him, 'Where is your furniture?' My Master, Sadhu Vaswani, said, 'Where is yours?' The Frenchman said, 'I'm here as a traveller, my furniture is in my residence in Paris.' Sadhu Vaswani told him, 'I too am a traveller, my furniture is in my home!'

Terry – The first part of my adult life was spent in trying to accumulate furniture. Then I discovered that I don't want it. The rest of my life has been about letting go of all of it.

Dada – Our furniture is not merely chairs and tables. It is what we stuff our mind with. That too is part of our furniture. And you are blessed.

Terry – Very blessed to be here right now.

Dada – To be at the right place, at the right time, always.

Terry – I forget that often, though.

Dada – But there is one who keeps on reminding you. He is with you. And you hear His call. (*Dada looks deep into his eyes. Then silence.*)

Terry – It is a challenge for those of us in a human body.

Dada – Not many of us realize the worth of the human birth. Thales is regarded as one of the seven wise men of ancient Greece. They put to him this question, 'What are the three great blessings of life?' His response was, 'One, that I have been born a human being and not an animal; two, that I have been born a man and not a woman; and three, that I am born a citizen and not a villager.'

The same question was put to Sri Sankaracharya, the great teacher of India. He replied, 'One, that I am born a human being; two, that by God's grace I have received *mumukshutva* (the desire for liberation, for freedom from desires); and three, that I have come in contact with a man who walks with God, who talks to God, who lives in constant fellowship with God.

Terry – I am glad I have found all three. I see why you are called the pilgrim of love.

Dada – I would not know what love is.

Terry – It is something you radiate. It is like a fish. It does not know that it is in water.

Dada (pointing to Keidi) – She is like a fairy.

Keidi – Oh thank you. I don't have wings.

Dada – You'll have wings! God gave wings to everyone, to some the wings are visible, to some they are invisible. The wings of wisdom, the wings of thought, and the wings of imagination. We can fly. We will never be bound.

Keidi – I like to write children's books and children's stories.

She asks if Dada has childrens' books. Dada says he does and requests Krishna to give them to Keidi.

Dada – Life itself is a story. It keeps on unfolding day after day. And in the story of my life your visit today will be an important chapter.

Terry – Mine too.

Keidi – Actually, at one point, I wasn't planning to come and visit you because of the cost and the time involved. But then Terry and I saw a video of you speaking. And the video on the computer opened on its own and you said, 'Do not have regrets. You must act in the moment. You must do what's in your heart.' That is why, in the end, we came here.

Dada – I feel so grateful to God that he has brought you here. I shall cherish this moment, this day. Ah yes!

Terry – That is what *we* are supposed to be saying.

Dada – We speak for each other. What we need is an understanding heart and not an understanding brain. Then we speak for each other. The words that are on these lips, come out of those lips.

Dada sits with a small group of devotees on the seashore in Puerto Rico. The wind is blowing through his hair. Behind him the waves are crashing against the rocks while the blue-green waters of the Caribbean Sea heave restlessly. Against that background Dada shares his thoughts with his companions:

> I sometimes feel that service is the rent we have to pay for dwelling in the human body. So long as we continue to live in the human body, so long we must continue to serve. Life fulfils itself truly in service of the forsaken and the forlorn, and service of the

lonely and the lost and service of the poor and broken ones.

I am reminded of a moving incident in the life of Gurudev Sadhu Vaswani. One day a man came to him and said to him, 'Dadaji, today has been the luckiest day in my life. I have earned three lakhs of rupees in one day.' So Sadhu Vaswani asked him, 'My brother, today did you give food to a hungry one? Did you give water to a thirsty one? Did you give a piece of cloth to a naked one? Did you offer some words of comfort to someone in need of comfort? Did you bring joy into the life of someone who was in need of joy?' The man replied, 'I never thought of these things.' 'Then,' said Sadhu Vaswani, 'today has been a lost day. Today has been a wasted day.'

My friends, we have wasted so many of our days. Let us make the most of what remains to us.

During the drive home, one devotee comments on the many problems that she has been facing over the last one year.

Dada – Problems actually become doors through which God enters our life. We have enclosed ourselves in a shell, which has kept God out of our life. Problems come and crack that shell. They open the way for God to enter our life. And what more do we want?

Dada's enthusiasm and love for adventure make him a fearless and tireless participant in all kinds of expeditions and travels. In Alaska, he poses for photographs in the snow with a number of people. While there are endless instructions from the person behind the camera, he waits patiently with his radiant smile until all are satisfied. Never is there even a flicker of impatience on his face.

At every moment he is fully alert to all that is going on. When someone is taking photographs and slowly walking backwards, it is Dada who alerts him or her that there is a step or a gradation and that the person should be careful. Never, even for a moment, does he lose awareness of those around him, despite the fact that it is he who is in need of physical care.

On a visit to Disneyland in Orlando, Dada takes delight in riding a little motorized scooter. Even though he is in his nineties, he seems completely indefatigable. He is ready to try everything, including the most nerve-wracking rides. At the end of the day when everyone is tired, Dada is ready to freshen up and go to the theatre.

Back in Pune for his birthday celebrations, Dada looks forward to the questions that Bollywood star, Aamir Khan, will put to him before a huge audience. The Dalai Lama is the chief guest on the occasion. A little before the event, Krishna notices a big stain on Dada's white shawl. She hastens to get another one. Dada simply takes off the shawl, turns it over and wears it again. 'You are worried about the stain, isn't it? Well now it can't be seen.' The epitome of simplicity, he loses little time in what he considers to be trivial matters.

Aamir Khan – So many of us come to ask you things. Some come with a clean heart, others with not such a clean heart. How do you distinguish, or do you not distinguish?

Dada – I do not distinguish. To me you all are images of my Master. That is why I bow down to all of you.

Aamir Khan – You have spoken of the three kinds of love. You are clearly in the third kind of love. My question is, were you ever in the first kind of love? We are all very curious to know that.

Dada – Yes, before I entered the intermediate class. I had my own dreams and one of them was this, the first kind of love. But that is an old story. It is an old birth. *(Laughs!)*

Aamir Khan – I want to know all about it but not in front of them! (*Pointing to the audience*)

Dada – I don't mind telling them for that was not I. It was somebody else.

Dada laughs heartily and his eyes twinkle with mischief.

Aamir Khan – How do you relax Dada?

Dada – My whole life is a relaxation. I do not know what it is to be tense. You teach me how to become stressful. Will anyone of you teach me? Sometimes stress is good.

Aamir Khan – What is the happiest moment of your life?

Dada – Now!

Aamir Khan - What is your favourite book? I love reading. Would you recommend any book for me to read?

Dada (pausing for a moment) – I have thousands of books but if there is one book to be chosen among them, then my vote goes to the *Bhagavad Gita*. It contains the wisdom of all the scriptures.

At the World Parliament of Spirituality, Hyderabad, Dada has a private meeting with two Italian ladies, members of a spiritual community in northern Italy.

Woman 1 – We are ambassadors of six hundred people.

Dada – But do you know from where we come? We come from God.

Woman 2 – Oh yes! For sure! (*They laugh.*)

Dada – God is our homeland. Yes, we are all pilgrims. Our pilgrimage is to the eternal place where our home is. Now we are wanderers. We are wandering here, wandering after shadow-shapes that come and go. Our home is there. So you are not from Italy. You are from God.

Woman 1 – Thank you for your wisdom. We feel really privileged to be here. And we would like to invite you to visit us. We would like to show you something so close to your vision, which makes us feel so connected to you all. We have excavated with our hands from deep in the mountain a big temple. The art of this excavated temple depicts many things that connect us. So we really would like to invite you.

Dada – The true temple is the temple of the heart. Keep it pure, keep it undefiled. God will come and stay there. You are divine, she is divine (*pointing to each one of them in turn*) because in the cave of the heart, God dwells. So when we do *namaskar*, we do namaskar to Him who is in the cave of the heart. We are carriers, Christophers. St Christopher carried Christ. Each one of us is carrying Christ. We are Christopher. There are things that a Christopher must not do.

Both women – For example?

Dada – For example, a Christopher will not speak an untruth. Truth is God. People say God is truth, but truly, Truth is God. People say God is love, but truly, love is God. Love is not a quality, love is God Himself. Whenever you see love, bow your heads.

They immediately fold their hands and bow before him. Krishna is asked to give them a set of books each.

Later in the evening, Dada sits surrounded by devotees, followers, and others drawn to him.

Devotee – Why is it that when I sit in your company I feel so energized, so inspired, so full of love, so charged? What is happening at the astral and causal levels in me? What are you doing?

Dada – Every person is vibrating to a particular frequency. I may speak to you goodie goodie words, but if my vibrations are not in tune with the words that I speak, then my words will have no effect on you. Your frequency must increase. We have so many *maunis* (saints who remain silent) in the world; they don't speak. They merely vibrate. We have to improve our vibration; firstly through prayer, secondly through fellowship, thirdly through selfless service, and fourthly through the regulation of thoughts.

Devotee – So what happens when I am in your presence? Do my vibrations change?

Dada – Yes, vibrations have an effect on vibrations. And that is why people like to be in the company of holy ones because they help you to face your karma. It is like a surgeon performing an operation. He gives you an anesthetic and then performs the operation, and you don't even know that something happened to you. So this is the anesthetic procedure: the company of the saints.

Devotee – But Dada, you said that saints can change the karma of a person.

Dada – Yes, they can but they don't usually do so; because karma is not punitive, it is reformative. So the saint knows that it is good for the person to pass through this karma. It will enrich his spiritual life.

Devotee – But sometimes they have done it, isn't it?

Dada – They have. Sometimes when they find that at that

point of time a person has become too weak then the saint gives him a push.

Devotee – So in that case, is the karma postponed or diminished?

Dada – A saint can postpone karma, he can cancel it out by taking it on himself and he can reduce it. This is the true sacrifice because the saint takes upon himself the load and he takes it voluntarily. It is not put upon him. There was a holy man, he prayed to God, 'Lord you have forgotten me, you have not sent me any trouble for a whole week!'

Devotee – Does that mean Jesus Christ carrying the cross represents his taking upon himself the karmas of his age? What is the real significance of the cross and crown of thorns?

Dada – I think Jesus wanted to show that to live is to carry the cross. To live is not to enjoy. We have not come to this world to have pleasures. We have not come for *preya* (short-term pleasures), we have come for *shreya* (long-term good) and shreya is carrying the cross.

Devotee – And what is the symbol of the crucifixion?

Dada – To me, crucifixion is just like cement; glue that joins you to the Beloved.

Devotee – You mean through sorrow and intense suffering you reach the Beloved?

Dada – No, you do not regard it as sorrow and suffering. If you asked Mansur, the Persian mystic, 'What were the happiest moments of your life?' he would tell you, 'When I was sent up the gallows.' Because that joined him to the Beloved. Otherwise there was always some little gap.

Devotee – That is so frightening!

Dada (laughing) – That applies only to the body. Such people have risen above the body. If something happens to my sweater, I don't mind it. A true seeker does not consider life as a cross. His dimensions are different.

Dada is having an informal satsang in Hong Kong. A young man comes with his wife. It is his birthday and he asks for a message from Dada.

Dada says, 'You should give *me* a message. It is your birthday.' Then, handing over a gift to him he says, 'Dive! We float on the surface. We have to dive. Within us there are Pacific and Atlantic oceans and Indian oceans in abundance. If only we give up the limitation that we have imposed on ourselves on account of the physical body.

A restless-looking young man pushes forward and asks, 'Dada what is the best lesson to learn in life?'

Dada – Perhaps the best lesson that 99.9 per cent of us have to learn, is the lesson of humility: egolessness.

Young man – How should we learn this lesson? What should we do?

Dada – What Sadhu Vaswani emphasized again and again was that we must always occupy the lowest place. The ego wishes to get a place in the front row but we must always seek the lowest place. The second thing we must learn is to listen more and talk less. The third is, if somebody is relating his experience to me and I interrupt him to tell him, 'I have a better experience than you.' That is inflating one's ego. Likewise, there are many such points. However, the ego can get completely annihilated only by the Guru and by no one else. If the Guru will have mercy on us, we too will become egoless.

A man arrives with a bulky package and offers it to Dada. 'Hare Ram, Hare Ram!' exclaims Dada surprised at the size of the package.

Visitor – It's a blanket. I liked it and bought it for you. Please use it Dada.

Dada – I will use it today. In fact, I am going to rest now and will use it right away.

A young woman asks, 'Dada what are your views on divorce?'

Dada - I am not for divorce. All that you experience in life is based on karma. And perhaps all that you have to go through with your spouse is based on such karma.

Young woman – Is divorce not also a part of karma?

Dada – Divorce I think is taking the law in your own hands. Once married, always married. If you divorce – I know there are conditions when it is simply impossible – but, still, I feel it is better to pay off in this very birth and be free than to keep on postponing. But I know it is very difficult for a woman, especially for a woman who can think, a woman who is educated. It is very difficult, but I am not for divorce.

Young woman – And what do you think about abortion?

Dada – Abortion is perhaps the worst thing that could happen to a society. It is the mother, herself, killing her own child. That is the limit. The mother is the giver of life.

Young woman – But what about cases where women have been raped in war?

Dada – I believe life is a gift of God and over life only He has command.

Young woman – One last question, Dada. What do you think about sati?

Dada – I was in Gwalior when a press correspondent asked me the same question. I said I have no objection to sati provided you have satto also, i.e. if the wife dies, then the husband also immolates himself on the funeral pyre! If you are ready to do that, then I have no objection.

Dada rises from his chair with the help of Krishna and Gulshan. 'Thank you everyone for having come. I have been enriched by your presence,' he says with folded hands and a radiant smile.

26

THE ROLE MODEL

Happiness belongs to those who live for others!

J. P. Vaswani

Dada Jashan has lived a life of total renunciation without taking formal sanyasa. Nevertheless, he has still had to fulfil certain family obligations as and when the need has arisen. Above all, he remained a devoted son until the end of his mother's life.

While his mother, Krishnadevi, enjoyed good health, she would attend the daily satsang at the Mission in Pune, which was not far from her apartment. Whenever Dada entered the satsang, he would first bow to his mother and seek her blessings. In 1977, Krishnadevi was detected with cancer of the stomach. Soon she was unable to attend satsang anymore. Dada Jashan would then visit her every day, whenever he was in town. When he was on his travels, the ladies of the satsang would take care of her.

Once, while Dada was away to Delhi, Krishnadevi mentioned to one of the devotees that she wished Jashan was with her because she felt that her end was fast approaching. This was conveyed to Dada the same evening over the telephone. Dada cancelled the rest of his trip and flew back to be with her. During the last fifteen days of her life Dada did not move out of her home. He devoted himself completely to his mother, feeding her, comforting her, taking short naps in her room while she slept. Repeatedly she would say to him, while shedding tears, that her life had been completely fulfilled for she realized that he was a *Mahasant* (great saint). Despite not having got married, he had always been there for her when she needed him. And, above all, he had brought meaning, comfort, and joy into countless lives.

Before passing away, Krishnadevi called her third son, Hiro, to her side. Placing his hand in that of Dada Jashan's she said, 'Take care of him when I am gone.' She died peacefully on April 14, 1977, at the age of eighty, in the arms of her beloved son, showering blessings upon him.

For twelve days, after Krishnadevi's passing away, all the traditional ceremonies were performed and the age-old customs strictly observed. There was continuous chanting, prayer offerings, and the feeding of the poor, the birds, the cows, and the fish. Dada gave a daily discourse on the topic 'Life after Death'. Through his own life, Dada has shown how respect for the past is the most important. Without knowledge of and respect for one's cultural and spiritual heritage, a society tends to lose its moorings.

Soon after Krishnadevi's death, Hiro, the younger brother of Dada, had a series of strokes and was bedridden for the remaining fourteen years of his life. There came a stage when he even lost his speech and the ability to eat. Despite this extremely painful situation, his mind remained clear and unaffected. Those who took care of him, as also devotees who visited him regularly, were amazed to note how he remained ever cheerful and optimistic right through those long years of physical helplessness. Dada Jashan, whenever he was in town, visited him every day, and would spend an hour with him, regardless of how busy his own schedule was. Hiro passed away suddenly while Dada was out of town. But

Dada was there the next morning to perform his brother's last rites.

In 1958, Ram, the second son of Krishnadevi, got married in Mumbai. Dada Jashan had not wanted to attend the wedding. Sadhu Vaswani was ailing and Dada was loath to leave his side even for a minute. However, Sadhu Vaswani had insisted that Dada Jashan, as the eldest son of the family, be there at the wedding to give his brother away. So Dada drove to Mumbai, attended the marriage ceremony, and left immediately after that, returning to Pune in the early hours of the morning. Similarly, Dada took care of his sister Hari Vaswani, affectionately called Dadi Hari, during the last days of her life.

Dada Jashan had seen his own Guru perform all his filial duties. Sadhu Vaswani had obeyed his mother and remained in his career during her lifetime, even though his heart had been elsewhere. While she lay dying, he had personally nursed her, bringing her comfort and solace. Before dying, she had placed the hand of her unmarried daughter, Papur, in his hand, entrusting her to his care. In 1965, when Papur passed away, Sadhu Vaswani personally performed her last rites, even though his health was frail. Duty to the family and obedience to the parents were values that both Master and disciple have held sacred.

Once, a mother asked Dada, 'If I as a householder, grow in the spirit of detachment, will I be able to care for and love my children in the same manner as I am doing now?'

'Yes,' answered Dada. 'When you grow in the spirit of detachment, you will be able to do your duties better, and in a more fulfilling manner. As a parent, you will not be attached to the child, and so, will perceive with a better and greater perspective, the welfare and growth of the child.'

To another devotee, he said, 'There is no conflict

between God and duty. The very first step to God, affirms the *Bhagavad Gita*, is the performance of one's duty to the best of one's ability. Never stray from the path of duty, but offer every little thing you do to God. Practice His presence in your daily life. As you attend to your daily chores, let this aspiration spring from your heart: For Thy sake, O Lord! For Thy sake alone.'

To bring home the point, Dada Jashan has often pointed out how, in the long course of Indian history, devotion and obedience to the parents has been upheld as a sacred duty by all the great spiritual masters. Take the case of Adi Shankara, the great Hindu reformer and missionary of the 8th century CE. As a sanyasi, he was, strictly speaking, not permitted to perform any rites because he had renounced family and all attachments. Yet, he broke with tradition to cremate his mother, showing society that a son's filial obligations are as sacred as his spiritual attainments; that it is not rules and rituals that are important, but the spirit in which they are obeyed that is of relevance. Similarly, Sri Rama also demonstrated in his life, how his father's words were sacrosanct, to be obeyed with gratitude and reverence, even when they implied his own personal discomfort and hardship.

Once, on entering the satsang hall as usual, Dada spotted a little boy dressed in rags sitting outside the satsang hall. The child had obviously been drawn by the kirtan. He was curious to know what was happening but dared not enter the hall. Dada promptly walked to the end of the hall and, to the amazement of the little boy, took him by the hand and brought him into the hall. There he made the child sit comfortably beside him, telling him with his loving smile, 'Aap to mere bhai hain (you are my brother).' Not ever having been treated in such a manner by a stranger, the little urchin's eyes filled with tears of gratitude and love. At the end of the satsang he was given a generous helping of prasad.

When Dada spends time in other cities of India or abroad, he pays special attention to the domestic helpers of the household. Once, in Mumbai, to the complete surprise of his hostess, Dada stated that on a particular day, he and his party from Pune would cook the food and serve it to the domestic helpers. Both the hostess and the helpers were shocked, for no one had ever thought of such a thing. This is particularly so in India where one tends to have a distinct class division even in households where the helpers are well treated and taken care of. Dada, however, was adamant. He assured the hostess that she would not experience any painful consequences of this act. It was important, he stressed, to make such a gesture once in a while. 'Who knows,' he said, 'by what karmas they have become our servants; and how do we know that by our karmas we may not become their servants in the next life. Therefore, it is important to sow good karma.'

So the women disciples, Piya Uttamchandani, Gulshan Dudhani, and Krishna Kumari Thadani prepared paani puri, dahi vada, chole bhature, and other delicacies. What Dada is particular about is that the food should be cooked personally and not simply ordered from outside; for the offering of prasad implies the offering of one's own loving effort and time. The helpers insisted that they would eat in the kitchen seated on the floor. They simply refused to sit at the table. Dada personally served them, assisted by his disciples. The helpers were also given the day off and Dada assured them that his disciples would serve the hosts themselves.

Here too, Dada Jashan was following the example of his beloved Master. While he had been the principal of Mahendra College, Patiala, Sadhu Vaswani would make it a point to prepare a vegetable biryani every Sunday and he would feed all his domestic staff. He strongly believed that since they took care of him six days a week, it was important for him to take care of them on the seventh day.

According to some members of Dada's entourage, Dada often offers fruit and other goodies to domestic helpers of his various hosts around the world. Once, a Spanish helper in the US, mentioned to a disciple of the Master, that she had found Dada cutting an apple. He had asked her to sit down opposite him. He had fed her with two slices of apple and had given her two more for her to take to her two children. She had been so moved by his love and tenderness. At other times when helpers come into Dada's room to clean the bathroom or empty the waste paper basket, he slips chocolates into their hands, or gives them something for their children.

On another occasion, during a trip to Saurashtra, Dada expressed the desire to visit the home of Raju, the driver, who had taken him to various places in the region. Raju was delighted. Dada sat on the simple floor of Raju's home and relished the peanuts Raju offered him. After a little kirtan that sanctified Raju's humble abode, Dada exclaimed with delight, 'We are today in Raju Bhavan which is as good as being in Raj Bhavan (the name of the Governor's residence in every state)!' Raju was overcome with emotion. To top it all, Dada, before leaving, handed him some gifts and then bowed before him seeking his blessings.

Opportunities to help others present themselves in all parts of the world, and Dada makes the most of them. Once, in Connecticut, Dada was returning from his usual morning walk when, outside the house where he was staying, he saw some workers loading what seemed to be a huge pile of garbage bags on to a truck. To the immense astonishment of all, Dada rushed to them and started picking up bags and loading them on the truck. Those with him, naturally felt compelled to help alongside their Master. In a few minutes, the task was done and the garbage collectors were delighted and touched. Dada had found a place in their hearts!

Or the time when the party was travelling through some rural areas in India, and Dada noticed a man tottering under the weight of the cart he had to pull. Dada noticed that the man was headed in the direction of a steep incline. Realizing that it would be extremely strenuous for him make it on his own, he stopped the car, got down, and went to lend a hand to the poor man. In moments, the steep incline was covered.

Numerous are the examples of how Dada Jashan has demonstrated through his actions that abundance is a state of being. There is always something to share with another, always something to give to another – a comforting pat on the shoulder, friendship and love, a helping hand to make the task less difficult. Above all, he demonstrates how the same light, the light of God, shines in all beings and that in serving others we draw closer to the source of light. Through his life he also demonstrates that his own life is lived for others and that in reaching out to those that need help lies his own complete fulfilment.

This great sensitivity to all around him is not restricted to human beings alone. Dada is the greatest friend and well-wisher of every creature that walks this Earth. Nothing is too small, too insignificant for his attention. Every creature merits compassion, friendship, and service.

While out on his evening walk in Pune, once, Dada heard the agonized howl of a dog. It had been run over by a passing vehicle. Rushing to it, he gently lifted up the injured animal and laid it on one side of the road. Finding that life was fast ebbing out of it, Dada recited a few shlokas from the *Bhagavad Gita*, while caressing its head, offering comfort to it in its last moments.

Dada Jashan cannot turn his face away when any creature is in distress. He personally does whatever he can to help. Once a big yajna was to be performed in Pune and it was known that four goats would be sacrificed on the occasion. Just as Gautama Buddha had appealed to King Bimbisara to refrain from sacrificing goats for a yajna, offering his own head instead, so also did Dada personally meet the pandits in charge of the yajna, pleading for the lives of the goats to be spared and offering to take the place of the animals. Unlike King Bimbisara who had heeded a similar plea by Gautama Buddha 2,500 years ago, sparing the animals and also taking the vow of vegetarianism, the pandits in Pune were unrelenting. It took a long demonstration by hundreds of Dada's devotees for them to finally give in and call off the yajna.

On another occasion, while awaiting a ferry in Hong Kong, Dada saw a case of live fish destined for a restaurant. He promptly bought it, carried it on board the ferry and in the middle of the sea, released the fish, granting them a new lease of life.

Festivities and celebrations of days sacred to the great ones of East and West are an integral part of the Mission programmes. For Dada Jashan, however, each celebration represents not just a remembrance, but an actual experience of the spiritual journey of that saint. When the birthday of

Chaitanya Mahaprabhu, the 15th century bhakti saint from Bengal, is celebrated, Dada completely enters the spirit of Chaitanya. For the whole month, he chants the famous kirtan *Hari bol!* All his talks pertain to the life and thoughts of Chaitanya. He lives immersed in the joy and ecstasy of Chaitanya's bhakti.

Similarly, in the Christmas season, Dada is filled with the spirit of Jesus. During this period, all his teachings are based on the New Testament. He quotes Jesus, talks of his life and his relationship with his disciples, of his extreme suffering on the cross, and of his legacy to suffering humanity. When Dada celebrates the life of Adi Shankara, he discourses on Advaita Vedanta and from his lips flow commentaries on the Upanishads, the *Bhagavad Gita,* and on the four yogas. On the occasion of Guru Nanak's birthday, Dada opens a grocery shop *(modi khana),* even as Guru Nanak did, selling groceries to members of the sangat. The goods they purchase are then handed over to the poor. All talks to the sangat during this period are based on the *Japji Sahib* and the *Sukhmani Sahib.* And Dada keeps repeating the mantra *satnam shiri waheguru.* Thus does Dada revel in bliss and ecstasy, identified with all the various spiritual figures who have appeared in the long course of history, in different countries, and who have all brought their own particular flavour to the history of humanity.

For the followers of Dada, all aspects of spirituality manifest in their Master. Dada revels in the great fountain of devotion, drinking of its divine waters in different tongues, and in myriad ways, showing how all paths lead to the same pinnacle of bliss and fulfilment. He shows how all temperaments are not alike, but that each individual may choose his own path and follow it with sincerity and dedication. All that matters is love, love, and love. For that is the key to unlock the ultimate door that separates the individual from the Beloved.

Dada is comfortable and completely at ease in any religious milieu, so completely is he able to identify with the essence underlying each scripture, each faith, and each tradition. Once a Muslim associate of Dada invited him home to bless his daughter on her first fast for Ramazan. Dada accepted with enthusiasm. When he reached the home, it happened to be the time for namaz and all the men present rushed to an allocated spot and started their ritualistic prayers. Unfazed, Dada readily joined them. He knelt and bowed like them and prayed in the same respectful manner as the others. The host was deeply moved by Dada's demonstration of kinship. A few of the men present felt that a *pir* had come in their midst to bless the evening and make it unforgettable.

Until ill health prevented him, Dada went for regular walks. According to Dada, 'Long, solitary walks are both a physical and a spiritual exercise. They give strength to the lungs and they build up our spiritual muscles. Life is a battlefield, and spiritual strength is needed. The rishis of India named it *atma shakti:* the power of the Spirit. He who has it is able to face the foe with ease and grace.'

Even during his numerous travels, long, brisk walks were part of his daily routine, and if that walk happened to be along a coastline or in the mountains, he would consider himself especially blessed. He loves nature and beauty. To him beauty is not enjoyment. Beauty is shakti, spiritual energy, vitality, an emanation of Krishna, the Beloved.

Periodically, Dada also feels the need to go into retreat with nature. In India, his favourite retreat is at Lonavala, between Mumbai and Pune. Here in solitude, when he was stronger, Dada would spend time climbing mountain slopes and sitting in silent reverie along rivers and on rocks, communing with the trees and flowers, the stars and streams. From nature, he claims, he has learnt his greatest lessons, and from nature he has received his most priceless gifts. For, it is while sitting amidst nature that the most exquisite songs have sprung from his heart. These *banis* have been jotted down by disciples whenever they were present and set to tune and sung at prayer meetings. Nature has been the greatest giver of emotional and spiritual nourishment to him.

Dada's lifestyle is one of utmost simplicity. His meals consist of fruits, salad, curds, a little bowl of cooked vegetable, a small chappati, and a cup of dal. He insists on cutting his own fruit, which he does with meticulous precision. 'There are a hundred and one ways of doing a thing, but only one way is the best. See that you do everything only in the best way possible,' says Dada repeatedly. Every little thing he does shines with beauty and perfection. There is never haste in his gestures and never any impatience or annoyance.

When people attribute his good health to his simple eating habits, he points out that it is not what he eats as food, which is the most important thing. 'More than the food, it is my thoughts and feelings that reflect on my health. Good thoughts and good feelings make one healthier than all the nutritious food that one eats.'

Until his heart problem, Dada treated all the little ailments of the physical body with home remedies or with homeopathic medicine. And these home remedies were prepared under his personal supervision. It is only since he had his heart surgeries that he is compelled to take allopathic medicines.

Every day Dada spends some time writing and reading. His personal library of several thousand books covers virtually every subject. He reads constantly from the life or teachings of different saints. This, he says, has a purifying influence on the mind and, consequently, on one's dream consciousness. The books that he has found especially helpful are *The Imitation of Christ* by Thomas à Kempis, *The Gospel of Sri Ramakrishna* by Swami Nikhilananda, and Sadhu Vaswani's *Gita: Meditations* and *Thus Have I Learnt*.

To the extent possible, Dada believes in doing his own work. When he was younger he would sweep and clean his own room. Until 1998, he used to sleep on the floor. A simple rug covered with a sheet and a pillow was all that he used. It is only after the heart operation, when doctors told him that getting up from the floor put a strain on the heart, that he started sleeping on a bed. He is known for his great punctuality. 'Even if I am five minutes late,' says he, 'I have wasted not only five minutes of my time, but five minutes of the precious time of many other people!'

Just as the body needs adequate and timely food for sustenance, just as the emotions and the intellect need food for their sustenance, so also does the soul require silence and meditation for its sound health. However pressing be the commitments of the day ahead, Dada never misses his early morning period of silence; his appointment with God, as he calls it. This is the auspicious hour of the day when there is a descent of holy vibrations from above and the mind is undisturbed and peaceful. This communion with God is the real meaning of good health.

Despite a packed day with appointments and invitations, meetings and satsangs, talks and guidance to devotees from around the world, he maintains a healthy and hearty sense of humour.

'Which is the most important of the five senses?' someone asked Dada, at a question-answer session.

'The most important of the senses is the sixth one,' came the reply.

'Which is that one?'

'The sixth sense is the sense of humour! Wear a smile and you have friends. Wear a scowl and you have wrinkles!' he says. 'Which would you rather have?'

His ready wit and repartee make even the shortest conversations with him truly scintillating. A devotee once asked, 'Dada, which is the best balm?'

In a flash came the reply, 'Of course, Hare Krishna, Hare Ram!'

He is also a master of the subtle pun. As he was leading an inspection team through the college once, one of the visitors wanted to know which was the largest room in the college. 'The room for improvement!' came Dada's inimitable answer!

On another occasion, he was asked which was the best city he had visited, he answered, 'May I tell you, the best city is simplicity!'

With gentle humour he tides over strained situations between people, and relaxes them. He is able to laugh with others and, more importantly, he is also able to laugh at himself. Once, he was present at a gathering of teachers, among whom his book, *Ten Commandments of a Happy Marriage*, was distributed. He remarked that it was indeed strange that a book on marriage should have been written by a confirmed bachelor like him! As people burst out laughing, the one who chuckled the most was Dada himself.

Dada does everything as though he has all the time in the world. He moves from one schedule to another effortlessly, and yet, at the end of the day, everything has been attended to. His tone, when he speaks, is ever gentle, sweet, and loving. Nothing seems to disturb his inner peace. And that is because when pressed by admirers to talk about his daily routine, he sums it up in just one sentence: 'My normal daily routine revolves round two things: let the heart keep on loving God and let the hands and feet be busy in rendering service to those in need, beholding in them pictures of God.'

With such an attitude, he is ever relaxed in body and mind, ever refreshed and alert. From observing him, his followers understand that what tires is the fever of activity for selfish interests. In so much of our thinking is brain-fatigue, nerve fatigue; for our thinking is not pure but selfish, separatist, combative, aggressive.

As a man with no possessions, he has the greatest possessions of all – peace and love. His shoulders carry no weight for he lives not for himself, seeks nothing for himself, and has only one desire, to serve his Master in everyone and everything. And that is why his mind is so crystal clear, his memory remains prodigious, his focus sharp. With a radiant glow on his face, his gliding graceful movements and his sharp wit, Dada proves that youth is not a matter of age, but a matter of mind.

27

IN THE COMPANY OF
SPIRITUAL MASTERS

*If in your thinking, there is no evil,
you verily dwell in Heaven!*

J. P. Vaswani

'What happens when two great spiritual masters meet?' a devotee once asked Dada.

'What happens when two wealthy people meet?' came Dada's instant reply.

'They talk about money,' said the devotee.

'It's the same with two spiritual Masters,' explained Dada. 'A person can give only what he has. Spiritual masters have spiritual wealth. You sit with them, you talk to them of worldly matters but they will give a twist to them. For them the body is only to be made use of. The body is like what the horse used to be in the early days – to take you from one place to another.'

Dada's numerous encounters with men and women of God have been captured on film. Below are some excerpts of these precious and moving moments of wisdom expressed both in words and experienced in silence.

The Dalai Lama was the chief guest at a function organized by the Sadhu Vaswani Mission on July 28th, 2013. Before the function, he and Dada spent a few moments together. The gist of the meeting is given below:

The two Masters sit facing each other. The Dalai Lama chuckles and pointing at Dada's face exclaims, 'Not much change! Ha! Ha!' Then, leaning forward, he tweaks Dada's nose. Both chuckle with delight. The Dalai Lama holds Dada's folded hands between his own two hands.

The Dalai Lama – The world needs people like you who are dedicated to peace and compassion through education. Your whole life, I admire. You dedicate it for others. I appreciate it.

Dada – My hope is not in politics. It is in education. Through education India has to become new, through the right type of education.

The Dalai Lama – That's right! That's right!

Dada – Not the education that is being given today in schools and colleges: the type of education that you, too, envisage.

The Dalai Lama – Absolutely right. The so-called modern education is about material values. Ancient Indian education dealt with the heart. We need to revive that. We need a blend of modern education and spiritual education: the traditional ancient Indian values. That I think is very important. We need both.

Dada – The two centres of character building are the school and the home.

The Dalai Lama – That's right.

Dada – The leader of the home is the mother. Therefore educate the girl.

The Dalai Lama – That's right.

Dada – Here we have institutions for girls – schools for girls, colleges for girls.

The Dalai Lama – So this is the moment to educate for awareness about the value of affection, of compassion. In my own opinion, women have more potential to offer these. Biologically, the mother provides us immense affection. That's very important. Women should play an active role in the promotion of human values.

Dada – Therefore, here we say that the woman soul will lead us upwards, onwards, Godwards.

T. T. Rangarajan or Rajan (as he is known) is a New Age Guru and the founder of Alma Mater, an organization dedicated to self-mastery and holistic personality development. He specially comes to meet Dada for the first time in 2011.

Rajan – There is no gap between what you are and what you say. Because the message and the messenger are one and the same, the message is so empowering.

Dada – Better than speaking is thinking, better than thinking is doing, but better than doing is being. It is *being* that counts. Better than being is non-being: *Fanah*, the extinction of the ego. There are very few who have achieved this. We should touch their feet, we should kiss their feet.

There was once a king called Ferdinand who went to visit a disciple of St Francis. Both had been classmates at one time. While one went on to become a king, the other became a devotee of God. So, on this visit of the king, the two spent two hours together. Neither spoke a word. Finally the king got up, bowed and left. People gathered around the disciple of St Francis and asked, 'How did the king greet you? What did he say to you?' The disciple replied, 'What he told me, I know. How he greeted me I know. We did it all in silence.'

With that, Dada lapses into silence. Both remain in silence for several minutes.

Rajan – I just like to come and sit in silence with you. I don't want to disturb you. I love you very much.

Dada (stroking his hand lovingly) – How can you disturb me? You come to bless me. You come to remove all disturbances.

They again lapse into silence while Dada continues to stroke his hand.

Rajan – There is so much ecstasy. You are in perpetual ecstasy.

Dada – The person who speaks means something else and the one who listens understands something else. But silence can never be misunderstood. The great ones communicate in silence. That is true telepathy.

Dada keeps stroking Rajan's hand, which is on Dada's knee. They remain this way in silence. Then suddenly Dada stops and both remain still with eyes closed. Dada is in deep meditation. Then Dada opens his eyes and so does Rajan.

Rajan (getting ready to leave) – Do you also have only 24 hours, or more than that?

Dada – I have unlimited time. God has so blessed me that I am never in haste. Time is a tyrant. It is one of the killers of humanity. So many people are dead because of time. Time and the telephone are both killers of humanity. And now we also have the computer.

Rajan – And all three are now available in one device – the three-in-one killer!

Dada – In the West they call the TV an idiot box.

Rajan – But it does serve some good purpose. It was on TV that I first saw you! It was early in the morning, around 3:30 a.m., during *brahma muhurta*. I saw you just for three minutes. And after that I have only seen you here. In those three minutes you said that Sadhu Vaswani used to say that God upsets your plans to execute his plans for you. What you said in those three minutes I have conveyed to about a million people already.

Dada – His plans are perfect. Sadhu Vaswani also said that every disappointment is his appointment.

Rajan – I just want to sit in silence with you for some time and then go.

Rajan holds Dada's hand with both his hands and with bended head. Then both embrace for long moments in silence. Then Dada once again draws Rajan to him in a tight embrace. Rajan tears himself away, as though reluctant to leave.

Dada meets Dadi Janki, the Spiritual Head of the Brahma Kumaris. Dadi Janki clasps his hands between her own and they remain like that for some time in silence looking into each other's eyes. Then she puts her arms on his shoulders and says, 'Mera bhai (my brother).' So much love is visible.

Dadi Janki – Recently I participated in an interfaith dialogue. I was seated between a Christian and a Buddhist. There were wonderful discussions, but until we recognize the One, we know nothing. If they don't understand this, no matter what they may know, it changes nothing. When

I go around the world and they ask me or tell me that I am a Hindu, I say no. I am not a Hindu, not a Christian, not a Muslim, and am nor a Buddhist.

Dada – Mai insaan hoon (I am a human being).

Dadi Janki (offering Dada a bouquet of roses) – There was a person in Ahmedabad who had become very pure. She came to the Mahatma and said, 'I have brought you roses. The thorns in the roses do prick you, but that is part of life. Those thorns refine you.'

Dada – There was a Mahapurusha once called Luther Burbank. He was an American botanist and horticulturist and he had a rose garden. He gave his roses a lot of love and always spoke to them sweetly. He would tell his roses that they should grow without thorns. That was his daily prayer. And miracle of miracles, in all the roses that bloomed, there was not even one thorn! They are known as Burbank's roses.

Dadi Janki – Wonderful!

Dada – Man's love can do such wonders.

Dadi Janki – It can create a rose without thorns.

A devotee – Dada we want to be roses without thorns.

Dada – You *are* roses without thorns. Now you should learn to live like lotuses in the lake. Living in the world, you must not let the world live within you.

(After a pause, turning back to Dadi Janki) *Dada –* I always walk at your feet.

Dadi Janki – We walk together. We are brother and sister since childhood.

Dada – No I am not worthy of that. I walk at your feet. That is true.

Dadi Janki – Let us walk and laugh together.

Dada – Yes we are together since childhood but I can never reach where you have reached.

Pointing to Krishna, Dadi Janki suddenly says, 'The *paaras mani* (the philosopher's stone) converts iron into gold. In the same way, in the company of Bhagwan, this iron has become gold. What a great work this is.

Dada (looking at the followers of both Masters that are present) – You are all yogis and about to become yogis. That is our divine destiny.

Then everyone closes their eyes and sits in complete silence for a while. Dada is wheeled away by the doctor attending on him.

At the World Parliament of Religions, Australia, 2009, Dada meets Sri Sri Ravi Shankar. Both join hands, laughing with delight. Then they hug each other. Dada places Sri Sri Ravi Shankar's hands on his head. Both laugh with so much joy.

Dada (to those standing around) – I have to learn the art of living from him. That is the great need of the world today, the art of living. The art of speaking everybody knows.

SSR – I don't know the art of speaking.

Dada – That is good. You are the art of arts!

Sister Shivani of the Brahma Kumaris, well known for her talks on the television, visits Dada for the first time in Pune in 2011.

Sister Shivani – I seek your blessings.

Dada – I want *your* blessings.

Dada (with folded hands and in a gentle, humble tone) – Teach me something. What is the lesson that you will teach me?

Sister Shivani (smiling) – We learn so much from you. Just looking at you and being in your presence, we get so much.

Kneeling at Dada's feet, Sister Shivani offers him gifts from Dadi Janki. There is a book titled *In God's Heart.* 'That is where you stay Dada,' says Sister Shivani.

Dada (chuckling) – I stay at the lotus feet of the Lord.

Sister Shivani – You stay in his heart. That is why we can feel this love.

Dada asks Krishna to start reading to him from that book. Dada listens with great attention, eyes closed.

Dada – Where does spirituality begin and where does it end? Spirituality begins with humility and spirituality ends in humility. What are we? We are nothing. *(Looking at Sister Shivani)* You are an exception. You are something.

Sister Shivani (smiling and shaking her head gently) – We all are nothing – *naa ham, naa ham, tuho, tuho*. That was a mantra that Sri Ramakrishna gave to his dear ones. 'Go and meditate upon it,' he would tell them.

Then Dada asks Krishna to offer some books to Sister Shivani. She is given the latest books. One of the books is entitled *All Will be Well in 2012.*

Sister Shivani – What a perfect title. Yes, all will be well. Shiv Baba says that the Golden World has to come down. While everyone is worrying about 2012 and creating fear that the world will come to an end, Baba says the world is not coming to an end.

Dada – People are also right. Because the world, as we know it, will come to an end. A new world is in the making. It will manifest itself, yes, yes.

Then Dada hands over to Sister Shivani a CD, *Jeeyo aur Jeene Do*, prepared by Krishna Kumari.

Dada – We took it for granted that you belong to the community. 'Ani' as a suffix suggests a Sindhi identity. So I took it for granted that you were Sindhi. But you belong to no community. You are above communities.

Sister Shivani – Baba always teaches us that we are beyond the body: no caste, no religion. Here in our family we have a very sweet custom. We don't know each other's surnames. So I don't know which caste anyone comes from. It is only one Baba and all his children.

Dada – You don't know her surname but you know her Sir's name. *(Everyone laughs)* And that is all that we need to know.

He hands over another two books of selected writings. 'This is one of Sadhu Vaswani's writings. The other one is of his servant's.'

Dada asks for her books to be packed for her. He puts a white shawl around her shoulders and also hands her a coconut. Then he offers her a packet of prasad for Dadi Janki.

Dada – How can you leave me?
Sister Shivani – We are always all together.

As she bows down in reverence, Dada reaches for her feet. She stops him.

28

IN THE REALM OF ECSTASY

*Man lives not by the beats of his heart, but by the
grace of God. Alone the grace of God sufficeth.*

J. P. Vaswani

There are three types of spiritual journeys according to Dada. The first one is the journey away from God, on which most of us are. The second is the U-turn, the awakening, or the journey back to God. The third journey begins when one realizes God or the Self. It is the journey in God. This third journey is what constitutes true spiritual life. What this journey is cannot be described by words, for it lies in a realm that is beyond the mind and intellect. It belongs to the realm of the transcendental. Therefore, this third journey is one that must be experienced to be understood. It is a state of supreme bliss.

This beatific state, however, can be somewhat gleaned from Dada's songs and poems, which are, invariably, outpourings from that state of exultation. Several of the compositions in his vast collection called *Anjali Sangraha* speak of the realm of ecstasy. In one such song, Dada describes the experience as 'flying in *chidaakasha* (inner universe)'. 'Nothing affects me,' sings Dada, 'I am attached to no one. Nothing belongs to me. I am flying in chidaakash!'

Dada's exalted state of consciousness also becomes evident in moments of intense physical pain and suffering. There have been times when his doctors and close disciples have felt that while physically present, mentally he is somewhere else. The descriptions they offer are just brief, totally inadequate observations of a state to which few aspire, but which only a minuscule number are blessed enough to reach.

In May 2010, Dada had an accident and the following months were what any normal person would consider an ordeal of excruciating pain and suffering. In the course of a Sadhana Camp at a large resort in Panama, Dada enthusiastically joined a group of children playing ping-pong. While making a strong swing, he tripped over his shawl and fell backwards, breaking his right shoulder and right femur. His right elbow was shattered and the right wrist, too, was fractured. The resort was an hour's drive from Panama City. The road was largely a dirt track filled with potholes. The pounding rain only made matters worse. In these conditions Dada was driven to the Panama City. The merciless jostling of the van due to the unevenness of the road caused intense pain. Each time the words 'Sri Ram', 'Om', or 'Hari Bol' would escape Dada's lips. After receiving first aid at Panama City, Dada was flown by an ambulance plane to Chicago, nine hours away.

The numerous fractures in an already frail body, aged ninety-two years, did not augur well. The doctors who accompanied Dada feared the worst. Despite it all, Dada remained conscious throughout this long journey. As the pain increased he could be heard repeatedly exclaiming, 'Thank you, God! Thank you, God! Thank you, God!' With a heart overflowing with gratitude he bore witness to what Meister Ekhart in the 16th century referred to as the importance of positivity. According to Meister Ekhart, even if in all your life you have offered only one simple prayer – Thank you God, Thank you God – then your coming on this Earth is not in vain. This was the prayer that sprang spontaneously to Dada's lips through the worst conditions and circumstances of life.

The flight was long and, at times, Dada would turn to his doctor-cum-disciple, Harish Wadhwani, requesting him to chant three bhajans that are offerings of gratitude to the Lord. Blessed with a mellifluous voice and the ability to compose music, Wadhwani had set these songs written by Dada to music. These bhajans he was asked to sing repeatedly over the next ten days – in the plane, in the ICU, and in the hospital ward.

Dada was admitted to the Rush Medical Center in Chicago. Two days later, his shoulder and hip were operated upon simultaneously. The surgery on the elbow was scheduled some days later. During this entire period of physical agony, Dada's mind appeared to soar to an exalted plane of consciousness. His face seemed to have a dazzling lustre and with a blissfull gaze in his eyes, he kept repeating the words, 'Beautiful! Beautiful!' It was clear that while doctors and disciples saw only suffering, he was seeing something quite different. At other times, he would exclaim, 'I see a light, the radiance of which dazzles, but it is a soft, white light. The brightness of the sun seems pale, but it is so calm and cool.' To his grieving followers, his radiant smile was like the lotus that blooms in the dark night.

On 18th May, Dada underwent a second operation for an elbow replacement. The surgery was successful but shortly thereafter Dada had a stroke. His left side, shoulder downwards, was affected. So, while the right side had recently been operated on and was recovering, the left side of his body was now paralyzed because of the stroke. That made physiotherapy very difficult and, yet, it was essential, both for the stroke as also for the limbs that had been operated.

When Dada was told about the stroke, he instantly said, 'It is a gift from God and I am the chosen one.' For the next two weeks, although he was immobile on the bed, Dada never lost his sense of humour. Jokingly he would say that the Lord had made him as helpless as a newborn baby. His doctors and disciples would humorously retort, 'Now you have to live another ninety years!' It was heart-warming to hear the familiar chuckle.

Physiotherapy was resumed after two weeks. Initially, even sitting on the bed was excruciatingly painful. By and by, progress was made. When the physiotherapist would say, 'Walk one step,' Dada would say, 'No I will walk two.' And when she would say, 'Walk ten steps,' he would say, 'No, I will walk twenty.'

Through this entire trying period of three months, Dada asked for a continuous chanting of the Lord's name. In between he would also ask to hear songs from the *Nuri* and *Anjali* rendered by one of the disciples. And, it was during this period of intense physical agony that a series of new songs flowed out of Dada in one nectarine stream of bliss. These were quickly jotted down and set to music by a gifted disciple. In one he rejoices in the new lila that God played for him, describing how, thereby, God, exalted a sinner like him.

On the 40th day, Dada was brought outside on his wheelchair. Thereafter, he would spend a couple of hours everyday in the open, under the beautiful trees in a big garden. Harish Wadhwani describes his experience with Dada during this period:

I think he used to leave his body and go. I used to refer to him then as Dada 1 and Dada 2. Dada 1 was the person I was treating and seeing physically. Dada 2 was another form, which from time to time used to come and speak through him. The reason I say that is because during his recovery phase, Dada was not talking at all. One afternoon in Chicago, the weather was very good so I said to Dada, 'Why don't I take you out for a walk in the wheelchair?' Whenever he is with nature he opens up. He agreed. So we went down and I parked his wheelchair under the shade of a tree hoping that Dada would now open up. I coaxed him to give us a message for the day. Dada just kept nodding his head. Then, all of a sudden, a transformation came over him and he started speaking. And he spoke for nearly 20-25 minutes. It was a proper *upadesh*. Now who was this, who came and spoke through him? Then this started becoming a regular phenomenon. Dada would say, 'I don't want to speak,' and he would go into silence. And then, suddenly, there would be a different Dada. And the voice energy would change. The outcome of these talks was the book *Gateways to Heaven*.

From the wheelchair, Dada graduated to the walker, and then to the walking stick. Recovery spanned several long months. One of the nurses taking care of Dada in Chicago one day, jokingly, said to him, 'Dada I believe you should not play ping-pong anymore as this was the initial cause of his accident.' With a big smile and a twinkle in his eyes he retorted, 'That is the first thing I shall do when I am back.' And, in fact, in 2013 when all was well again, Dada revisited Panama. He reminded the child he had been playing ping-pong with when the accident happened that they needed to finish their game. And they did.

Dada is never tired of repeating that those whom God loves the most get the maximum suffering. He quotes the Koran and some Sindhi Sufi poets who claim that those whom God loves, He slays. When questioned why bad things happen to good people while others who are evil have the best in life, he replies, 'Bad things happen to good people so that they may grow better, nobler, purer. Even as gold is burnt in the crucible to be cleansed of its dross, even so good people are chosen to burn in the fire of suffering, and so become pure as thrice-burnished gold.'

In his typical way, he relates a little story to illustrate this point. In the epic *Mahabharata*, after the war is over and Krishna is about to depart, Kunti asks him for a boon. She requests that she might always have some little suffering, for in suffering, she says, the Lord is remembered. In pleasures and enjoyment He is forgotten.

Many are the instances of Dada's immense physical suffering. Earlier in 1972, at the age of 64 years, he came down with an ischemic heart attack. In 1998, at the age of 80 years, Dada went in for a quadruple bypass surgery in Washington. He has osteoporosis, neurological difficulties, and some other medical problems as well. He has been hospitalized several times but has welcomed and endured physical pain even as the great spiritual Masters Ramakrishna Paramahamsa, Bhagwan Ramana Maharshi, and Sadhu Vaswani have done before him. 'Not many,' he explains, 'know the value of suffering. It was an Indian saint who prayed: "Lord grant me starvation and sickness and suffering and ignominy!" Those are things that are of real value to those that know.'

Dada believes that every moment, every experience in our lives is planned by God and is for our good. Disciples and devotees of Dada, however, believe that whenever sufferings come his way, they are because he takes upon himself the karmas of others. And, by taking up their problems, he teaches people how to live with faith, surrender, and gratitude.

Medically speaking, there are things that the numerous doctors attending on him have not been able to explain. For instance, his post-surgery stroke in Chicago did not affect his head and neck at all. It was only the shoulder down that was affected. Moreover, to recover from total paralysis of the limbs at the age of ninety-two in such a short while defies science.

Dada's will power is also quite exceptional. It enables him to do what most patients would be incapable of doing. One of the senior neurologists attending on him describes how a week before his 96th birthday in 2014, Dada was admitted to the intensive care unit of a hospital in Pune. He had a tube in his throat through which he was being fed. He had IV fluids going into his body and he was taking innumerable drugs. Despite that state of health, he convinced the doctors that he would go home on 2nd August, his birthday. Numerous followers had come from all over the world to meet him and he could not bear the idea of disappointing them.

From the ICU, Dada came straight before a gathering of about seven thousand people. In nine short minutes (the maximum time allotted to him by the doctors) he gave a powerful message to the sangat. The gist of it was: 'Each one of you has the power to change the world. Don't think that you are insignificant. In whatever field of activity you are, you have the power to change the world.' Dada's mental faculties were crystal clear and no one could have imagined that just the day before he had been delirious.

On another occasion, in May 2014, Dada was visiting Dubai en route for the US when he developed severe pain in the back. During a function on his first day in Dubai, he had spent one hour bending forward touching the heads of devotees in blessing. That caused him strain in the lower back. He was prescribed complete bed rest for a few days. Thereafter, when he felt some improvement, instead of returning to Pune, as advised by the doctors, he insisted that they move forward to the US as scheduled. His concern was for the hosts who had organized the programme and for the numerous ardent devotees who awaited his visit.

Those attending on Dada seek to attribute his phenomenal physical and mental power to various factors. Some believe that he has an exceptionally active brain, a highly developed spiritual personality and an extremely wide knowledge base. Others consider that the immense power of his mind comes from positive thinking his entire life; and that positive thinking has made all the difference to thousands of people all over the world. Yet others speculate that Dada has little or no body awareness. Once when he seemed to be in considerable distress, a doctor asked him whether he was having a headache. Dada responded, 'No, I don't have a headache, but I have heartache because of the suffering of people around me.'

On another occasion, because of severe physical discomfort, Dada could not sleep. When asked about it, he replied, 'What disturbs me the most is the fact that those attending on me cannot sleep.' Doctors have described how when Dada is not listening to the recitation of the holy name or a bhajan, he is reading. And when he is unable to read, he has someone read to him.

Dada's secret in dealing with anything unpleasant and painful is summed up in his own words: 'Agree with the adversary, as it is said. Do not resist anything. Move forward to greet every experience of life: pleasant and unpleasant: with the words: I accept! I accept! As I have already said, in everything that happens, there is a meaning of God's mercy. And everything that comes from God is good. Realizing this, it will not be difficult for us to handle every situation in a loving way.'

Dada's positive attitude is something that he explains to others at length:

> Firstly, we must be careful to see that we always have a constructive, a positive attitude towards life. By positive attitude, I do not mean that life does not have a negative side. Life does have a negative, dark side. Life is full of difficulties and danger, trials and tribulations. But the man with the positive approach refuses to dwell on the negative side of life. Surrounded by the most adverse conditions, he will look for a place to stand on. Conditions all around him may be frustrating, but he will not give up. He will continue to expect the best results. And this is an inviolable law of life: what you expect persistently comes rushing to you. We only draw to ourselves that which we think of all the time. Our thoughts are magnets. Through our thoughts we draw to ourselves conditions and circumstances of which we keep on thinking all the time.
>
> The second point in the formula is that we must not offer resistance to life. Life has given us many things. Some of them are good; some of them are not as good. I must accept them all and make the most

of them. Of course, I must not be fatalistic. I must not take things lying down. But if, in spite of my best efforts, I am not able to achieve the desired results, I must accept the situation. Acceptance is not a passive thing. To accept truly is to accept in joy. To accept is to triumph over the circumstances and not let them touch the joy and peace of the soul. Resistance inevitably leads to wastage of energy, which could be used to constructive ends. Do your very best to achieve the desired results, but if in spite of your efforts you fail, let that not depress you. The great cosmic power that controls the universe knows what is good for you. So accept, and rejoice!

It is easy to be grateful to God when the going is easy, but may I say to you, you must be grateful to Him even when the going is tough. You may be suffering, you may be facing obstacles, you may be stumbling at every step, but you are still alive; while there is life, there is hope! As a human being you are the crown of God's creation. And you can think; you can reason; you can reflect; you can laugh and cry!

All these examples demonstrate that there is complete integration between Dada's thoughts, words, and deeds. Never does he offer any advice or guidance to anyone without having first practiced it himself. The most difficult teachings are those that are part of his everyday life. In the hospital, those taking care of him recalled his words:

There is one teaching to which I try to bear witness in deeds of daily living: In God's providence, all is well, all was well, all will be well, both tomorrow and a hundred years hence! In every so-called misfortune, calamity, adversity, and illness, there is the merciful hand of God. God always means well by us. Every experience He sends us is meant to teach us a lesson, which we need to learn. On the surface, it may appear to be a misfortune, a calamity, but within, it is a hidden treasure of wisdom we need to unfold. Therefore, I go about as a child. The child is never worried. The child knows its mother is near. It has not to fear. The child lives a carefree life. Have you ever seen a child keeping aside a portion of his lunch for the night meal? The child is sure his mother will provide. Faith in the divine providence is very necessary. But this does not happen without the grace of the Guru. As long as He will pour His grace on me, so long will I continue to be like this. If, even for a moment he withdraws His grace, I do not know what will happen.

Dada's many ordeals have touched and transformed the lives of his caregivers offering them a new direction and perspective on life.

In 1998, when he arrived in Washington one Friday afternoon for his heart surgery, he met with Dr Augusto Pichard who was scheduled to operate on him the following Monday. That same night, however, Dr Pichard claims he had a dream in which Jesus appeared before him. Deeply moved, he visited Dada the next morning telling him that he felt Jesus had come to him in the form of Dada. Today, both the doctor and his wife have become followers of Dada. They regularly attend Dada's sadhana camps in the US and both have turned vegetarian.

On the last day of Dada's stay at the hospital in Washington, numerous members of the staff turned up to meet Dada in the course of the day, to receive his last message. It was clear that they had been deeply touched by him, each in his or her special way. Nancy Schaffer Lodding, Director of Residential Services at the hospital in Washington Medical Center, says, 'Every time I meet with Dada, he has wisdom to share. He shares God's grace and a sense of peacefulness. It has been an amazing experience for me. And I have come to love Dada. I have come to love the members of his family. I even brought my dog to meet him and be blessed.'

If caregivers have been touched by close contact with Dada, his many trials and recoveries have brought new life and vigour into the spiritual life of numerous followers around the world.

Dada's recovery from multiple fractures in 2010 was followed by many moments of euphoria. When, on being discharged from the hospital, he flew to New York to celebrate his 92nd birthday, thousands of people came every day for his talks and the associated events. Kajal Chandiramani, a singer from Mumbai, was specially flown in to New York to perform. The highlight of her performance was the rendering of one of Dada's compositions from *Anjali* called *Chhori na chada jain*. It is a song of supplication by a woman mendicant at the door of her master – *O Lord*, she pleads, *do not abandon this one at your door*. Kajal's soul-stirring rendering of this song, full of pathos and yearning brought tears to Dada's eyes, so much so that at the end of the song Dada insisted on being helped up from his wheelchair. Taking off his shawl, he draped it around her shoulders. The atmosphere was highly charged that evening and there was hardly a dry eye in the audience. Something profound had happened. Few could describe it, but experience it they all did.

Later, Dada explained that the reason why he had been so overcome was because Kajal's devotion was so intense that, as she sang, Dada saw his Master standing before him as large as life.

In the same way when Dada returned to the Mission on his birthday, 2nd August 2014, directly from the ICU, there was surge of spiritual energy, an elation that was almost ethereal. To the thousands that were waiting to catch a glimpse of him, it was as though Lord Rama was returning to Ayodhya after fourteen long years in exile.

Dada entered the hall to the sound of the conch, clapping and chanting: *Bhalee aayein, dadal shah, jeetu aayein* (Welcome O King of our hearts, the uncrowned king of our hearts, you have come to your own home. May your lilas continue.) Euphoria had gripped each and every one present in the hall. People were dancing and weeping; those who were usually timid insisted on singing on the mike; those who were reserved were laughing and hugging others; the more boisterous ones were so overcome with emotion that they could only stand as though stunned with rapture on their faces and tears streaming down their cheeks. It was a sacred moment, when the Guru's presence made each one present feel whole and healed after months of longing and dejection.

Pierre Teillard de Chardin has eloquently stated that, 'We are not human beings having a spiritual experience. We are spiritual beings having a human experience.' Ordinary people, alas, are not aware of this. Exalted beings such as Dada, however, are ever conscious of their own divinity as well as the divinity of every sentient being and insentient object. That is why people are drawn to them even as honeybees to the nectar.

Saints of God come not to reform society but to usher in

a new and better world. By their very presence, they silently and peacefully set in motion a new mode of thinking and being. Through their own lives they become gentle catalysts of profound and abiding change. So subtle is this process that many remain unaware of their transformation until they are well established on the path to Truth. Thus, the presence of saints is the greatest *tirtha*, the highest pilgrimage, for they constantly radiate peace, love, and timelessness. And no one who comes in contact with them returns untouched.

Dada Jashan is a towering figure in the spiritual firmament of the 20th and 21st centuries. Steeped as he is in God-consciousness, he is a window to that state of bliss that surpasseth all understanding, the Godly state described by all the scriptures of the world. He is the manifestation of Lord Krishna's promise in the *Bhagavad Gita* that He will take form again and again, age after age, to destroy evil and to protect the good. He is the assurance that divine guidance will always be available to those who seek it, and that salvation is certain for all those that surrender to the Divine Will.

Books by J. P. Vaswani

7 Commandments of the Bhagavad Gita
10 Commandments of a Successful Marriage
108 Pearls of Practical Wisdom
108 Simple Prayers of a Simple Man
108 Thoughts on Success
114 Thoughts on Love
A Little Book of Life
A Little Book of Wisdom
A Simple and Easy Way to God
A Treasure of Quotes
Around the Camp Fire
Be An Achiever
Be in the Driver's Seat
Begin the Day with God
Burn Anger Before Anger Burns You
Comrades of God – Lives of Saints from East & West
Daily Appointment with God
Daily Inspiration (A Thought for Every Day of the Year)
Daily Inspiration
Destination Happiness
Dewdrops of Love
Does God Have Favorites?
Empower Yourself
Finding Peace of Mind
Formula for Prosperity
Friends Forever
Gateways to Heaven
God in Quest of Man
Good Parenting
How to Overcome Depression
Highway to Happiness
I am a Sindhi
I Luv U, God!
India Awake
Joy Peace Pills
Kill Fear Before Fear Kills You
Ladder of Abhyasa
Lessons Life Has Taught Me
Life after Death
Life and Teachings of Sadhu Vaswani
Life and Teachings of the Sikh Gurus: Ten Companions of God
Living in the Now
Management Moment by Moment
Mantras for Peace of Mind
Mantra for the Modern Man
Many Paths: One Goal

Many Scriptures: One Wisdom
Nearer, My God, To Thee!
New Education Can Make the World New
Peace or Perish: There is No Other Choice
Positive Power of Thanksgiving
Practice the Presence of God
Questions Answered
Saints for You and Me
Saints with a Difference
Say No to Negatives
Secrets of Health and Happiness
Shake Hands with Life
Short Sketches of Saints Known & Unknown
Sketches of Saints Known & Unknown
Spirituality in Daily Life
Stay Connected
Stop Complaining: Start Thanking!
Swallow Irritation Before Irritation Swallows You
Teachers are Sculptors
The Goal of Life and How to Attain It
The Highway to Happiness
The Little Book of Freedom from Stress
The Little Book of Prayer
The Little Book of Service
The Little Book of Success
The Little Book of Yoga
The Magic of Forgiveness
The Miracle of Forgiving
The New Age Diet: Vegetarianism for You and Me
The Perfect Relationship: Guru and Disciple
The Terror Within
The Way of Abhyasa (How to Meditate)
Thus Have I Been Taught
Tips for Teenagers
What you would like to know about Karma
What you would like to know about Hinduism
What to do when Difficulties Strike: 8 Easy Practical Suggestions.
Why do Good People Suffer?
Women: Where Would the World be Without You
You are not Alone: God is With You!
You can Change your Life: Live–Don't Just Exist!
Why be Sad?

Books by J. P. Vaswani

Story Books:
100 Stories You Will Never Forget
101 Stories for You and Me
25 Stories for Children and also for Teens
Break the Habit
It's all a Matter of Attitude!
More Snacks for the Soul
Snacks for the Soul
The Heart of a Mother
The King of Kings
The Lord Provides
The Miracle of Forgiving
The One Thing Needful
The Patience of Purna
The Power of Good Deeds
The Power of Thought
Trust Me All in All or Not at All
Whom do you Love the Most
You can Make a Differenc

In Hindi:
Jiski Jholi Mein Hain Pyaar (Dada J.P. Vaswani
    His Life and Teachings)
Pyar Ka Masiha (Pilgrim of Love)
Sadhu Vaswani: Unkaa Jeevan Aur Shikshaayen
    (Sadhu Vaswani His Life and Teachings)
Aalwar Santon Ki Mahan Gaathaayen
Brindavan Ka Balak
Santon Ki Leela
Bhakton Ki Uljhanon Kaa Saral Upaai
Dainik Prerna (Daily Inspiration)
Krodh Ko Jalayen Swayam Ko Nahin (Burn
    Anger Before Anger Burns You)
Prarthna ki Shakti
Shama Karo, Sukhi Raho
Safal Vivah Ke Dus Rahasya (10
    Commandments of a Successful Marriage)
Atmik Jalpaan (Snacks for the Soul)
Atmik Poshan (More Snacks for the Soul)
Bhale Logon Ke Saath Bura Kyon? (Why Do
    Good People Suffer?)
Mrutyu Hai Dwar... Phir Kya? (Life After
    Death)
Chahat Hai Mujhe Ik Teri Teri! (Hindi
    Booklet)
Ishwar Tujhe Pranam (Begin the Day with
    God)

In Marathi:
Krodhala Shaanth Kara, Krodhane Ghala
    Ghalnya Purveech (Burn Anger Before Anger
    Burns You)
Sufi Sant (Sufi Saints of East and West)
Jyachya Jholit Aahay Prem (Pilgrim of Love)
Mrutyu Nantar Che Jeevan (Life after Death)
Karma Mhanje Kay? Samjun Ghayaych?
    Karma (What You Would Like To Know
    About Karma)
Yashasvi Vyavahik Jeevanchi Sutre (10
    Commandments of a Successful Marriage)

In Kannada:
Burn Anger Before Anger Burns You
Life After Death
Why do Good People Suffer
101 Stories for You and Me
Tips for Teenagers

In Telugu:
Life after Death
Burn Anger Before Anger Burns You
What you would like to know about Karma

In Spanish:
Mas Respuestas de Dada (Dada Answers)
    Todo es Cuestion de Actitud! (It's all a
    Matter of Attitude)
Mas Bocaditos Para el Alma (More Snacks
    for the Soul)
Bocaditos Para el Alma (Snacks for the Soul)
Inicia Tu Dia Con Dios (Begin the Day with
    God)
Cita Diario Con Dios (Daily Appointment
    with God!)
El Buen Cuidado De Las Hijos (Good
    Parenting)
L'Inspiration Quotidienne (Daily
    Inspiration)
Aprenda A Controlar Su Ira (Burn Anger
    Before Anger Burns You)
Queme La Ira Antes Que La Ira Lo Queme
    A Usted (Burn Anger Before Anger
    Burns You)
El Bein Quentu Hagas, Regresa (The Good
    You Do Returns)

Books by J. P. Vaswani

Mata al miedo antes de que el miedo te mate
(Kill Fear Before Fear Kills you)
Encontro Diario Com Deus (Daily
Appontment With God)
Sita Diario ku Dios (I Luv U, God!)
Vida despu'es de la Muerte (Life After Death)
Mas Cerca Oh Dios De Ti ! (Nearer My God
To Thee)
Tiene Dios Favoritos? (Does God Have
Favorites?)
Lo Que a Usted Legustaria Saber Sobre el
Karma (What you would Like to Know
about Karma)
101 Historias Paraa Ti Y Para Mi (101 Stories
for You and Me)
Simplemente Vegetariano (Simply Vegetarian)
10 Mandamientos Para Un Exitoso
Matrimonio (10 Commandments of
Successful Marriage)
Maneje su Vida Momento a Momento
(Management Moment By Moment)
Deje De Quejarse Y Empiece a Agradecer!
(Stop Complaining Start Thanking)
Asi Nos Han Ensenado! (Thus I have been
Taught)
Tu Puedes Marcar La diferencia (You Can
Make A Difference)

In Arabic:
Daily Appointment with God
Daily Inspiration
Thus Spake Sadhu Vaswani

In Chinese:
Daily Appointment with God

In Dutch:
Begin De Dag Met God (Begin the Day with
God)

In Bahasa:
Life After Death
Musnahkan Kemarahan Sebelum Amarah
Memusnahkan Anda (Burn Anger Before
Anger Burns You)
A Little Book of Success

A Little Book of Wisdom
Menulis Di Atas Pasir (It's all a Matter of
Attitude)

In Gujrati:
It's all a Matter of Attitude
Ishwar Se Dainik Bhet (Daily Appointment
with God)
Life After Death
Flowers & Fruits

In Oriya:
Snacks for the Soul
More Snacks for the Soul
Why Do Good People Suffer
Burn Anger Before Anger Burns You
Pilgrim of Love
Life after Death
Prathna Ki Shakti

In Russian:
What you would you like to know about Karma
Burn Anger Before Anger Burns You

In Sindhi:
Why do Good People Suffer
Burn Anger Before Anger Burns You

In Tamil:
Why do Good People Suffer
Burn Anger Before Anger Burns You
Snacks for the Soul
It's all a Matter of Attitude
More Snacks for the Soul
Secrets of Health and Happiness
10 Commandments of a Successful Marriage
Kill Fear Before Fear Kills You
Daily Appointment with God

In Latvian:
The Magic of Forgiveness

In French:
Burn Anger Before Anger Burns You

INDEX